THE WORLD TURNED UPSIDE DOWN:
Maintaining American Leadership in a Dangerous Age

Preface by Joseph Nye and Condoleezza Rice
Edited by Nicholas Burns, Leah Bitounis, and Jonathon Price

CONTRIBUTORS INCLUDE:

Madeleine K. Albright, Stephen E. Biegun, Nicholas Burns, Richard Danzig,
John Deutch, John Dowdy, Michèle Flournoy, Michael Froman,
Stephen Hadley, Christopher Kirchhoff, Anja Manuel, Joseph Nye,
Condoleezza Rice, Carla Anne Robbins, David E. Sanger,
David Shambaugh, Dov S. Zakheim, and Philip Zelikow.

To: Walter Isaacson

You have taken the Institute to new heights, and have done it with grace. We at the Aspen Strategy Group have benefited from your leadership and salute you.

Published in the United States of America in 2017 by The Aspen Institute

Printed in the United States of America
ISBN: 0-89843-670-2
Wye Publication Number: 17/018

Cover design by: Steve Johnson
Interior layout by: Sogand Sepassi

aspen strategy group

Aspen Strategy Group Leadership

CHAIR EMERITUS

Brent Scowcroft
President
The Scowcroft Group, Inc.

CO-CHAIRS

Joseph S. Nye, Jr.
University Distinguished Service Professor
Emeritus
Harvard University

Condoleezza Rice
Denning Professor of Global Business
Stanford University
Stephenson Senior Fellow
Hoover Institution

DIRECTOR

Nicholas Burns
Roy and Barbara Goodman Family Professor
of the Practice of Diplomacy and
International Relations
Harvard University

DEPUTY DIRECTOR

Jonathon Price
Deputy Director
Aspen Strategy Group

SPECIAL PROJECTS OFFICER

Leah Bitounis
Special Projects Officer
Aspen Strategy Group

ASPEN INSTITUTE PRESIDENT

Walter Isaacson
President and CEO
The Aspen Institute

MEMBERS

Madeleine K. Albright
Chair
Albright Stonebridge Group

Graham Allison
Douglas Dillon Professor of Government
Harvard Kennedy School

Zoë Baird
CEO and President
Markle Foundation

Stephen Biegun
Vice President
Ford Motor Company

Kurt Campbell
Chairman and CEO
The Asia Group

James Cartwright
Harold Brown Chair
Center for Strategic and International Studies

Eliot Cohen
Professor
Johns Hopkins SAIS

Richard Cooper
Professor
Harvard University

Acknowledgements

The Aspen Strategy Group (ASG) has spent more than thirty years bringing together a bipartisan group to reflect on the nation's most pressing international relations and national security challenges. Every summer, we ask our group to discuss and debate one major issue. This year, we focused on the challenges to the liberal world order that was constructed in the aftermath of World War II.

The Aspen Strategy Books series are a reflection of our annual discussions, and this publication is a direct result of our August 2017 meeting of experts and thought leaders in Aspen, Colorado. These papers provide insight into our discussions—the way the group wrestled with the diverse array of challenges. Each of us made a conscious effort to question our underlying assumptions and challenge each other to be open to the real changes that need to be made. As always, our goal in this process was to provide practical, honest, and constructive insight.

We hope this book provides some clarity on these issues along with possible paths forward.

In light of these emerging challenges, fostering such discussions is even more important. We are indebted to our partners, whose investment in ASG makes these meetings possible. We are grateful to Robert Abernethy, Robert and Renee Belfer, Howard Cox, Dick Elden, Gail Engelberg, Adam Metz, Francis Najafi, Lynda and Stewart Resnick, Robert Rosenkranz and Alexandra Munroe, Leah Zell, the John Anson Kittredge Educational Fund, the Markle Foundation, McKinsey & Company, the Pritzker Family Foundation, the Segal Family Foundation, and the Stanton Foundation. Without their support, this book would not have been possible.

In addition, we are grateful to the many people who labored over this text. These include the authors for contributing their ideas and putting pen to paper, Gayle Bennett for proofreading and editing every page of this publication, Steve Johnson for his creative talents on the cover, and Sogand Sepassi for designing the interior layout.

We are also indebted to our Brent Scowcroft Fellows, Anand Raghuraman, Ariel Fanger, and Kajsa Mayo, who spent many hours reviewing this manuscript to ensure its quality. They are all bound for distinguished careers in foreign affairs, and we look forward to reading their own papers someday.

We would be remiss not to thank our leadership. Joe Nye, one of the original founders of the group, continues to lead ASG as co-chair and exemplifies the bipartisan spirit of the group. This year, Condoleezza Rice assumed her role as ASG co-chair, following the inimitable Brent Scowcroft. She has already reminded us all why she was one of America's finest secretaries of state.

Finally, as noted in our dedication, we must thank Walter Isaacson, who has led the Aspen Institute so ably these last fourteen years. He has provided the physical and intellectual space for this group to grow and flourish. As we inscribed with a haiku on the leadership award we gave him this year:

At home with Wynton
Jobs, Einstein or Da Vinci
Who Else? But Walter.

Though we will miss his wise counsel and leadership at the Institute, we know we can count on his example and presence as we move forward.

Contents

Preface 11
Joseph S. Nye, Jr. and Condoleezza Rice

Foreword 13
Nicholas Burns

The Ninth Annual Ernest May Memorial Lecture 17
The Idealism of What Works
Philip Zelikow

CHAPTER 1
US Trade Policy Toward Asia: Strategic Questions 33
Michael Froman

CHAPTER 2
Restoring the Case for Free Trade 47
Stephen E. Biegun

CHAPTER 3
**Real News, Fake News: The Assault on Truth, the Free Press,
and the Liberal Order** 65
Carla Anne Robbins

CHAPTER 4
**Short of War: Cyber Conflict and the
Corrosion of International Order** 77
David E. Sanger

CHAPTER 5
**An Even Flatter World:
How Technology Is Remaking the World Order** 91
Christopher Kirchhoff

CHAPTER 6
**An Irresistible Force Meets a Moveable Object:
The Technology Tsunami and the Liberal World Order** 99
Richard Danzig

CHAPTER 7
**Maintaining America's Lead in Creating and
Applying New Technology** 117
John Deutch and Condoleezza Rice

CHAPTER 8
**China's Economic March:
Will It Undermine the Liberal World Order?** 123
Anja Manuel

CHAPTER 9
China and the Liberal World Order 139
David Shambaugh

CHAPTER 10
More Tooth, Less Tail: Getting Beyond NATO's 2 Percent Rule 151
John Dowdy

CHAPTER 11
NATO and Its Authoritarian Member States 167
Dov S. Zakheim

CHAPTER 12
**Russia's Campaign Against American Democracy:
Toward a Strategy for Defending Against, Countering,
and Ultimately Deterring Future Attacks** 177
Michèle A. Flournoy

CHAPTER 13
Modernizing the International System: What Needs to Change? 189
Stephen Hadley

CHAPTER 14
Modernizing the Liberal Order: What Needs Fixing? 219
Madeleine K. Albright

Preface

Joseph S. Nye Jr.
Co-Chair, Aspen Strategy Group
University Distinguished Professor
Harvard University

Condoleezza Rice
Co-Chair, Aspen Strategy Group
Denning Professor of Global Business
Stanford University
Stephenson Senior Fellow, Hoover Institution

Next year, we will commemorate the seventieth anniversary of the Marshall Plan. This plan ushered in a new era of international cooperation and signaled the beginning of what we now know as the liberal world order. As the premier global power, the US has led this rules-based world order since its inception.

Within this framework, the Aspen Strategy Group discussed America's national security architecture during our 2016 annual summer meeting in Aspen. As we looked back on 9/11, our prolonged involvement in Afghanistan and Iraq, cyber issues, and threats posed by Russia and China, we hoped to modernize our decision-making calculus.

A year later, our conversation is different; while we still reflect on our foreign policies, the framework within which we have been operating for the past seven decades has been called into question. During the last twelve months, forces of nativism, populism, and isolationism have gained ground in various places around the globe. The new administration has questioned the benefits of certain international institutions and agreements. Russia has launched multiple covert actions aimed at destabilizing democracy. And China has continued to exert its growing economic power in East Asia, Central Asia, and Europe through the expansion of the One Belt, One Road initiative.

Our conversation this summer focused on re-examining our assumptions about the liberal world order and reflecting on the challenges outlined above. As uncertainty in many of these areas threatens the existing world order, our presenters discussed how to manage points of instability and where positive opportunities exist within them.

Our nonpartisan group is made up of current and former government officials, business leaders, and journalists who have spent their careers working on American foreign policy. While our members hold varying political beliefs and have different ideas for America's trajectory, together we confronted a multitude of questions and put forward a number of practical ideas.

The discussions prompted a wide range of questions. Will the revised order be more diffuse and proliferated with less agreement on core principles? Will the idea of community or competition prevail in relationships between nations, and which idea will the United States prioritize? And finally, can and will Donald Trump lead this new order? It is still early days, and the answers to these questions remain unclear.

However, it was clear for many that we must modernize the current world order, and that the US, as the largest economic and military power, will continue to play a central role. Many believed that the concerns of ordinary Americans must be better taken into account in our trade policies. But many issues related to jobs and insecurity arise from technological change that is not related to trade. There was a general apprehension that technology, which has been a central aspect of the liberal world order for the past 70 years, may be now be undermining it. Many also agreed that we must not underestimate the importance of a well-resourced US government that can assemble teams of enormous depth to successfully deploy national security strategies.

The book features essays based on our summer discussions, which covered securing the US trade position in Asia, the assault on truth and the free press, cyber's impact on national security, China's place in the world order, and the crisis in the transatlantic alliance, and the threat of a revisionist Russia. We concluded the workshop by discussing the aspects of the liberal world order that must be changed to account for these rapidly developing national security challenges.

As a convening body, we continue to believe that face-to-face dialogue is a necessary means to developing successful foreign policy. As a nonpartisan organization, we believe that our group's value is the ability of its members to come together to express their views, to learn from one another, and ultimately to begin a national conversation among students, young leaders, and policy makers on the challenges ahead. We hope this book provides a starting point for such a conversation.

Foreword

Nicholas Burns
Director, Aspen Strategy Group
Roy and Barbara Goodman Family Professor of the Practice of Diplomacy and International Relations
Harvard University

When the Aspen Strategy Group first met in the summer of 1984, its founders— Brent Scowcroft, Bill Perry and Joe Nye— likely never dreamed that members at a future meeting would actually worry that the liberal world order might be at risk. But that was our focus at our annual summer conference in Aspen, Colorado this year.

In this book, we aim to conduct an intensive, frank and serious examination of the health of the liberal order, the many challenges to its future and, in particular, the changes the US must make to preserve its indispensable global leadership role. While our main focus is on how to preserve a liberal, democratic world with the US at its center, we also look to identify what needs to be renovated, up-dated and changed altogether so that it may endure far into the future.

This book has been written in the spirit of non-partisanship that has been the Aspen Strategy Group's tradition for over three decades. All of us know all too well that this is a particularly divisive and bitter time in American politics. We also know America has been at its best when we pull together across party lines to agree on common prescriptions to fix what is ailing our foreign and defense policies. This was one of the great achievements of the Truman, Vandenburg, Marshall and Eisenhower generation when it created the American-led global order following the Second World War.

The crisis in the liberal order is dominating discussions among government officials and academic experts around the world and in our own country.

Professors Hal Brands and Charles Edel pose a question that offers a good framework for this publication:

"Are we living through an era that resembles the 1930s, when authoritarian leaders were on the march, democratic leaders failed to stand up to them, the international system buckled, and the world was dragged into war? Or are we living through something more like the late 1970s, when America, recovering from its long engagement in a losing war and pulling itself out of a prolonged economic slump, began to take the course corrections that allowed it to embark on a period of national recovery and reassert its international ascendancy?"

These are key questions for all of us seeking to understand the future of American foreign policy under the leadership of President Donald Trump.

There is no question that the US faces a multiplicity of challenges today from a resurgent Russia in Europe and the Middle East and a more assertive China in the South and East China Seas. There are dangers to the future of democracy, particularly in Europe and even the US itself, from right-wing populism. Many are concerned that technological change is acting as a leveling force to reduce and limit the power of nations like the US and to empower renegade regimes like North Korea as well as terrorist groups. Commentators like David Brooks fear even the values of the Enlightenment are under assault in the US and other democratic countries.

The Trump Administration's America First policy, of course, is at the very center of this international debate. President Trump and his leadership team came to Washington with new and often radically different ideas about American leadership in the world.

The President's persistent criticism of NATO and the EU during the campaign and early in this administration has led to concern that he views the European allies, particularly Germany, more as economic competitors than strategic partners. Those who champion free trade worry the Administration is abandoning a decades-long strategy that has produced historic global growth and expanded US influence on every continent. The President's immigration and refugee restrictions have forced Europe to assume a much greater burden when there are more refugees and internally displaced people in the world today than at any time since the summer of 1945. US withdrawal from the Paris Climate Change agreement and the possibility of leaving the Iran nuclear agreement worry American allies and many in our own country who understand the perils of America withdrawing from its global leadership role.

For many of Trump's critics, the greatest worry is that America will cease to be the linchpin of a vast international system as it has been for the past seventy years— the Alliance leader, coalition builder, trade hub and open defender of democracy and human rights.

The Trump Administration rejects this criticism and argues that President Trump's policies will strengthen America rather than weaken it by restoring lost American influence and power in the world. They maintain that "America First does not mean America alone." Many Trump supporters echo Gary Cohn and General H.R. McMaster, who argued in a May 2017 Wall Street Journal op-ed that "the world is not a 'global community" but an arena where nations, nongovernmental actors and businesses engage and compete for advantage". This evolution of an inward-looking nationalist and self-centered America has only deepened the debate about America's long stewardship of the liberal order.

With political battle lines thus drawn, critics and defenders of the Trump administration are contesting a fierce debate in America about the future of American foreign policy.

The Aspen Strategy Group examines in this book the state of the international liberal order with all of these questions in mind. The issues explored in this book include: the internal dynamics of the Trump presidency, and its effect on the US relationship with its allies; the ever-increasing pace of technological innovation (both in the consumer and military spaces) and its effect on governance, privacy, and security; shifting domestic politics between the liberal world order's historical champions (the US, UK, and other allies); and authoritarian states such as China and Russia that repudiate the essential values of the liberal order—democracy, civil freedoms, human rights, and the rule of law.

I concluded from our discussions that the world still needs the strong, active and purposeful leadership of the US. The liberal order is not coming to an end, but it needs to evolve with changing times. And, while it is experiencing a great internal debate about the wisdom of President Trump's foreign policy, the US is likely to remain the most powerful force for good for decades to come. We at the Aspen Strategy Group hope this book will help to shed light on this vital issue.

"So much of the divide between antiliberals or liberals is cultural. Little has to do with "policy" preferences. Mass politics are defined around magnetic poles of cultural attraction. If Americans engage this culture war on a global scale, I plead for modesty and simplicity. As few words as possible, as fundamental as possible."

—PHILIP ZELIKOW

The Ninth Annual Ernest May Memorial Lecture
The Idealism of What Works

Philip Zelikow
Professor
University of Virginia

Editor's Note: Philip Zelikow presented the annual Ernest R. May Memorial Lecture at the Aspen Strategy Group's August 2017 Summer Workshop in Aspen, Colorado. The following are his remarks delivered at the meeting. The Ernest May Memorial Lecture is named for Ernest May, an international relations historian and Harvard John F. Kennedy School of Government professor, who passed away in 2009. ASG developed the lecture series to honor Professor May's celebrated lectures.

I start with a Tale of Two Prophets. This tale comes from that terrible and glorious decade, the 1940s. The two prophets predicted the future of freedom.

My first prophet was a man named James Burnham. In 1941 Burnham was thirty-five years old. From a wealthy family—railroad money—he was a star student at Princeton, then on to Balliol College, Oxford. Burnham was an avowed communist. He joined with Trotsky during the 1930s.

By 1941 Burnham had moved on as he published his first great book of prophecy, called *The Managerial Revolution*. The book made him a celebrity. It was widely discussed on both sides of the Atlantic.

Burnham's vision of the future is one where the old ideologies, like socialism, have been left behind. The rulers are really beyond all that. They are the managerial elite, the technocrats, the scientists, and the bureaucrats who manage the all-powerful enterprises and agencies.

You know this vision. You have seen it so often at the movies. It is the vision in all those science fiction dystopias. You know, with the gilded masterminds ruling all from their swank towers and conference rooms.

It's a quite contemporary vision. For instance, it is not far at all from the way I think the rulers of China imagine themselves and their future.

In this and other writings Burnham held up Stalin's Soviet Union and Hitler's Germany as the pure exemplars of these emerging managerial states. They were showing the way to the future. By comparison, FDR's New Deal was a primitive version. And he thought it would lose.

Burnham's views were not so unusual among the leading thinkers of the 1940s, like Joseph Schumpeter or Karl Polanyi. All were pessimistic about the future of free societies, including Friedrich Hayek, who really believed that once-free countries were on the "road to serfdom." But Burnham took the logic further.

Just after the Second World War ended my other prophet decided to answer Burnham. You know him as George Orwell.

Eric Blair, who used George Orwell as his pen name, was about Burnham's age. Their backgrounds were very different. Orwell was English. Poor. Orwell's lungs were pretty rotten and he would not live long. Orwell was a democratic socialist who came to loathe Soviet communism. He had volunteered to fight in Spain, was shot through the throat. Didn't stop his writing.

Orwell was profoundly disturbed by Burnham's vision of the emerging "managerial state." All too convincing. Yet he also noticed how, when Burnham described the new superstates and their demigod rulers, Burnham exhibited "a sort of fascinated admiration."

Orwell wrote: For Burnham, "Communism may be wicked, but at any rate it is *big*: it is a terrible, all-devouring monster which one fights against but which one cannot help admiring." To Orwell, Burnham's mystical picture of "terrifying, irresistible power" amounted to "an act of homage, and even of self-abasement."[1]

Burnham had predicted Nazi victory. Later, Burnham had predicted the Soviet conquest of all Eurasia. By 1947 Burnham was calling for the US to launch a preventive nuclear war against the Soviet Union to head off the coming disaster.

Orwell saw a pattern. Such views seemed symptoms of "a major mental disease, and its roots," he argued, "lie partly in cowardice and partly in the worship of power, which is not fully separable from cowardice."

Orwell thought that "power worship blurs political judgment because it leads, almost unavoidably, to the belief that present trends will continue. Whoever is winning at the moment will always seem to be invincible."

Orwell had another critique. He deplored, "[t]he tendency of writers like Burnham, whose key concept is 'realism,' is to overrate the part played in human affairs by sheer force." Orwell went on: "I do not say that he is wrong all the time. ... But somehow his picture of the world is always slightly distorted."

Finally, Orwell thought Burnham overestimated the resilience of the managerial state model and underestimated the qualities of open and civilized societies. Burnham's vision did not allow enough play for "the fact that certain rules of conduct have to be observed if human society is to hold together at all."[2]

Having written these critical essays, Orwell then tried to make his case against Burnham in another way. This anti-Burnham argument became a novel. The novel called *1984*.

That book came out in 1949. Orwell died the next year.

By that time, Burnham had become a consultant to the CIA, advising its new office for covert action. That was the capacity in which Burnham met the young William F. Buckley. Burnham mentored Buckley. It was with Buckley that Burnham became one of the original editors of the *National Review* and a major conservative commentator. In 1983 President Reagan awarded Burnham the Presidential Medal of Freedom.

Not that Burnham's core vision had changed. In 1964 he published another book of prophecy. This was entitled *Suicide of the West: An Essay on the Meaning and Destiny of Liberalism*. The Soviet Union and its allies had the will to power. Liberalism and its defenders did not. "The primary issue before Western civilization today, and before its member nations, is survival." (Sound familiar?)

And it was liberalism, Burnham argued, with its self-criticism and lack of commitment, that would pull our civilization down from within. Suicide.

So was Burnham wrong? Was Orwell right? This is a first-class historical question. Burnham's ideal of the "managerial state" is so alive today.

State the questions another way. Do open societies really work better than closed ones? Is a more open and civilized world really safer and better for Americans? If we think yes, then what is the best way to prove that point?

My answer comes in three parts. The first is about how to express our core values.

American leaders tend to describe their global aims as the promotion of the right values. Notice that these are values in how other countries are governed.

President Obama's call for an "international order of laws and institutions" had the objective of winning a clash of *domestic* governance models around the world. This clash he called "authoritarianism versus liberalism."

Yet look at how many values he felt "liberalism" had to include. For Obama the "road of true democracy" included a commitment to "liberty, equality, justice, and fairness" and curbing the "excesses of capitalism."[3]

What about our current president? Last month he urged his listeners to be ready to fight to the death for the "values" of the West. He named two: "individual freedom and sovereignty."

A week later two of his chief aides, Gary Cohn and H.R. McMaster, doubled down on the theme that America was promoting, with its friends, the values that "drive progress throughout the world." They too had a laundry list. They omitted "sovereignty." But then, narrowing the list only to the "most important," they listed "[T]he dignity of every person … equality of women … innovation … freedom of speech and of religion … and free and fair markets."[4]

By contrast, the antiliberal core values seem simple. The antiliberals are *for* authority … and *against* anarchy and disorder. And they are *for* community … and *against* the subversive, disruptive outsider.

There are of course many ways to define a "community." Tribal … religious … political … professional. It is a source of identity, of common norms of behavior, of shared ways of life.

Devotees of freedom and liberalism do not dwell as much on "community." Except to urge that everybody be included. And treated fairly.

But beliefs about "community" have always been vital to human societies. In many ways, the last 200 years have been battles about how local communities try to adapt or fight back against growing global pressures—especially economic and cultural, but often political and even military.

So much of the divide between antiliberals or liberals is cultural. Little has to do with "policy" preferences. Mass politics are defined around magnetic poles of *cultural* attraction.

If Americans engage this culture war on a global scale, I plead for modesty and simplicity. As few words as possible, as fundamental as possible.

Certainly our history counsels modesty. Americans and the American government have a very mixed and confusing record in the way we have, in practice, related values in foreign governance to what *our* government does.

Also, until the late nineteenth century, "democracy" was never at the core of liberal thinking. Liberal thinkers *were* very interested in the design of *republics*. But classical liberal thinkers, including many of the American founders, always had a troubled relationship with democracy. There were always two issues.

First, liberals were devoted, above all, to liberty of thought and reason. The people were often regarded as intolerant, ill-informed, and superstitious—unreliable judges of scientific truth, historical facts, moral duty, and legal disputes.

The other problem is that democracy used to be considered a synonym for mob rule. Elections can be a supreme check on tyranny. But sometimes the people have exalted their dictators and have not cared overmuch about the rule of law.

It therefore still puzzles me: Why is there so much debate about which people are "ready for democracy"? Few of the old theorists thought any people were ready for such a thing.

It was thought, though, that any civilized people might be persuaded to reject tyranny. Any civilized community might prefer a suitably designed and confining constitution, limiting powers and working at a reliable rule of law.

By the way, that "rule of law" was a value that Mr. Cohn and General McMaster left off of *their* "most important" list. Yet is anything more essential to our way of life?

Aside from the relation with democracy, the other great ideal that any liberal order finds necessary, yet troubling, is the one about community: nationalism.

Consider the case of Poland. For 250 years, Poland has been a great symbol to the rest of Europe. For much of Polish and European history, nationalism was an ally of liberalism. Versus Czarist tyranny, versus aristocratic oligarchs.

But sometimes not. Today Poland's governing Law and Justice Party is all about being anti-Russian, anti-Communist, and pro-Catholic. They are all about "authority" and "community." At the expense of … ? Poland's president has just had to intervene when the rule of law itself seemed to be at stake.

We Americans and our friends should define what we stand for. Define it in a way that builds a really big tent.

In 1989, working for the elder President Bush, I was able to get the phrase "commonwealth of free nations" into a couple of the president's speeches. It didn't stick.

Nearly twenty years later, in 2008, the late Harvard historian Ernest May and I came up with a better formulation. We thought that through human history the most adaptable and successful societies had turned out to be the ones that were "open and civilized."

Rather than the word "liberal," the word "open" seems more useful. It is the essence of liberty. Indian Prime Minister [Narendra] Modi uses it in his speeches; Karl Popper puts it at the core of his philosophy; Anne-Marie Slaughter makes it a touchstone in her latest book.[5] That's a big tent right there.

Also the ideal of being "civilized." Not such an old-fashioned ideal. It gestures to the yearning for community. Not only a rule of law, also community norms, the norms that reassure society and regulate rulers—whether in a constitution or in holy scripture.

Chinese leaders extol the value of being civilized; naturally they commingle it with Sinification. Muslims take pride in a heritage that embraces norms of appropriate conduct by rulers. And, of course, in an open society, community norms can be contested and do evolve.

The retired Indian statesman Shyam Saran recently lectured on, "Is a China-centric world inevitable?" To Saran, "A stable world order needs a careful balance ... between power and legitimacy. Legitimacy is upheld when states, no matter how powerful, observe ... norms of state behaviour." India, Saran said, had the "civilizational attributes."

So that is my first suggestion—to simplify yet balance our expressions of core values.

My second suggestion is to think strategically about where or how the US can promote such a world.

Strategically, we could ask: Where can we do the most to tilt the balance toward an open and civilized world? What states or regions or issues are pivotal? Where can US actions have catalytic impact?

Especially since 9/11, the danger of catastrophic terrorism has turned America's global strategic priorities upside-down. The terrorists tend to flourish in the broken "wilderness" areas of the world. These are just the places that therefore are *least* likely to change the course of world history in any positive way.

These places draw huge amounts of our attention, resources, and energy. From the perspective of global strategy, not only is this all playing defense, it is actually anti-strategic. The *most* important power in the world concentrating on the least important places.

I get that the defensive effort is important. My well-documented track record working on terrorism issues goes back more than twenty years. Ash Carter, John Deutch, and I first published on a new threat we called "Catastrophic Terrorism" back in 1997, and you know of my work with the 9/11 Commission. But the US government's leaders should never forget that, from the perspective of global strategy, this part of its work is fundamentally reactive and fearful.

You can't win if you don't put points on the board. And reactive defense does not put points on the board. It does not *advance* aspirations to build an open and civilized world.

This is one more way that the narrative discourse about "liberal world order" becomes ... a policeman's sort of narrative. A rather weary and overburdened policeman at that, and handling a complicated home life.

And the narrative is a bit imperial too. Not in a way to envy. More like the British colonial secretary who commented in 1902 about feeling like "the weary titan."

Indeed, anyone reading the papers assembled for this conference might feel rather like the British diplomat who, in 1907, noted to his colleagues that, "It has sometimes seemed to me that to a foreigner reading our press the British Empire must appear in the light of some huge giant sprawling over the globe, with gouty fingers and toes stretching in every direction, which cannot be approached without eliciting a scream."[6]

To think about this more strategically, try out a different mindset ... one that turns that "policeman of the world order" image inside-out. Or maybe I should say outside-in.

Start out there, with whatever foreign country or region one might think is troubled and important. Start in whatever area you deem crucial, like Brazil or Mexico or Egypt or Turkey or Pakistan or Indonesia. Then, from the perspective in that country, look at what issues actually dominate much of their daily lives.

Then ask yourself, which foreign countries matter the most to solving these problems? After doing that, try to size up just where or how America can fit in.

The so-called "world order" is really the accumulation of such local problem-solving.

In this construct, power and persuasion come mainly by example. Because people see what works ... or what fails. Inspired ... or alarmed, they make their local choices ... which accumulate.

How might an American statesman think this way? Consider the example of George Marshall. He thought this way. Here is a Tale of Two Marshall Plans.

The second half of 1947 was a busy time. Supposedly the Truman administration had just announced a Grand Strategy of Containment.

The most direct threat to that grand strategy was in Asia. There the most populous country on earth—China—was gravely threatened by Soviet-supported Communists. China mattered. In 1941 American concern for China had been a major reason for the war with Japan. America had just promoted China to lead world-power status, insisting that it be one of the five permanent members of the new UN Security Council. And here it was under direct armed attack, with the issue still very much in doubt.

Next, on the other side of the world, there was the threat of economic collapse and communist domestic subversion in Western Europe, even as Eastern Europe was practically being written off.

In the second half of 1947 plans were put together for both of these problems— China and Western Europe. Both plans called for massive, conditional assistance.

The China plan was much less expensive, but it included a significant military advisory effort. It had been put together by a mission out there led by General Albert Wedemeyer, a man Marshall knew well and had picked for the job. The Wedemeyer report was supported by the Joint Chiefs of Staff.

The Europe plan had been suggested in a Marshall speech at Harvard. But, as summer rolled on, there was no plan there. A European committee on economic cooperation was trying to put something together. It didn't seem to be going well, but they kept trying.

In the autumn of 1947 Marshall made his decision. Just to give a sense of some of the other things on his plate, during the same weeks the US also decided not to help establish a peacekeeping force for the partition of Palestine, and gave up on trying to prevent the impending war there.

Marshall analyzed the plans for Europe and China. He knew both regions really well, especially China. He decided to lower expectations for the China plan and put all his chips on the one for Western Europe.

Now, one might think there would be some problems with a containment strategy that starts off by allowing Communist conquest of the world's most populous country. But Marshall and his colleagues made—explicitly—some very tough and controversial choices about what mattered most, what they thought the local governments could and could not do, and how US action was most likely to make a difference in those local stories.

Marshall had explained his mindset. In a nationally broadcast radio address he said that, "Problems which bear directly on the future of our civilization cannot be disposed of by general talk or vague formulae—by what Lincoln called 'pernicious abstractions.' They require concrete solutions for definite and extremely complicated questions."[7]

Analyzing those questions, Marshall chose. They chose Western Europe as their preferred testing ground. Doing so, Marshall and his country regained the strategic initiative. They promoted the idealism of what works.

Today the US must make strategic choices about what places or issues will advance our narrative.

Now I come to my third answer as to how to prove the possibilities for an open and civilized world. I want to talk about the disproportionate role in history played by what I call, "catalytic episodes." The postwar recovery of Western Europe was one.

Much of history is punctuated by catalytic episodes. After they happen, people interpret them to construct narratives about past and future.

Such episodes are usually quite complex and contingent. Few outsiders and even most insiders do not understand what really happened.

They will nevertheless be dramatically simplified into catchphrases and axioms. In this way, intricate, half-understood policy moves, good or ill, can mold mass culture.

All world orders are an accumulation of the ways people and their institutions try to solve their era's problems. A deep system-wide crisis occurs when people, people all over the world, no longer think the old order, the old examples, work. Catalytic episodes usually emerge from a sort of systemic crisis.

When such a crisis comes in the modern world, there can be upheavals—often violent—all over the world. For example, as the world became more deeply interconnected during the nineteenth century, probably the largest and most violent systemic crisis occurred between 1854 and 1871.

You all know about the American Civil War, though its global causes and connections may not be as familiar.[8] And you probably know about some of the wars in Europe throughout this period. But the largest civil war of that age was in China. Another huge struggle wracked the Indian subcontinent. Another transformed Japan. The Mexicans shot their foreign emperor and created a republic. And there was more.

This systemic crisis had catalytic episodes that seemed to show the world "what works" and what didn't. The American Union. German unification. By 1871 the world believed that the constitutional nation-state was the New Thing. So, for instance, right after the Japanese civil war had ended, the winning side modeled Japan's system of government on the German one.

Again, after World War I and World War II people everywhere argued about whether the total state, or the managerial state, was the new wave of the future. An alternative was social democracy, pioneered during the 1930s by much-discussed examples in the United States and Sweden.

In such times of crisis there are global "elections." Just as American elections have "swing states," global elections have swing regions, or swing "issues."

For instance, in the late 1970s and early 1980s, capitalism was in an obvious global crisis. "Can Capitalism Survive?" cried a *Time* magazine cover from 1975. "Is Capitalism Working?" asked another cover in 1980.

So let's recall a couple of catalytic episodes that changed the global narrative.

In East Asia: Mao died in 1976. China was divided among competing visions. In 1978 Deng Xiaoping and his allies started a pivotal turn. They rejected the Soviet model. Why? Looking around, they were influenced less by the example of the United States and more by examples nearby: Japan, South Korea, and (whisper it) Taiwan. US policy did do a lot to set the background conditions for *their* achievements. Isn't it ironic that, in the very years these US policies produced world-historical results, those very policies were being trashed in America itself.

In the Atlantic world: During the 1970s social democracy was sputtering on both sides of the ocean. The Bretton Woods system had put national economic autonomy ahead of the free movement of global capital. That system had collapsed. Galloping inflation joined with high unemployment. Labor strife was endemic. Protests and terrorism wracked Western Europe. There were also the twin energy shocks.

But capitalism rebooted during the late 1970s and early 1980s. Led from Europe at least as much as from the United States, leaders threw their weight behind a new and freer economic orthodoxy of hard money and open capital markets. National economic "sovereignty" declined, but global investment and commerce took off.

Here too Americans played a vital part. Yet it was the Europeans who were in the swing states. Socialism was contesting the future not only of France but was also of Italy and Spain. As 1982 began, Margaret Thatcher carried the torch but was barely surviving in office. West Germany became an anchor, finding common cause with French technocrats like Jacques Delors, who preferred the Single European Act to the path of independent socialism.

This too was a battle of ideas. The victory of what the Germans called the *Tendenzwende* (change of course). A colossal political fight over NATO deployment of US nuclear missiles, an initiative pioneered by a German chancellor, became a central, symbolic battle.

In 1982 and 1983 the swing states of Europe made their choices, as the Chinese were making theirs. These choices turned the tide in a global election.

Orwell had not foreseen this. In 1947 he thought the world would divide into the spheres of two or three Burnhamesque superstates. These would have "a semi-divine caste at the top and outright slavery at the bottom, and the crushing out of liberty would exceed anything that the world has yet seen." Orwell held out only a small, wistful hope that perhaps Europe might develop an *alternative*, "to present ... the spectacle of a community where people are relatively free and happy and where the main motive in life is not the pursuit of money or power."[9]

One can make a fair argument that the Cold War ended precisely because this happened, because such promising alternatives were, in fact, created. It is too easy just to concentrate on communism's failings, the weakness of its managerial states. Wars, even Cold Wars, are not just lost. They have to be won.

Such were the positive alternatives consolidated in another catalytic episode, the whirlwind of diplomacy in 1989 and 1990, with the coda of the decisive defeat of aggression in the Gulf War of 1991. Some of us here played a part. And the world stepped forward into another era.

Let me offer another personal example of this kind of positive, catalytic policy making. Many of you are familiar with the huge, controversial move in 2005, the civil nuclear deal with India. This episode became catalytic, transforming our relations with India and India's place in the world. I worked on this at the State Department.

Take a moment to consider that genesis, the creation of the India move. The move became public in July 2005. But the genesis occurred between February and April of that year. Note: at that time there was no big "India threat." The move was a bit reactive, but only in an incidental sense, in that our thinking was spurred by a problem of how to present or offset a forthcoming transfer of F-16 aircraft to Pakistan. That spur, though, just opened up broader thinking about how a positive strategic opportunity might change the whole conversation, with wide rippling effects over space and time.

Condi Rice does not discuss this genesis phase in her memoir. But it was one of her finest episodes as secretary of state, precisely because she embraced a kind of strategic thinking that was so very different from the reactive, defensive playbook.

Apply this idea of "catalytic construction" to the world today.

The world has entered a new major era in its history. The 1990s were a transitional time, with the new era taking form early in this century. The political side of that story is obvious enough. But the socioeconomic dimension is even more important.

The fundamental shift is the digital revolution and the rise of a networked world. This really started to take off during the decade of the 2000s. It is still in its early stages. It is a bit akin to the period of the 1880s and 1890s during the takeoff of the Second Industrial Revolution. As with that revolution, this digital revolution is beginning to transform the structure and organization of society and communities in deep ways.

The challenges and opportunities are not the same as they were in the 1970s and 1980s. Our governing systems are not nearly keeping pace.[10]

The United States can take the lead here in America. Our own institutions are decaying. But little is being done to renew them. Meanwhile opioids, much coming from China, are the leading cause of death of Americans under 50.

Looking at other countries or regions around the world, probably all of us share some sense that the world is slouching toward another cycle of grave systemic crisis. The last three years have been disheartening.

Everyone here can reflect on unease in global capitalism, global environment, mass migrations, cyberspace, advances in biological engineering, trends in mass media and culture, the implosion of the Arab and Muslim world, and other problems in Eurasia, East Asia, Latin America, or Africa.

It is hard for me to see how American effort in the world is purposefully directed in any meaningful way.

Also, as a government, the US is not well informed or well equipped for strategic works of catalytic construction. Here we are in this information age, with our $70 billion intelligence enterprise, and as a government and as a country I feel we are less able to reconstruct the policy-making world in the really crucial, swing countries than we were in Marshall's time seventy years ago. And US capacities for working with foreigners to solve their problems were also smarter and more functional seventy years ago than they are now.

That does not mean Washington is not busy. A poorly functioning government is not inert. Instead, it lives the life of a pinball. The life of a pinball can feel quite busy. So many bright lights, so noisy, so bounced about.

Maybe any more constructive moves just have to wait a few years. Yet it does seem to me that the world is drifting toward a truly massive general crisis.

Every one of America's major adversaries now has the strategic initiative. They— Russia, Iran, China—are currently better positioned to set the time, place, and manner of engagement, including political engagement. On every vector, we react.

Blustery declarations, backed by unsustainable commitments, do not regain the strategic initiative. Instead they invite the exemplary humiliation, this American generation's version of Britain's "Suez" moment, that some of our adversaries will eagerly try to arrange.

Suppose, instead of just reacting episodically, the United States and its friends wanted to go on offense, so to speak, and seize the strategic initiative. My little reading of history suggests a checklist of three strategic questions.

1. Set priorities. What battleground issues or states are most likely to influence this generation's global election about prospects for an open and civilized world, including the pivotal battlegrounds for the future of governance here in America?

2. Think outside-in. Out in those states, out in the world of those issues, are there catalytic possibilities? How do *they* see their situation? What (and who) are the critical variables in *their* choices?

3. US efficacy. In that context, where or how can the US really make a strategic difference?

These are exactly the kind of questions Marshall and his colleagues analyzed in 1947. They are also just the kind of questions the Bush administration analyzed during 1989 and 1990.

Here are a few candidate focal points for catalytic initiatives.

Which developed countries may model ways to adapt successfully to the digital revolution? Fareed Zakaria just noted that Canada has been immune to "populism" not because the Canadian people are immune from our culture war, but "rather because for the last 20 years, they have pursued good public policy."[11]

If, as Fareed says, "we now live in a post-American West," how do we size up the prospects and variables in the efforts of Macron and his partners to reboot Europe's political and economic model? I see no evidence of a real Atlantic agenda.

China's future course is not set. So what are the crucial and foreseeable way points ahead? On which can the US make a difference? Ditto for India.

In the Arab and Muslim world? Is there any state that could develop in a way that inspires wide hope across the Arab and Muslim world? The giant Saudi domestic experiment? I don't know. And the US now seems overweighted on the Gulf, underweighted in the pivotal potential of Baghdad and Cairo. No one should underestimate what Iraqis have accomplished in the last two terrible years. And what about Widodo in Indonesia? Couldn't that be exemplary?

In Latin America, again perhaps defense can turn to offense. As Mexico descends into another abyss of violence and faces a crucial election, what about instead playing offense toward a North American vision? Brazil's crisis might be an opportunity. The Pacific Alliance countries—Mexico, Colombia, Peru, and Chile—also offer inspiration.

To boil my argument down to two sentences: If you don't like Burnham's vision then you better build and spotlight Orwell's alternatives. Outsiders will only understand the results, the vivid results.

Philip Zelikow is the White Burkett Miller Professor of History at the University of Virginia, where he has also served as dean of the Graduate School and director of the Miller Center of Public Affairs. His scholarly work has focused on critical episodes in American and world history and on the history and practice of American foreign and military policy. Before and during his academic career he has served at all levels of American government. His federal service has included positions in the White House, State Department, and the Pentagon. His most recent full-time position was as the Counselor of the Department of State, a deputy to Secretary Rice. He also directed a small and short-lived federal agency, the 9/11 Commission, as well as an earlier bipartisan commission, this one on federal election reform and chaired by former presidents Carter and Ford, that led to the Help America Vote Act of 2002. A former member of the Intelligence Advisory Boards both for President Bush and for President Obama, he is currently a member of the Defense Policy Board. He is a member of the Aspen Strategy Group.

[1] George Orwell, "James Burnham and the Managerial Revolution," [1946] and "Burnham's View of the Contemporary World Struggle," [1947] in Sonia Orwell & Ian Angus, eds., *The Collected Essays, Journalism & Letters: In Front of Your Nose*, vol. 4 (Boston: Nonpareil, 2000), 169, 170, 325.

[2] Ibid., 173, 324, 179-80.

[3] Quoting Obama's last major foreign policy addresses: "International Order" December 6, 2016; "Authoritarianism Versus Liberalism," September 20, 2016 (to the UNGA).

[4] Trump address in Warsaw, July 6, 2017; Gary Cohn and H.R. McMaster, "The Trump Vision for America Abroad," *New York Times*, July 13, 2017.

[5] Karl Popper, *The Open Society and Its Enemies* (Princeton: Princeton University Press, 2013, orig. 1945); Anne-Marie Slaughter, *The Chessboard and the Web* (New Haven: Yale University Press, 2017).

[6] Thomas Sanderson, commenting on Eyre Crowe's 1907 analysis of Anglo-German relations, quoted and usefully put in context in Zara Steiner, *The Foreign Office and Foreign Policy, 1898-1914* (Cambridge: Cambridge University Press, 1969), 69.

[7] Marshall radio address of April 15, 1947, quoted in Philip Zelikow, "George C. Marshall and the Moscow CFM Meeting of 1947," *Diplomacy and Statecraft* 8, no. 2 (July 1997): 97, 116.

[8] The American Civil War arose from uncontrollable desires and fears about the expansion of slavery. The drive for such expansion had global causes: the takeoff of slave-produced Southern cotton as a crucial global commodity, when combined with the (mainly British) tools of the First Industrial Revolution and the associated global transport revolution. See, e.g., Sven Beckert, *Empire of Cotton: A Global History* (New York: Penguin Random House, 2014).

[9] George Orwell, "Toward European Unity," [1947] in Sonia Orwell and Ian Angus, eds., *The Collected Essays, Journalism & Letters: In Front of Your Nose*, vol. 4 (Boston: Nonpareil, 2000), 371, (emphasis added).

[10] A broad agenda for adaptation of the American economy to the digital revolution was offered by a group organized by the Markle Foundation, Rework America, in *America's Moment: Creating Opportunity in the Connected Age* (New York: Norton, 2015). I held the pen for this group work. Other especially insightful works include James Bessen, *Learning by Doing: The Real Connection Between Innovation, Wages, and Wealth* (New Haven: Yale University Press, 2015); Edmund "Ned" Phelps, *Mass Flourishing* (Princeton: Princeton University Press, 2013); Suzanne Berger and the MIT Task Force on Production in the Innovation Economy, *Making in America: From Innovation to Market* (Cambridge: MIT Press, 2013); and Gary Pisano and Willy Shih, *Producing Prosperity* (Cambridge: Harvard Business Review Press, 2012). Crucial information about business developments is being regularly published by the McKinsey Global Institute, such as its pathbreaking report on *Manufacturing the Future* (2012). And inspiring local and state innovations have been called out in a series of *Atlantic* essays by James Fallows and his colleagues, including the cover story of that magazine's March 2016 issue.

Figures like US Senator Mark Warner, Purdue University President Mitch Daniels, and Arizona State President Michael Crow have tried to drive a national agenda with titles like "Capitalism 2.0" and the Aspen Institute's Future of Work Initiative. So far, none of this has meaningfully worked its way into the national agendas of political leaders of either party.

[11] He added: "Canada's economics, health care, banking and immigration policies have been inclusive and successful." Fareed Zakaria, "What Happens When Liberty Fails to Deliver," *New York Times*, July 25, 2017.

"By focusing on bilateral deficits as the ultimate metric of trade policy success or failure, the Trump administration is potentially setting itself up for failure."

—MICHAEL FROMAN

US Trade Policy Toward Asia:
Strategic Questions

Michael Froman
Distinguished Fellow
Council on Foreign Relations

There is little debate about Asia's importance to the United States. It is the focus of some of our strongest alliances. It is the locus of some of our most serious national security challenges. And it is absolutely central to our economic well-being. Asia is home to some of the largest and fastest-growing markets in the world, some of the greatest sources of innovation, some of the most important segments of the global supply chain, and some of the most significant sea lanes of commerce and communication. The United States is a Pacific power. Our national security and economic interests are inextricably linked to those of the region. And it is difficult to imagine the US retaining its competitiveness if it were to find itself excluded from markets representing more than half the world's population.

These factors were central to the Obama administration's rebalancing strategy toward Asia: a raising of our military profile in the region (e.g., deployment of troops to Darwin), a deepening of our political engagement with key partners (e.g., presidential participation in the East Asia Summit and annual summits with the Association of Southeast Asian Nations [ASEAN] leaders on maritime security and other issues), and arguably most importantly, a step-change in our economic involvement in the region through the negotiation of the Trans-Pacific Partnership (TPP).

But it appears that TPP is not to be, at least for the US under the Trump administration. What happened, what does it mean for US trade policy toward Asia going forward, and what are the strategic implications of the choices ahead?

The Road Not Taken

TPP would have created the largest free trade area in the world, representing about 40 percent of the global economy.[1] It would have disproportionately benefitted US exporters since the US economy is already quite open—our average applied tariff is 1.4 percent,[2] 80 percent of our imports from TPP countries already come in duty-free, and we do not use regulations as a disguised barrier to trade—but our trading partners maintain much higher barriers to their markets.

Vietnam's 100 percent tariff on Harley-Davidson motorcycles would have been completely eliminated.[3] Japan's 38.5 percent tariff on beef would have been reduced to 9 percent.[4] The barriers to Canada's dairy and poultry market—which were not addressed in the North American Free Trade Agreement (NAFTA)—would have been broken down. The non-tariff barriers to Japan's auto market would have been addressed. For the first time in any trade agreement, TPP would have created disciplines on currency practices. These specific examples are instructive because, at various times, candidate and then President Trump has cited each of them when describing the unfairness in our trade relations with other countries. All of them would have been addressed by TPP.

Similarly, when it came to rules, TPP would have imposed the most stringent labor and environmental obligations of any trade agreement in history and made them fully enforceable, including by trade sanctions, helping to level the playing field between our workers and workers abroad. (Mexico, the target of much of the Trump administration's ire, would have been obligated to fundamentally reform its labor practices, much along the lines that organized labor and its supporters in Congress have been demanding since NAFTA first went into place.) It would have strengthened intellectual property rights protections and their enforcement, while ensuring that the benefits of innovation—whether in the pharmaceutical sector or on the internet—were broadly shared. It would have put in place comprehensive market disciplines on state-owned enterprises and, very importantly, defined for the first time a set of norms for the digital economy consistent with the ecosystem that has led to so much innovation in the United States. In sum, TPP would have ensured that the rules of the road for arguably the most important region in the world would have broadly reflected US values and US interests.

That is why TPP ultimately enjoyed such broad support across a wide range of stakeholders: from the Business Roundtable and the US Chamber of Commerce to the National Association of Manufacturers and the Farm Bureau, from the Coalition of Services Industries and the Financial Services Roundtable to the Internet Association and TechNet. It was not just large, multinational companies that supported TPP: the National Small Business Association—and small businesses in every state, ranging from a garage door manufacturer in Tacoma to a wastewater treatment equipment manufacturer in Cleveland—endorsed it. Hispanic and Asian chambers of commerce endorsed it. Bipartisan groups of governors and the US Conference of Mayors endorsed it. TPP was supported by both internet platform companies and content creators, such as the movie industry, two groups that rarely agree. It was the first trade agreement to be fully supported by the domestic textile industry and the apparel importers, and it was supported by both the association of footwear manufacturers and the footwear importers. Even traditionally import-sensitive interests, such as the dairy farmers and the auto parts manufacturers, supported it.

The number of companies that worked actively against it, such as Philip Morris International and the Ford Motor Company, were relatively few and fairly isolated. The broad support across the economy was noteworthy given the array of different interests that often make it difficult for consensus to form on major legislation. While no stakeholder group got 100 percent of what they sought across 100 percent of the agreement, the vast majority saw that they were much better off with TPP than without it—a fact they are seeing play out in real time as competitors from other countries take market share that could have been theirs and as the rules that would have played to the benefit of the US economy, such as those defining an innovative digital ecosystem, are being set aside in favor of more statist, mercantilist models.

And it was not just the business community that saw the value in TPP. A number of environmental stakeholders viewed the environmental obligations—from the disciplines on illegal fishing to the commitments on wildlife trafficking—to be game changers. So did some of the more thoughtful people on labor and human rights issues—even if their organizational politics did not permit them to make a public endorsement.

That said, over the course of the 2016 presidential election, the conventional wisdom was that TPP was dead. Candidate Trump tapped into isolationist, nativist, and protectionist sentiments, and TPP was a casualty. Candidate Clinton—under populist pressure from both Bernie Sanders and Donald Trump—determined that the agreement she once promoted as the gold standard no longer met her requirements for support. While the small but critical mass of pro-trade Democrats in Congress remained largely supportive, the majority of Democratic Party activists—if the number of signs on the floor of the Democratic Convention were any indication— were strongly against it. Mainstream Republicans and their congressional leaders, long the foundation of support for trade, felt boxed in by candidate Trump and went largely silent. The business community made a judgment that if President Trump delivered on tax reform and regulatory relief, they were generally willing to bite their tongues and look the other way on his trade and, to a certain extent, immigration policies.

In fact, the underlying politics of trade are more complicated than the conventional wisdom. According to Gallup, more Americans are "pro-trade" now—fully 72 percent—than any time since the 1970s.[5] The most pro-trade cohort in America are young Democrats; the least, middle-age Republicans. While there is no doubt a wide range of polls to cite, according to the Chicago Council on Global Affairs, fully 74 percent of self-identified Clinton supporters and 56 percent of Sanders supporters supported TPP. Even 47 percent—close to half—of Trump supporters supported TPP.[6] Still, the passion of the opponents far outweighed the passivity of the supporters, allowing President Trump to withdraw from TPP on his third day in office, fulfilling a promise to his base.

The Implications of Retreat

President Obama and his administration warned that failure to move forward with TPP would undermine US credibility in the Asia-Pacific, sideline US economic interests as the rest of the world moved on without us, and create a void in leadership that China would be all too willing to fill.

That, unfortunately, is exactly what is playing out in real time. President Trump's decision to withdraw from the TPP sent shockwaves through the capitals of our allies and partners across the Asia-Pacific region. Leaders from Japan to Singapore to Australia explicitly questioned whether the US could be counted upon on issues of national security if it could not deliver on trade. Outside the region, Europeans linked the US withdrawal from leadership of the global trading system with the withdrawal from the Paris Accord and some equivocation over NATO as proof points that the US might no longer be a reliable partner.

In many respects, the Trump administration's withdrawal from global leadership has been a wake-up call to the rest of the world. It has spurred other countries to show leadership and take action they might not otherwise have done. In that regard, as others step up (e.g., on defense spending), there may well be some positive consequences.

When it comes to trade, though, the rest of the world is moving on, as expected, without the United States. With US participation in TPP on the shelf, Japan moved quickly to complete a drawn-out trade negotiation with the EU, giving European farmers, ranchers, and businesses the access to that critically important market they had promised the US in TPP. At the same time, the TPP-11 (the TPP countries other than the United States) are actively considering putting TPP in place without us—to secure at least for themselves the benefit of both the rules and the market access commitments that were made in those negotiations. The EU is proactively pursuing trade or investment agreements with Mexico, Australia, New Zealand, India, China, ASEAN, MERCOSUR, and the Gulf Cooperation Council. The Pacific Alliance countries of Mexico, Peru, Colombia, and Chile continue to deepen their regional integration as they reach out to New Zealand and Australia to cement ties. Africa is deepening its regional economic communities and is pursuing tripartite and continental-wide free trade negotiations. Canada is considering launching a free-trade agreement negotiation with China.

And, as expected, China has stepped in to fill the void. At Davos in January 2017, President Xi declared China to be the leader of the open, global economy—notwithstanding its actual highly protectionist, statist, mercantilist posture on trade and investment.[7] Between the One Belt, One Road (OBOR) initiative, the Silk Road Fund, the Asia Infrastructure Investment Bank (AIIB), the assertions of sovereignty in the South China Sea, and the negotiation of the Regional Comprehensive Economic Partnership (RCEP)—the regional agreement spanning sixteen countries from India to Japan, which China has been helping to lead—China has a coherent and long-term regional strategy that it is executing with a fair degree of success.

Now, the question is whether the US has a regional strategy and can execute on it. On the trade front, beyond making clear its preference for bilateral over multiparty deals, the Trump administration has not yet laid out a clear alternative to the Obama rebalancing strategy, nor a clear response to China's regional integration strategy.

The Trump administration has made clear that its top trade priority is the renegotiation of NAFTA and, failing that, US withdrawal from it. It has also expressed interest in amending or withdrawing from the Korea-US Free Trade Agreement (KORUS). While the Trump administration has made noises about the possibility of negotiating some sort of bilateral trade agreement with Japan, it is unclear whether the administration considers that a priority, and Japan remains skeptical of that effort.

But there has been little discussion about what to do vis-à-vis the Asia-Pacific more generally, beyond bringing down bilateral trade deficits. This includes not only the other TPP countries, such as Vietnam, Malaysia, and New Zealand, with whom we do not already have free trade agreements, but also more than a dozen other countries that expressed an interest in beginning consultations toward possible participation in TPP. Nor has there been a clear articulation about how trade fits into a broader strategic vision for the region.

The Centrality of China

To the degree that there has been a focus on trade policy toward Asia, it has centered on China. Though, while there has been a lot of talk and some action, the underlying strategy remains unclear.

There is no doubt that China remains a major economic challenge for the United States. Every administration has tried its hand at restructuring the dialogue with China, worked to find sources of leverage and pressure, used incentives of engagement to encourage reforms, and deployed enforcement actions to underscore the seriousness of the effort. But the China problem persists.

The Trump administration continues to wrestle with its approach to China. During the campaign, candidate Trump highlighted the problem of China as an almost existential threat to the United States, but at Mar-a-Lago, President Trump declared that we had a great relationship with China and continues to lavish praise on President Xi.[8]

Throughout the campaign and up until early April, candidate and President Trump criticized China for manipulating its currency, but when it came time in mid-April to decide whether China was actually a currency manipulator, the determination was negative.[9]

There have been a number of public statements about the importance of being tough on enforcement with China. Thus far, the administration has launched a number of studies and investigations but has yet to take action. And on some of the most systemically important enforcement actions it inherited, such as the WTO case against China for using state-owned banks to provide subsidized financing to promote overcapacity, the Trump administration has failed thus far to follow through.

That said, the Trump administration has already made its mark on US-China trade relations. First, President Trump made an explicit linkage between economic and national security interests in a manner that previous administrations had assiduously eschewed. He declared that he would not find China to be a currency manipulator in part because we needed China's help on North Korea, and if China helped us on North Korea, it would get a better trade deal from us.[10] What trade deal he was referring to remains a bit of a mystery. A free trade agreement? A bilateral investment treaty? Less aggressive enforcement actions? But the willingness to subjugate domestic economic interests to China's cooperation on stabilizing the situation on the Korean Peninsula—which, of course, is in China's national interest as well—was noteworthy.

The other element of the Trump administration's approach to China was its focus on a 100-day plan. The first outcome of that process was a list of measures that had largely been agreed to and announced before—in some cases, a number of times before. That said, some of the commitments had new deadlines, giving hope that we will see progress in implementation.

As part of this package of repackaged deliverables, the US lent its credibility to China's strategic vision for the region by "recognizing its importance" and sending a senior official to participate in President Xi's landmark OBOR summit.[11] On the one hand, this was a low-cost concession: given that this initiative—like the AIIB—was going to move forward with or without us, participating in the summit was only an acceptance of that reality. On the other hand, given that the administration turned away from major planks of the rebalancing strategy toward Asia without putting forward an alternative strategy, lending US credibility to China's regional strategy was not trivial. Symbolism matters, perhaps especially in that region of the world, and the Trump administration sent a powerful signal that was interpreted by many in the region as US acquiescence to China's leadership of this all-important region. In 2014, Sandy Berger noted that the orientation of the Asia-Pacific region was still uncertain: it could be transpacific or China-centric in character. Currently, it certainly looks like it is heading toward the latter.

Indeed, one of the most striking ironies of the Trump administration's trade policies is that China has been the greatest beneficiary. Withdrawing from TPP, threatening to withdraw from KORUS, and raising questions about the reliability of the US as a partner in the eyes of our allies and partners in the region—precisely at a time when China has put forward an impressive array of soft- and hard-power initiatives—has fundamentally damaged our relative standing in the region and made it more difficult for those in the region looking to mitigate China's dominance to find a way to do so.

Having undermined efforts to balance China's influence in the region, the question now is how the Trump administration can influence China's behavior itself. China is nothing if not pragmatic. It has indicated that it understands President Trump to be a "deal maker" and that it is perfectly prepared to cut a deal with him, while steadily pursuing its own long-term objectives. As one senior Chinese official noted earlier this year, the Chinese understand how important "tweetable deliverables" are to this president, and they are prepared to provide such deliverables as it becomes clear what the administration actually wants.

China has tried this shopping list approach in the past: tell us what you want us to buy, tell us where you want us to invest, and we will make sure you have successes to point to. China can buy its soybeans and corn from us or from South America. It can buy airplanes from us or from Europe. It can buy tractors from us or from Japan and South Korea. It can buy its liquefied natural gas from us or from others. China would be quite happy to commit to buying a certain amount of each of these exports from us and to commit to invest tens of billions of dollars in Midwest manufacturing companies or US infrastructure assets.

And what's wrong with that approach? President Trump could point to individual micro-successes, convince his supporters that he has dealt effectively with the China problem, and even potentially have a marginal, temporary impact on the bilateral trade deficit. But if the shopping list approach comes at the cost of pulling our punches in pressing China on fundamental economic reforms, including intellectual property theft, forced technology transfer, indigenous innovation, predatory industrial policy, subsidies that encourage excess capacity, and a fundamental asymmetry in the manner in which we participate in each other's economies, then the benefits will be short-lived and come at a high price.

China would like nothing more than for the US to accept "tweetable deliverables" in exchange for standing down in challenging these broader economic policies, let alone Taiwan, Tibet, and human rights. Here, the Trump administration will face a critical choice, one that may come down to how it measures success.

Metrics and Unintended Consequences

Thus far, the Trump administration has put an overwhelming emphasis on reducing bilateral trade deficits as it focuses on its trade policy. The administration has made clear that countries with which we have a trade deficit will need to renegotiate trade agreements (if they have one with us) or take other actions to balance our trade—or face the consequences.

But Economics 101 teaches us that imbalances are a reflection of a number of macroeconomic factors, such as differential growth rates and savings and investments rates. At the margin, to the degree that a bilateral trade deficit reflects barriers to our exports or dumping of the other country's exports, that certainly is a legitimate area of focus for trade policy, including enforcement actions. But by focusing on bilateral deficits as the ultimate metric of trade policy success or failure, the Trump administration is potentially setting itself up for failure.

For example, if the Trump administration is successful in achieving its objective of moving the US from 1.9 percent growth to 3.0 percent growth on a sustained basis, we could well see larger trade deficits than we do now. Indeed, our trade deficit widened when we added 22 million new jobs in the 1990s; we ran a sizable trade surplus during the Great Depression.[12] Few would trade the economy of the 1990s for that of the 1930s.

Focusing on the trade balance as the only or primary metric creates a risk that we will see some short-term unsustainable successes (e.g., selling a few more planes, which would no doubt be a good thing) while letting China off the hook on the fundamental reforms of Chinese economic policy needed to ensure a more fair and level playing field. Those reforms were the focus of the Obama administration's approach to China, whether it was getting China's government to stop approving foreign participation in large sectors of the Chinese economy through the Bilateral Investment Treaty (BIT) negotiations or eliminating indigenous innovation policies that put our companies and their workers' intellectual property at risk or ensuring that science, not protectionism, determined the approval of agricultural imports.

The Path Forward

What should the Trump administration do going forward? First and foremost, it should decide whether it will settle for "tweetable deliverables" or whether it will insist on systemically important economic reforms. A trade agreement is different from a purchase and sales agreement. It may be harder to negotiate, but it provides longer-term dividends. Eliminating excess capacity, disciplining industrial policies, and encouraging China to take global norms seriously should remain important US policy objectives.

Of course, the US must remain prepared to use our enforcement tools—not in a manner that invites a trade war, but strategically to eliminate unfair trade practices and secure concessions on the systemically important reforms. In that regard, the administration should be as explicit as possible about what is expected of China and the costs of failure in making concrete progress.

Beyond China, the Trump administration needs to decide what its economic engagement with the rest of the region will be. An amended KORUS and a periodic dialogue between Vice President Pence and Japan's Deputy Prime Minister Aso are hardly a substitute for TPP. It could well be that the Trump administration does not see it as a priority to have a substitute, that it is comfortable looking inward and allowing China to pursue its approach without a counterbalance.

However, to the degree that the administration understands how important it is to US exporters (and the workers who produce those exports), as well as our allies and partners, that there be an alternative model to China's, it should build on the foundation TPP laid as it negotiates or renegotiates "good" trade deals. As Secretary of Commerce Ross and USTR Ambassador Lighthizer have indicated, much was done in TPP that should be harvested.[13] It is in our interest—and particularly in the interest of small businesses—that a single set of high-standard rules be adopted as broadly and consistently as possible.

The Open Strategic Question

Beyond the specifics of trade, the Trump administration needs to determine whether it wants to provide allies and partners in the region with an alternative to China's leadership and, if so, what form that alternative will take. President Xi has signaled that China intends to turn the OBOR initiative into a new building block of global architecture, not unlike the G-20, a forum that would continue to meet and take on issues not just related to its initial mandate—infrastructure development across the region—but broader issues as well. The Trump administration will need to determine what role the US should play in the region and, therefore, whether and what alternative is necessary. It would be of little utility to try to oppose the OBOR initiative, but that does not mean that we should cede the field entirely to China.

There is no doubt that early actions by this administration have raised serious questions about US leadership in the region and more generally, but the rest of the world still very much wants the US to be involved and be a partner. The challenge now for the Trump administration is to develop a coherent regional strategy and to turn some of the uncertainty and unpredictability it has precipitated into meaningful negotiating leverage.

If it can do so, it has the potential to mitigate some of the damage that has been done and potentially reassert US leadership. Doing so, though, requires careful and disciplined execution. It is still relatively early days.

Michael Froman is a distinguished fellow at the Council on Foreign Relations and the James R. Schlesinger distinguished professor at the University of Virginia's Miller Center of Public Affairs. He previously served in President Obama's cabinet as the US Trade Representative. Key initiatives under his leadership included TPP, T-TIP, and an array of other negotiations; the monitoring and enforcement of US trade rights at the WTO; and Congressional passage of TPA, AGOA, GSP, and the Trade Facilitation and Trade Enforcement Act. At the start of the Obama Administration, Mr. Froman worked as Assistant to the President and Deputy National Security Advisor, where he was responsible for coordinating policy on international trade and finance, energy security and climate change, and development issues. He served as the US Sherpa for the G20 and G8 Summits. Earlier, he worked at Citigroup, including as CEO of its international insurance business, COO of its alternative investments business, and head of its infrastructure investment business. In the 1990s, Mr. Froman served as Chief of Staff and as DAS for Eurasia and the Middle East at Treasury. He also worked as a Director at the NEC and the NSC. Mr. Froman has been a White House Fellow, a Ford Foundation Fellow, a SSRC/MacArthur Foundation Fellow, and a Fulbright Scholar. He was selected by *Fortune* and *Politico* as one of their top 50 leaders in 2016. Mr. Froman, his wife, Nancy Goodman, and their two living children, Benjamin and Sarah, live in Washington. Mr. Froman received an A.B. from Princeton University, a D.Phil from Oxford, and a J.D. from Harvard, where he was an editor of the *Harvard Law Review*.

[1] Joshua P. Meltzer, "The Trans-Pacific Partnership Is a Win for All Parties," Brookings Institution, December 9, 2015, https://www.brookings.edu/blog/future-development/2015/12/09/the-trans-pacific-partnership-is-a-win-for-all-parties/.

[2] "Trans-Pacific Partnership: Leveling the Playing Field," Office of the United States Trade Representative, https://ustr.gov/sites/default/files/USTR-Tariff-Information-by-Sector-6115.pdf.

[3] Ylan Mui, "Trump Talks About His Concern for Harley-Davidson, But He Killed the Deal That Could Have Fixed Its Problems," CNBC, March 1, 2017, http://www.cnbc.com/2017/03/01/trump-talked-harley-davidson-but-he-killed-the-tpp.html.

[4] "Fact Sheet: Trans Pacific Partnership and Japan: Key Outcomes for Agriculture," US Department of Agriculture, https://www.usda.gov/media/press-releases/2015/11/19/fact-sheet-trans-pacific-partnership-and-japan-key-outcomes.

[5] Art Swift, "In US, Record-High 72% See Foreign Trade as Opportunity," Gallup, February 16, 2017, http://www.gallup.com/poll/204044/record-high-foreign-trade-opportunity.aspx.

[6] "Poll: Majorities of Americans Support TPP, Say Trade Is Good for US Economy," The Chicago Council on Global Affairs, September 7, 2016, https://www.thechicagocouncil.org/press-release/poll-majorities-americans-support-tpp-say-trade-good-us-economy.

[7] Noah Barkin and Elizabeth Piper, "In Davos, Xi Makes Case for Chinese Leadership Role," Reuters, January 17, 2017, http://www.reuters.com/article/us-davos-meeting-china-idUSKBN15118V.

[8] "Trump Hails 'Tremendous' Progress in Talks with China's Xi," BBC, April 7, 2017, http://www.bbc.com/news/world-us-canada-39517569.

[9] Ana Swanson and Damian Paletta, "Trump Says He Will Not Label China Currency Manipulator, Reversing Campaign Promise," *The Washington Post*, April 12, 2017, https://www.washingtonpost.com/news/wonk/wp/2017/04/12/trump-says-he-will-not-label-china-currency-manipulator-reversing-campaign-promise/?utm_term=.233695971120.

[10] Gerard Baker, Carol E. Lee, and Michael C. Bender, "Trump Says Dollar 'Getting Too Strong,' Won't Label China a Currency Manipulator," *The Wall Street Journal*, April 12, 2017, https://www.wsj.com/articles/trump-says-dollar-getting-too-strong-wont-label-china-currency-manipulator-1492024312.

[11] Ben Blanchard, Philip Wen, and Michael Martina, "US to Send Delegation to China's Belt and Road Summit," ed. Robert Birsel, Reuters, May 12, 2017, http://www.reuters.com/article/us-china-silkroad-usa-idUSKBN18816Q.

[12] Council of Economic Advisors and Office of the Chief Economist, "20 Million Jobs: January 1993-November 1999," US Department of Labor, December 3, 1999, https://clintonwhitehouse3.archives.gov/WH/EOP/CEA/html/20miljobs.pdf, 2.

[13] Andrew Mayeda and David Gura, "Ross Says TPP Could Form Starting Point for US on Nafta Talks," Bloomberg, May 3, 2017, https://www.bloomberg.com/news/articles/2017-05-03/ross-says-tpp-could-form-starting-point-for-u-s-on-nafta-talks; "Lighthizer Says Renegotiated NAFTA Could Go Beyond TPP Provisions," World Trade Online, March 20, 2017, https://insidetrade.com/daily-news/lighthizer-says-renegotiated-nafta-could-go-beyond-tpp-provisions.

"Before considering a way forward on trade, it is necessary to acknowledge that what ails trade policy is less about trade and more about blaming trade for what really challenges those most disaffected."

—STEPHEN E. BIEGUN

Restoring the Case for Free Trade

Stephen E. Biegun
Vice President
Ford Motor Company

It was a stunning rejection of decades of American leadership in liberalizing global trade. For the first time in memory, at a heated debate in Cleveland, Ohio, a major party candidate, who would soon go on to lead his party's ticket in the fall presidential election, openly rejected the North American Free Trade Agreement (NAFTA), a cornerstone of US, Canadian, and Mexican economic and political unity.

Fanning the flames of protectionism and seeking to tap into the political unrest and anger among working class voters who felt they were losing ground to foreign competition, the first-term senator from Illinois (yes, it was THAT president), clawed for political advantage at a pivotal moment in his presidential primary campaign by denouncing NAFTA and endorsing an ultimatum to Mexico to either renegotiate the agreement or see the United States withdraw (see the transcript of the Obama-Clinton debate).[1]

Unions cheered and the business community was aghast, not to mention the governments of Mexico and Canada. The potential cost and disruption to trade for major sectors of the US economy like agriculture and automobile manufacturing was calculated in the tens of billions of dollars. And the reaction from Mexico City and Ottawa was swift. In fact, it was later reported that candidate Obama was so concerned about the potential international fallout from the threat to withdraw from NAFTA that a senior economic advisor was quietly dispatched to Ottawa to reassure the Canadian government that the statement was just necessary campaign rhetoric; there was no intention to follow through on the threat. While this political feint eventually proved to be the empty campaign rhetoric that it was purported to be, it undoubtedly moved the nation, and the nation's politics, a step further down the road to NAFTA's potential undoing.

Clearly, the politics of trade in the Unites States are confounding to politicians and policy makers who want to pursue trade liberalization, even if they are reluctant to defend it on the campaign trail. Free trade agreements (FTAs) have plenty of supporters motivated by an ideological persuasion toward economic liberalization, intellectual conviction that freer trade produces better economic efficiencies and outcomes, geopolitical ambitions to cement international relations through trade agreements, or constituent private sector interests that benefit either from easier rules to export from the United States to other markets or even easier rules to import into the United States. Nonetheless, despite ample evidence and a broad consensus among economists that freer trade is good for the American economy, FTAs themselves increasingly have become ripe political targets.

One oddity around the politics of trade in recent years is the growing disconnect between Democratic and Republican elected leaders and the voting bases of their respective political parties. Over the past eight years, the Democratic Party establishment and its presidential candidates (at least during their campaigns) have at best soft-pedaled support for free trade negotiations and more often than not stridently opposed most FTAs. It is an article of faith inside the Washington Beltway that an FTA will only gain a majority of support in the US Congress by obtaining near-unanimous support from Republican legislators combined with a handful of Democratic votes. While undoubtedly a large part of this political inclination is driven by the desire of elected officials to curry favor from important constituencies like organized labor and other interest groups, it nonetheless stands in stark contrast to polling by the Pew Charitable Trust that shows 67 percent of Democratic or Democratic-leaning voters support the idea that FTAs are good for the United States.[2]

Not to be outdone, Republican Party presidential candidates (with one recent and notable exception) have seemingly treated support for FTAs as an article of faith, reflexively endorsing every free trade negotiation past, present, and future. And, as referenced already, Republican legislators have constituted the overwhelming majority of Congressional votes supporting most FTAs passed by the Congress. While this support is certainly in favor with well-moneyed corporations and business groups that tend to support Republican candidates, this voting also defies that same Pew polling data that shows just 36 percent of Republican or Republican-leaning voters believe FTAs are good for the United States (at 27 percent this lack of support is even more pronounced among Trump voters).

The political controversy around trade negotiations has many legitimate causes, from the poor quality of some agreements to weak enforcement to misplaced priorities (e.g., geopolitics over economic outcomes). Without a doubt, the seeming inability of FTAs to reduce the enormous and persistent annual US trade deficit of over a half trillion dollars per year has served to amplify discontent about FTAs. But the most devastating factor undermining public support for FTAs is the sense that they disadvantage the United States economically, and supporters of free trade have been unable to effectively address the anxieties of those negatively impacted by FTAs. Consequently, over the past two decades, free trade agreements have become more difficult and taken longer to negotiate and especially more difficult to pass through the United States Congress.[3]

The unpopularity of FTAs seemed to hit a climax in the 2016 presidential campaign, which resulted in the election of a harsh critic of the outcomes from past US trade negotiations. Immediately upon taking office in January, the new president announced the withdrawal of the United States from the Trans-Pacific Partnership (TPP), an agreement negotiated over eleven years among twelve countries seeking to create a giant trade bloc in the Asia-Pacific region. In July, the new president's trade representative requested consultations with the Korean government, with the aim of demanding renegotiation of the US-Korea Free Trade Agreement. Nine years after his predecessor trashed NAFTA in that Cleveland debate, the new president has reopened the beleaguered NAFTA agreement for renegotiation. And after almost four years of negotiations with the European Union, the US-EU Transatlantic Trade and Investment Partnership (TTIP) has run out of gas. The battle for trade agreements has ended, and the battle against trade deficits has begun.

All the trade chickens came home to roost in the negotiation of the TPP, an FTA that for many epitomized the collective misjudgments of trade negotiations over the preceding decades. TPP proved to be too big with too many members of vastly different attitudes toward free trade, too inconsequential in its expansion of trade volumes, and too controversial in its attempts to not only free up trade but also to regulate and in significant ways even limit certain trade. The TPP also was seen by many as falling short of addressing some of the most confounding trade barriers faced by America's largest sectors of exports (in particular ignoring currency manipulation). When it was finally concluded, the agreement fell flat with the American business community, the American public, the Congress, and, in the one area of bipartisan agreement in an otherwise extraordinarily divisive election year, the presidential candidates for both major political parties.

To be clear, the TPP did not die on January 23, 2017, when President Trump formally signed a presidential memorandum of withdrawal, nor for that matter did it die on November 8, 2016, when Donald J. Trump was elected the forty-fifth president of the United States. The TPP died on February 4, 2016, the day it was signed in Auckland, New Zealand, cementing its flaws and shortcomings. Back in the US, the TPP was dead on arrival.

Across the breadth of the US business community, a number of the nation's blue chip companies were either opposed or completely indifferent to the outcome of the TPP. Generally, the completion of an FTA by the United States government would be closely choreographed with the US Chamber of Commerce, which, in claiming to be the unified voice of thousands of American companies, would give a full-throated endorsement the moment the US government affixed its signature to the agreement. Instead, the TPP signing was met with weeks-long silence from the business community. Government officials anxiously lobbied companies and the Chamber to come forward with endorsements.

After the fact, negotiators made efforts to relitigate (if not renegotiate) controversial TPP provisions through understandings, side agreements, or promises to undo politically controversial provisions later. Ultimately, many companies reluctantly came on board, but the damage was done; even that corporate support became less about TPP as an agreement and more as a general effort to sustain momentum in global trade liberalization. Ironically, some holdout companies argued in effect that the reason they didn't support the TPP FTA in its current form was precisely because they supported free trade.

In fairness to the TPP, the agreement did contain hard-won provisions setting higher standards in a number of areas of trading behavior. It also reduced tariffs and opened new markets for US exports, especially agricultural goods. Still, for most observers—and Congressional supporters of the TPP—the analyses on net impact on trade flows were disappointingly small.[4]

Even more problematic, within the small overall gain in trade volumes, the United States' manufacturing sector specifically was expected to see a net loss in both exports and jobs, despite globally competitive products and costs. And there was not a single analysis that indicated the slightest impact on the persistent, decades-long trade deficit with Japan, the second largest economy in the TPP after the United States. In fact, there was near unanimity that the TPP simply locked in the status quo in trade with Japan—a $70 billion annual deficit.

A contributing factor to the TPP's underwhelming new trade volumes is that preceding US administrations had already negotiated high-quality FTAs with seven of the twelve members—Canada, Mexico, Australia, Brunei, Chile, Peru, and Singapore—and the low-hanging fruit already had been picked. Along with the United States, these seven countries with which the United States already has FTAs largely represent the core constituency for free trade in the Asia-Pacific region. In hindsight, had TPP negotiators stuck to the original purpose of building a critical mass by linking together into a single trading block the nations in the Asia-Pacific that embrace a high-level commitment to free trade, TPP would have already passed the Congress. And had that TPP been successfully concluded, it may have served its further purpose of creating enough incentive to attract other, less free-trade-oriented nations in the Asia-Pacific region to negotiate to those same high levels of ambition.

As for the remaining four TPP members with whom the United States did not already have FTAs, the reasons for the relatively small expected increase in trade volumes were pretty straightforward. New Zealand and Vietnam are small markets for US exports, and Japan and Malaysia simply do not embrace the model of free trade—and no amount of cajoling by US negotiators was going to change those realities. The choice of free trade negotiating partners matters.

In free trade negotiations, New Zealand has evermore been the bridesmaid and never the bride. Seemingly too small to be hugely interesting to the US economy, and having isolated itself at a critical moment in history through a key foreign policy choice during the Cold War, New Zealand has missed subsequent opportunities to be part of US trade priorities. Vietnam is a small market, which in the view of many, is held back by a socialist government that guides the economy with a heavy hand. Despite third-party concerns about Vietnam's deficient human rights and democracy record, some US corporations were interested in its market (and continue to be interested today). It should be understood though that this interest stems not so much because Vietnam is a market to which American exports would be sent but rather because it is a low-cost location to which US corporations could shift manufacturing in order to competitively reach other Asian, European, and possibly even US markets.

The biggest challenge to framing the economic benefits of the TPP definitely came with the inclusion of Japan and Malaysia, two of the largest economies in Asia—and ones in which the governments use policy tools and protectionist measures to prop up exports and promote domestic national champions and state-owned enterprises at the expense of importers. Japan and Malaysia made some grudging and even politically sensitive compromises to remain part of the TPP negotiation, but in the estimation of most in the US private sector, these measures on balance would be more likely to sustain the status quo in trade than improve it. It is the negotiator's conceit that all problems can be negotiated, but sometimes this is simply not true.

In fact, the greatest catalyst that might prompt governments like Japan's and Malaysia's to undertake deep, politically challenging reforms would be to expose them to the natural forces of markets themselves. But by leaving major trade-distorting policies untouched, the outcome of the TPP may well have shored up for another generation the flawed economic models that plague Japan and Malaysia in different ways today. And these compromises, which were necessary to get to a conclusion in a twelve nation FTA, in the end overshadowed the other potential economic and geopolitical benefits of the agreement. From a purely trade perspective, the larger size of the Japanese and Malaysian economies did not make the TPP more interesting. Instead, they made it more complicated and more controversial.

The most significant trade barrier omitted from the TPP negotiations—one frequently employed by Japan and, to a lesser extent, Malaysia—is currency manipulation. This is a hugely consequential issue affecting trade flows over many years and responsible for a substantial portion of the US trade deficit. According to a study by the highly regarded Peterson Institute for International Economics, the trade distortions caused by illicit, direct currency manipulation have cost the United States economy between one million and five million jobs and have added between $200 billion and $500 billion annually to the US trade deficit.[5] Yet, despite wide-ranging consensus among trade economists regarding its trade-distorting impact, and in defiance of specific rules in place at the International Monetary Fund (IMF) and World Trade Organization (WTO), a handful of governments have created huge imbalances in the global trading system by manipulating the relative value of their currencies.

A sizeable majority of members of both bodies of Congress and the past two US presidents have explicitly called for the inclusion of measures to deter currency manipulation in US FTAs. Yet, the US negotiators of the TPP chose to ignore these commitments. The failure of negotiators to include provisions against currency manipulation likely served as the single greatest factor in the TPP's failure.

While a reflexive desire for more liberalized trade and good economic outcomes are the traditional drivers for private sector support for FTAs, the argument most animating support from the foreign policy community is the geopolitical benefit of FTAs. Yet too often those arguments, made by worthy and respected voices with deep experience in international relations, sound like free trade is the country cousin of foreign aid programs. Intentional or not, the message that those most affected by poorly negotiated agreements hear is that US foreign policy interests are more important than their jobs.

If failure to include currency disciplines was the beginning of the downfall of the TPP, the agreement's fate was sealed when a combination of geopolitical ambition, hopeful legacy building, temptation to plow virgin soil, and the search for new markets led to a dramatic reinterpretation of the TPP's original purpose. Deviating from its trade-focused objectives, it was explicitly reconstrued as a tool to shore up the United States as an Asia-Pacific power, and cast as a means to curb China's mercantilist tendencies and slow the spread of Chinese influence. This new mandate was not shared by all of the TPP partners, certainly not explicitly, and it belied the fact that the only way to negotiate a successful outcome with the overly large group of TPP nations (with mismatched levels of support for free trade) was to lower ambition sufficiently to accommodate all.

A lesson that has been lost on many foreign policy-oriented supporters of FTAs is that geopolitics makes for lousy FTAs, but good FTAs can make for the best geopolitics. American autoworkers, who build high-quality, well-designed cars that can compete in the most open automotive market in the world, have a point when they ask why they're surrounded by imported vehicles from Asian markets in which American companies are actively blocked from competing. The geopolitical argument you would hear in Detroit, Michigan, is why is it that our sons and daughters are good enough to be sent as soldiers to defend Japan and Korea, and yet the automobiles we build in our factories are not?

The enthusiasm for geopolitical arguments among the foreign policy establishment is clearly lost on those who worry about the impact of FTAs on their jobs and livelihood. So, across several US administrations, the pedantic and somewhat patronizing admonishment from government officials to the private sector—and often among US companies themselves—is that more effort must be devoted to explaining to skeptical employees the benefits of FTAs so that they understand it's actually good for them. They are told that free trade literature shows they will all be better off in the long run and that they will be reeducated and retrained in order to participate better in the economy. And we are somehow surprised that they do not support FTAs.

Instead of talking more, trade negotiators and their corporate supporters would be much better served by listening more. What they would have heard is that it is unacceptable to have an FTA like the US-Korea Free Trade Agreement, which in its first five years produced a doubling of the US trade deficit with Korea, all the while the Korean government failed to implement commitments and used mercantilist tools to subsidize exports and block imports. And rather than speaking to those most impacted by bad trade agreements, perhaps (like our current president) they might have found it more beneficial to speak *with* them, much less *for* them.

With the current poisonous politics around trade agreements in the United States, combined with turbulent and shifting geopolitical dynamics in the Asia-Pacific region, the thought of a proactive strategy to expand the US trade position in Asia seems a bit Pollyannaish. In the next four years, Trump administration trade negotiations seem much more likely to focus on what it perceives as actions that will reduce trade deficits, neglected enforcement opportunities, and necessary repairs to existing trade agreements. In his administration's first foray into trade negotiations, the NAFTA renegotiation, the president has made clear that his highest priority is not the further opening of trade, per se, but instead rebalancing US trade flows to eliminate trade deficits with major trading partners. This priority will at some point shift to the Asia-Pacific region, where a similar approach is expected in the renegotiation of the US-Korea Free Trade Agreement.

Rebalancing trade deficits is a difficult goal to achieve without resorting to trade-*limiting* rather than trade-*opening* measures. This also represents a substantial shift in historical US trade policy, which will now determine the quality of an FTA's outcome based upon the impact on the US trade balance rather than on the degree of liberalization achieved within the negotiation. Such an approach no doubt will be controversial among trading partners and traditional supporters of FTAs, but it is also likely to win overwhelming public support in the US (and probably in Congress as well). Regardless of whether one views this shift in US trade policy as an unacceptable retreat or a necessary correction, it reflects the approach that many of America's Asia-Pacific trading partners have historically used.

Even if the next four years will be consumed by the priority of fixing or dismantling the existing trade infrastructure, it is still worth thinking through what else the United States might do to position itself for future opportunities. There are important lessons from the collapse of the TPP that should guide future efforts to reaffirm open trade and incentivize market opening in the Asia-Pacific. As past failures have indicated, securing the future US trade position in the Asia-Pacific region will require more than negotiating the same way and then hoping to make better arguments in favor of FTAs. Addressing the political and popular controversies around trade liberalization will require in equal parts better selection of negotiating partners, better negotiations, and better outcomes.

Before considering a way forward on trade, it is necessary to acknowledge that what ails trade policy is less about trade and more about blaming trade for what really challenges those most disaffected. The United States is sorely lacking a holistic approach to US tax and regulatory policies that considers the impact on US global competitiveness. The United States is lacking a coordinated infrastructure plan that should not only repair but also transform US infrastructure to speed the future development of the economy. Despite gargantuan efforts by the two previous administrations, reform efforts are still falling short on providing better and more accessible education and both the vocational and technical training opportunities that would bring broader segments of the US population into higher-paying employment. While bad trade policy should not be let off the hook, no trade policy—no matter how effectively negotiated—can overcome a broken tax code, a smothering regulatory system, decrepit infrastructure, or a broken education training system.

Likewise, while again not trade policy per se, the sluggish growth rate of the US economy over the past decade has eroded confidence, depressed wages, and increased pressure on the working middle class. Solutions may be out of reach absent other major domestic policy reforms, but it is possible to imagine that 4 percent economic growth in the United States would likely ameliorate many of the other controversies that have sapped popular support for FTAs. At the same time, such robust growth, and the attendant consumption that it would likely drive, would provide a far greater incentive to America's trading partners in the Asia-Pacific region to negotiate high-quality FTAs in exchange for greater access to the US consumer.

But, returning to reality, in establishing the United States' trading position in the Asia-Pacific region, there is no such thing as a blank sheet of paper to work with, particularly in the wake of the TPP's failure. There will be scars from the US withdrawal from the TPP, and some opportunities may be lost for the time being. Parallel geopolitical events or other ongoing trade negotiations will impact the range of future possibilities for better or for worse, and the current policy priorities of the US government, and others in Asia, probably mitigate against high hopes for early action on ambitious trade liberalization.

But as a start, next steps could include:

1. **Select the right negotiating partners.** The greatest advances in improving the US trading position in the Asia-Pacific region may, counterintuitively, be linking the countries with which the United States already has FTAs. While such an agreement would not likely create a substantial uptick in trade volumes, it might set trade policy ambitions at a sufficiently high level so as to serve as an antecedent for future successful negotiations. At some point, should circumstances permit, the United States would be well-served by returning to first principles on the TPP (i.e., negotiating among a group of

countries that embrace the highest level of free trading behaviors in order to create a critical mass that attracts other nations to likewise aspire to the same behaviors in order to gain market access).

An orthogonal approach to advancing the trade position of the United States in the Asia-Pacific region would be to restart US-EU negotiations on the TTIP agreement. This ambitious negotiation, which includes trading partners who embrace both open markets and free trade, sought to remove both regulatory and tariff barriers to US-European trade. If the US and EU are able to create the efficiency and scale of a combined market, it would strengthen the foundation of shared values that underpin the democratic free market orientation of the transatlantic community, including rule of law, transparency (i.e., anti-corruption), respect for private property (including intellectual property), and a limited role for government in the private sector. Moreover, the scale and attractiveness of a transatlantic marketplace could be exactly the incentive other trading nations need to make the tough choices to genuinely open their own markets. And this need not be limited to Asia-Pacific nations; it is easily conceivable that a union of TTIP and NAFTA would be a short step away (and possibly a solution to fitting a post-Brexit United Kingdom into the transatlantic and EU trading blocs).

2. **Reduce opportunities for non-tariff regulatory barriers (NTBs) to trade through mutual recognition.** Intentionally unique or opaque and shifting regulations can be more of a barrier to trade than tariffs. While tariffs, like any tax, can be priced into a good and passed on to consumers, a shifting regulation is an unsolvable barrier that most often causes potential importers to abandon markets altogether. All US FTAs should include provisions to mutually recognize or accept the largest possible range of regulations between or among negotiating parties. Once it is proven that regulations reach acceptable or equivalent outcomes, even if they differ in methodology, US policy should be that the United States will recognize such regulations— and trading partners must reciprocate.

3. **Include meaningful and binding disciplines against direct currency manipulation as a core component of FTAs.** Currency manipulation (specifically acting in violation of IMF rules to directly intervene in currency markets by using one country's national currency to buy, remove from circulation, and hold massive reserves of another country's national currency) is both a direct subsidy of exports and a de facto punitive tariff on imports.

In addition to negatively influencing trade flows, currency manipulation creates dangerous global imbalances with inflated reserves, distorted credit, and an over-dependence on export-driven growth by manipulators. These imbalances create property bubbles, deplete savings, and fuel the conditions that culminate in banking crises and recession.

Additionally, currency manipulation distorts trade by imposing artificial price points on goods. While some consumers can enjoy some cheap goods for a period of time as a result of currency manipulation, the larger economy faces deep disadvantages as overcapacity in the economies of currency manipulators are rewarded for overproduction (i.e., beyond a rational business case), shipping excess capacity, and the attendant pressure for restructuring economies that are otherwise healthy and competitive. Beggar-thy-neighbor currency manipulators appear to be exporting goods, but they are actually exporting unemployment.

Allowing currency manipulation to continue not only undermines the very concept of free trade, it destroys popular support for free trade precisely because it cheats comparative advantage, regardless of quality, product excellence, cost of manufacturing, or wage competitiveness of workers. (If you build the best product at the lowest cost and still lose your job, would you support free trade?) The argument that cheaper consumer prices justify currency manipulation suggests that the test for a winning case on free trade is not the forces of the market but rather the degree to which a government is willing to intervene in the market to produce a winning outcome. That is not free trade as envisioned by Adam Smith but rather the seventeenth century mercantilism of England. It is a theory, but if America embraces (or tolerates) that approach, don't expect free trade—and consumers will be much poorer for it.

IMF principles provide the basis for the criteria that should be surveilled when evaluating whether a trading partner is manipulating its currency. This includes:

- Protracted large-scale intervention in one direction in the exchange market;

- Excessive and prolonged official or quasi-official accumulation of foreign assets; and

- Large and prolonged current account deficits or surpluses.

To determine if a trading partner is in fact manipulating its currency in an IMF-prohibited manner, the following three-part test should be applied:

- Did the country have a current account surplus over the preceding six-month period?

- Did it add to its foreign exchange reserves over that same six-month period?

- Are its foreign exchange reserves more than sufficient as deemed by the IMF guidelines (i.e., the value of three months' imports)?

Whether one agrees on principal or accepts the necessity of such disciplines as a political imperative, absent enforceable action on currency manipulation, it seems very unlikely that an FTA will gain approval in the United States Congress.

4. **Pursue negotiations only on a bilateral basis with mercantilist trading partners.** While to some extent every country will seek to advantage its own interests in free trade negotiations, there are often wildly different levels of ambition in multinational free trade negotiations. In East Asia in particular, there are economies that have grown dramatically through the pursuit of mercantilist and protectionist policies and which seek to sustain those policies as much as possible under the cover of multinational negotiations. Negotiations with such economies are not so much free trade negotiations as reciprocal market access negotiations, more akin to an adversarial arms control negotiation—in which confidence building, transparency, inspection, and enforcement must be part of the toolbox. Bad actors in global trade that embrace an export-driven model that creates huge global imbalances through support for state-owned enterprises and national champions to protect markets at home, and use policy instruments like currency manipulation to advance beggar-thy-neighbor export policies abroad, should not be afforded the cover of multiparty negotiations.

5. **Improve consultation and transparency.** There is a persistent suspicion among many interest groups that US trade negotiators negotiate in secret in order to have more latitude to trade away American jobs and US sovereignty. This conspiratorial view is fed by the fact that trade negotiators do in fact meet in secret and that public consultations are often overly vague and generalized. More likely than not, what is actually being hidden is the true agenda of negotiators on both sides who are unwilling to publicly own up to what they are willing to give up or defend.

Reforms have been made over the years to bring in outside expertise to advise US negotiators in secret, first including industry lobbyists and then expanded to include labor unions and other interested groups. Still, even that has been criticized as playing favorites. A proposal on Capitol Hill worth considering is to publish publicly the updated agreement text after each negotiating round. Another more extreme idea would be to negotiate the agreements openly— on C-SPAN even. Seasoned negotiators will likely scoff that such ideas would make negotiations infinitely more difficult, but that may be beside the point if agreements otherwise don't get off the ground because of secrecy. As the old saying goes, sunlight is the best disinfectant.

6. **Demand fair competition rules.** One of the structural economic issues confounding both exports and investment in the global economy is the concentration of market power held by national champion companies and state-owned enterprises. Restrictive and enforceable antitrust or competition measures should be a boilerplate for US FTAs. Even outside FTAs, a means should be found even within existing trade enforcement authorities to isolate and treat separately such entities. Monopolistic companies do not operate under the rules of the free market, and they should not benefit from its open rules.

7. **Fight corruption.** Another structural issue hugely disadvantaging American companies in particular is trade distorted by corrupt behavior on the part of governments and competitors alike. While US companies have certainly been caught up in corruption scandals before, the key distinction is that they have been caught—and prosecuted. Under the Foreign Corrupt Practices Act, global corruption by US companies and individuals is illegal regardless of the jurisdiction in which it happens. Such penalties should be extended in equivalent form to every company in every country with which the United States negotiates an FTA.

8. **Enforcement, enforcement, enforcement.** Trade enforcement needs to be used as aggressively as possible to demonstrate to those negatively impacted by unfair trade practices that there is a virtue in having FTAs—that they provide tools to retaliate against cheating. Every president comes into office promising to fiercely defend US economic interests through diligent use of authorities to penalize trade cheating, but these authorities in reality are often blunt instruments with unintended consequences. They are difficult to use in a targeted manner and at times run contrary to the geopolitical

aims of the US government. Nonetheless, political will to use enforcement tools is essential not to destroy free trade, but to preserve it—and new tools including penalties against currency manipulation would help. FTAs likewise contain dispute resolution mechanisms, but these too are often time-consuming and cumbersome, creating a lengthy process of negotiation while allowing violators substantial time to disrupt trade flows before facing any consequences. In cases of trade violations, the first resort of trade officials is usually to seek to negotiate the problem away. But a sharp enforcement action may actually do more to sustain the integrity of an FTA by signaling clearly the level of compliance expected from countries enjoying favorable access to the US market.

9. **Get the economics right and the geopolitics will follow.** Perspectives differ vastly as to the "right" economics in an FTA. A corporation that intends to use the flexibility of an FTA to move all investment out of the United States and exclusively import goods back into the US might believe an FTA is great, but that company's workers (and many politicians) would certainly beg to differ. The driving national interest for an FTA might in part include alignment with the US government's foreign policy priorities, but if this argument is used to trump concerns over the economics of an FTA, it will be very hard to get Congress to support an agreement. Measuring the benefit of an FTA is complicated, but the central goal of good free trade negotiations should be to create more winners than losers through fidelity to the most complete possible removal of the barriers to the movement of goods and services. Some basic rules of thumb might be: 1) Does the agreement address the root causes of major trade deficits? 2) Does the agreement offer an opportunity to expand US exports in a manner approximately equivalent to potential imports? and 3) Does the agreement contain enforcement provisions that will either deter or effectively penalize noncompliance with the agreement's provisions?

10. **Trust the free market.** If a trading partner cannot make the tough choices to open its markets to trade, negotiators should not be shy about walking away. That status quo is costly and difficult to sustain for protectionist economies, and no agreement will always be superior to a bad agreement that sustains bad policies. As with any long negotiation, negotiators must be especially wary about allowing the completion of the agreement to become more important than its purpose. Fairly or not, this is how many critics of the TPP see its trajectory: an agreement originating with the sound concept

of tying together countries with high fidelity to the principles of free trade later retreated to lower ambitions and ultimately mutated into a tool to offset Chinese influence in the Asia-Pacific region. The very trade policy reforms that might be most confounding for China in the future (e.g., prohibiting currency manipulation or the denial of FTA benefits to state-owned enterprises) were either compromised beyond effectiveness or ignored altogether. Again, in the view of its critics, the TPP did not rectify the mercantilist and protectionist measures employed by governments like that of China. Instead, it accepted them. The favorable market access that is derived from an FTA, especially relative to competitors, might well lead a protectionist economy to a more ambitious approach the next time.

In light of the current politics surrounding trade issues, ambition for a grand new trade negotiation to provide a breakthrough in advancing the US trade position in the Asia-Pacific region by 2020 is likely a dead end. That is not to say, however, that the United States needs to stand still. Improving the US trade position in the Asia-Pacific region could include renegotiating the US-Korea FTA to make it more market friendly and possibly launch new, bilateral negotiations to rectify trade imbalances with Japan, Malaysia, Vietnam, and possibly China.

The most important work to be done to advance the US trade position in the Asia-Pacific is the routine, day-to-day blocking and tackling done by US trade negotiators and businesses in the whole gamut of global and Asia-Pacific multilateral bodies that help sustain global momentum on market opening. This includes the WTO and IMF, the Group of Seven and Group of 20, the Association of Southeast Asian Nations' (ASEAN) Regional Forum, and especially the Asia-Pacific Economic Cooperation (APEC). Within APEC there is a longstanding commitment to achieve barrier-free trade among its members through a Free Trade Area of the Asia Pacific (FTAAP). FTAAP has proven elusive and at times divisive, as the United States and China maneuver to give it an imprint of their preferred designs. Though advocates for the TPP claimed that the goal was to use the twelve-member TPP to advance the cause in a manner that could ultimately include the other nine APEC members, the withdrawal of the United States from the TPP does not spell the end of the FTAAP. With or without the United States in the TPP, achieving progress on the FTAAP is well worth continued effort.

Finally, trade negotiators and advocates for FTAs must be careful not to do more harm than good to the international trading system, much less to popular support for trade among the American people. At numerous turns, US TPP negotiators were warned that they could force the TPP negotiation to a conclusion but in so doing could drive public support for trade off a cliff. And that is exactly what happened.

Trade is actually much simpler than an ideological proposition, a geopolitical priority, or a philosophical disposition. Trade is a commercial transaction—the movement of goods and services between and among national markets. That is all. And the quality of FTAs can most sensibly be judged on the basis of whether they remove the government policy-inspired obstacles to the movement of goods and services. When rhetoric about trade and FTAs becomes theological, with statements like "belief in free trade," or when labels like "supporters of trade" (instead of supporters of *free trade agreements*) and "protectionist" are thrown about, the debate becomes even more intractable. It is in fact possible for one party to benefit and another to lose in the same agreement, regardless of the quality of the agreement. That is why FTAs are so hard to negotiate.

The United States economy has benefitted tremendously from global trade, and the strength and innovation of the US economy should give every confidence that this will remain true for the future. And negotiations to achieve freer trade will likely contribute to that future success of the American economy. But the trading policies of the United States will surely fail if they cannot win the support of the American people. The simple goal of good free trade negotiations should be to create more winners than losers through fidelity to the most complete possible removal of the barriers to the movement of goods and services. That will also be the test for many companies, and quite possibly the secret to winning back broad public support.

Stephen E. Biegun is a corporate officer and vice president for international governmental affairs for Ford Motor Company, overseeing all aspects of Ford's international governmental relations including the Company's business development, trade strategy, and political risk assessment around Ford's global manufacturing locations. Prior to joining Ford in 2004, Mr. Biegun was national security advisor to the Senate Majority Leader. Prior to that, he served in the White House from 2001-2003 as Executive Secretary of the National Security Council. Mr. Biegun also served fourteen years as a foreign policy advisor in the House of Representatives and Senate, including as Staff Director of The United States Senate Committee on Foreign Relations. Mr. Biegun was born in Detroit, Michigan, and is a third generation Ford Motor Company employee. He serves on the board of directors of the US-Russia Business Council, the US-Russia Investment Fund, The US-Russia Foundation on Economic Development and the Rule of Law, the Moscow School of Political Studies, and the Business Coalition for Transatlantic Trade. He graduated from the University of Michigan, where he studied political science and Russian language. He is a member of the Council on Foreign Relations and the Aspen Strategy Group.

[1] "The Democratic Debate in Cleveland," *New York Times* transcript, February 26, 2008, http://www.nytimes.com/2008/02/26/us/politics/26text-debate.html.

[2] Bradley Jones, "Support for Free Trade Agreements Rebounds Modestly, but Wide Partisan Differences Remain," Pew Research Center, April 25, 2017, http://www.pewresearch.org/fact-tank/2017/04/25/support-for-free-trade-agreements-rebounds-modestly-but-wide-partisan-differences-remain/.

[3] Caroline Freund and Christine McDaniel, "How Long Does It Take to Conclude a Trade Agreement with the US?" Peterson Institute for International Economics, July 21, 2016, https://piie.com/blogs/trade-investment-policy-watch/how-long-does-it-take-conclude-trade-agreement-us.

[4] "USITC Releases Report Concerning the Likely Impact of the Trans-Pacific Partnership (TPP) Agreement," United States International Trade Commission news release, May 18, 2016, https://www.usitc.gov/press_room/news_release/2016/er0518ll597.htm.

[5] C. Fred Bergsten and Joseph E. Gagnon, "Currency Manipulation, the US Economy, and the Global Economic Order," Peterson Institute for International Economics, December 2012, https://piie.com/publications/policy-briefs/currency-manipulation-us-economy-and-global-economic-order.

"France's experience shows that the Kremlin's hack-and-hype teams are by no means invincible and that voters and journalists, forewarned, may not be as credulous as we feared. The question now is how can democratic governments and societies push back more systematically against Russia's "weaponization of information"—while also protecting free speech and a free press."

—CARLA ANNE ROBBINS

Real News, Fake News: The Assault on the Truth, the Free Press, and the Liberal Order

Carla Anne Robbins
MIA Faculty Director, Marxe School, Baruch College
Adjunct Senior Fellow, CFR

The Kremlin has been waging information warfare, first against the former Soviet states then moving westward, for nearly a decade. Using its RT Network, Sputnik News, local language websites, troll factories, botnets, and sophisticated hacking operations, its goals are to sow suspicion within and among its neighbors, undermine confidence in democratic leaders and institutions, and divide the transatlantic alliance.

While Moscow's "political technologists"[1] tailor their messages for different audiences, certain themes are constant: Western governments are weak or unraveling; elections are rigged; God-fearing working people are under siege by migrants, terrorists, and "cosmopolitan" interests; and the news from "corrupt" "corporate" "mainstream" media can't be trusted.

Until the 2016 US elections, many analysts who followed Russia's disinformation campaigns in Ukraine and the Baltics with alarm still considered the United States and Western Europe invulnerable. Our democracies were too mature, our citizens too sophisticated, our media too diverse and too skeptical to be manipulated this way. We were wrong.

The January 2017 report by US intelligence agencies described a Putin-ordered "influence campaign" that blended hacking and overt messaging intended to "undermine public faith in the US democratic process, denigrate Secretary Clinton and harm her electability … [and] help President-elect Trump's election chances." The report also warned that Moscow would "apply lessons learned" in the US against "allies and their election processes." The Russians tried again in France this spring. This time, Emmanuel Macron's campaign—on alert after the US experience and with an assist from cyber and social media researchers—beat back a last minute dump of hacked documents.

France's experience shows that the Kremlin's hack-and-hype teams are by no means invincible and that voters and journalists, forewarned, may not be as credulous as we feared. The question now is how can democratic governments and societies push back more systematically against Russia's weaponization of information—while also protecting free speech and a free press, bedrocks of the liberal order that Vladimir Putin and other autocrats are so determined to discredit.

In more normal times the US would take the lead in developing this strategy. We have both the recent, bitter experience with Russian hacking and disinformation and the strongest legal protections in the First Amendment to ensure that any effort does not chill free speech.

Unfortunately, President Donald Trump is continuing to deny Russia's assault on the US electoral process. His relentless attacks on America's free press—"the enemy of the American people"—along with his attacks on the courts, nonpartisan pollsters, US intelligence agencies, the Congressional Budget Office, and other sources of independent information are reinforcing Putin's illiberal narrative. Ideas on how to challenge the Kremlin's information warfare campaign will have to come from groups outside the US government and from our allies.

The Message, the Medium, or Our Times?

What makes the Russian disinformation campaign so compelling? Is it the message? Is it the way the message is amplified on social media, where the price of entry and distribution are negligible? Or is the main problem that a small but worrisome percentage of Western audiences is so receptive to these messages—whether from the Russians; the conspiracy-mongering alt-right; Breitbart and Infowars; or even from what Vox's Zack Beauchamp calls the Russiasphere, "a fake news bubble" for a much smaller number on the left, who see Russia's hand everywhere in the Trump administration.[2]

Russia has its own far more profound economic, social, and political problems for which Putin has no answers. But the Kremlin's political technologists were ahead of Washington, London, and Paris in recognizing the anxiety and polarization building in the West and the power of technology to feed, exploit, and leverage those anxieties for political gain.

Gleb Pavlovsky, a Putin adviser and political technologist until his fall from grace, has explained that in the "new Russia" the Kremlin has given up trying to prove that anything is true. "Now ... you can say anything. Create realities."[3] Pavlovsky was talking about domestic Russian propaganda, yet the same description applies to many of the vile, absurd, but frighteningly powerful reality-bending stories pumped out by Kremlin-funded websites abroad and then amplified by Kremlin social media surrogates.

Recent pernicious gems from the European Union's weekly *Disinformation Review*: A story in Polish claiming that spreading Muslim culture has led 150,000 women in Sweden to undergo female genital mutilation. A story in Czech claiming that US ships are delivering migrants to Europe, and one in Russian claiming Ukraine's Health Ministry is selling organs. Stories in English and Finnish claiming that a German family "escaped" to Russia either because there were too many immigrants in Germany, or because German authorities were threatening to take away their grandchildren unless they stopped demonstrating against immigrants.

We know how Russian bots used Twitter during the US campaign to push out hacked DNC emails and fake news about Secretary Clinton's health. We are only now learning from the tech companies' testimony about a flood of Russian posts, tweets, videos, and ads—Facebook estimated 150 million users were exposed, Twitter reported more than 130,000 tweets, Google 1,100 YouTube videos—with ugly, inflammatory messages on the Black Lives Matter movement, gay rights, "sanctuary cities," Muslim refugees, and gun rights. The Special Counsel and Congressional investigations may find more efforts to "create realities" and sow division.

The Ecosystem

The declassified version of the January 2017 intelligence report on Russian meddling in the US election devotes as much space to an annex (first published in 2012) on the Kremlin's RT America TV network—"Kremlin's TV Seeks to Influence Politics, Fuel Discontent in US"—as it does to the report's findings. That says more about the intelligence community's dubious decision not to provide any supporting evidence on Russia's covert activities than it does about the transcendent power of RT. (The authors also accept RT's unsupported claims on audience numbers, while their concern about RT's anti-fracking coverage deserved the mockery it drew.)

Still, it is worth spending time on the RT website or cable channel (the latter is not that easy to access unless you're in a hotel) to get the flavor of what the Kremlin is pitching in English, French, Spanish, German, and Arabic at a self-reported budget of $300 million a year.

The network's slogan is "Question More," and "Fake News" (irony is not RT's strong point) is one of its favorite topics. In July 2017—around the time President Trump was retweeting a video of himself body-slamming a man with a CNN logo superimposed on his head—RT's flagship show *CrossTalk* devoted its full thirty minutes to the "Counterfeit News Network," asking "if CNN's evidence-free war on Donald Trump is really at the expense of real journalism."[4] RT's other go-to topics are stories about a West staggering under the weight of immigrant-driven sexual assaults and murders, corporate greed, "deep state" abuses, and any signs of discord in the transatlantic alliance. Like Breitbart and American news sites ranging from hard- to alt-right, RT is particularly focused on fictitious European "no-go zones" and the supposed unraveling of Sweden. RT's coverage of last summer's G-20 summit in Hamburg devoted more homepage attention to the anti-globalization street protests—including a live feed of the "chaos" and "carnage"—than to the actual meeting.

RT doesn't do a lot of reporting. It relies mainly on not-so-outside experts—a quick Google search usually leads back to RT or some other pro-Russian website—and a few high-profile commentators to carry it arguments. "America's most important intellectual" Noam Chomsky is a favorite ("If you criticize policies, you are anti-American. That only happens in dictatorships."—Chomsky to RT), and the Green Party's Jill Stein got a lot of airtime during the 2016 campaign. Stein, you may recall, was also at the Putin head table for RT's December 2015 anniversary gala, the one General Mike Flynn was paid $45,000 to address from the dais.

Starting in late 2015 then-candidate Donald Trump began drawing big RT headlines after he defended Russian President Vladimir Putin in two American television interviews.[5] ("Putin killed reporters? Prove it!"—Trump to ABC show host). Trump garnered even more attention, after he began declaring that the US political system is rigged. "He became a high-profile validator [for the] Russians' main narrative that US democracy is a stitch up, all fake," says Ben Nimmo of the Atlantic Council's Digital Forensic Research Lab, which investigates disinformation.[6] Hillary Clinton was the villain throughout, and stories about the email server were on nearly continuous play.

In May 2017, looking for a younger demographic, RT launched *FAKEbook Live*, a hipper, slyer weekly talk show streaming on Facebook, Twitter, and YouTube, with less obvious RT branding. Two millennial hosts take gleeful shots at President Trump, champion Julian Assange, and offer indulgent criticism for Syria's Bashar al Assad—"You can't back him up completely because he has made some huge mistakes." Their main message, again, is don't trust the US media, and especially not the "fake" *New York Times, Washington Post,* and CNN, whose many alleged sins include falling for the hype on Russian meddling in the US elections; conspiring to manufacture evidence of chemical weapons attacks in Syria; and failing to investigate the murder of a young

DNC staffer who, in the noxious imaginations of alt-right websites, RT, and Fox News until it retracted the story, was the source (rather than the Russians) of thousands of DNC emails.[7]

It is hard to assess the impact of such programming. The RT network doesn't report actual audience numbers, instead claiming that it has a potential reach of 700 million viewers in 100 countries. English-language RT has 2.2 million YouTube subscribers (more than three times Fox News, nearly four times NBC News and just behind CNN), but its most popular videos are clickbait: four-year-old footage of a meteorite crashing in Russia and six-year-old videos of the Japanese tsunami. RT political videos do land the occasional punch. An interview with Mohammed Daqneesh, the father of the young boy pulled from the rubble in Aleppo covered in blood and soot, denouncing his son's rescuers for "exploiting" him for anti-Assad propaganda has been seen more than a half million times in different RT formats and via reposts on right-wing and other conspiracy-promoting websites. FAKEbook Live's most popular show, however, had 7,800 YouTube views as of mid-October.

None of this sounds like the stuff of grand conspiracy. But RT and Sputnik are only the most visible parts of a much larger ecosystem that gathers, shapes, and promotes information in a strategy that Nimmo describes as "vilify and amplify."

In Ukraine, nonstop Russian propaganda, delivered by Kremlin-financed satellite TV and websites and picked up by sympathetic local news outlets and social media operations, are intrinsic parts of a hybrid warfare strategy that also includes cyber and kinetic military attacks. Fake news regulars include stories of drunken Ukrainian leaders, fascist cabals, human rights abuses (a viral report that Ukrainian soldiers crucified a Russian-speaking three-year-old was first broadcast on Russian state television and the "witness" later unmasked as an actress), and betrayal by and corruption from the West (visa-free travel to the EU will increase sex trafficking).

How much have Russian campaigns of hacked, hyped, and faked news contributed to the rise of populist governments in Hungary and the Czech Republic? How much popular anger can Russia turn against NATO troops in the Baltics or Poland, where stories about drunken alliance soldiers raping local girls or crashing their jeeps into families are staples? How much damage can Russia's continued vilification do to pro-Europe leaders including Germany's Merkel or France's Macron? There is no way of knowing, just as there is no way of knowing for certain if Russian interference changed the outcome in the US election. The continuing flood of stories and cyber intrusions suggest the Kremlin believes it is worth the continued investment.

The French 'Lessons Learned' and Where Do We Go from Here?

To remind, some nine gigabytes of hacked emails and files from the Macron campaign—with supposed revelations of offshore accounts and tax evasion—were dumped on the internet a day and a half before French voters went to the polls. The press stayed away, and Macron overwhelmingly defeated his populist far-right opponent, Marine Le Pen, a Putin favorite.

There are a variety of explanations for what went right in France—some *sui generis*, some that may provide useful lessons.

The data was dumped just hours before a pre-election news blackout, suggesting that the Russians were scrambling after underestimating Macron's political chances. Anticipating trouble, French news organizations were already part of a multinational joint fact-checking experiment. They followed the election commission's order to keep to the blackout and not report the contents of the hack. Their forbearance was likely reinforced by warnings from the Macron campaign that some of the documents in the dump were faked. The campaign would later explain that it too had prepared by creating false email accounts with faked information to complicate hackers' efforts.

Researchers also played an important role in debunking the hacks. With the French press silent, the data was pushed back to France by Russia's Sputnik News and by Twitter users in the United States. While cyber researchers had warned in April that the hacking group targeting the Macron campaign appeared to be the same one responsible for the breach at the Democratic National Committee, the Atlantic Council's Digital Forensic Research Lab moved quickly to identify the sources of the #MacronLeaks social media campaign.

As Ben Nimmo explained in an article on Medium, they tracked the #MacronLeaks hashtag, as it reached "47,000 tweets in just three and a half hours," back "through a machine analysis ... to the Twitter account of Jack Posobiec, the Washington, DC, bureau chief of an obscure, alt-right website, theRebel.media."[8] That information, shared widely with the press, appears to have further undermined the credibility of the hack.

While the Russians are unlikely to procrastinate again, the French experience suggests the importance of preparation, the value of public awareness in encouraging healthy skepticism, and the role cyber and social media researchers can play in helping journalists identify the sources of information—and amplification.

Strategies for Pushing Back

There are a host of ideas on how—and how hard—to push back against the Russian disinformation campaign. The challenge is coming up with strategies that don't also constrain free speech—a real danger.

Peter Pomerantsev and Michael Weiss, who raised an important early alarm[9] about the Kremlin's "weaponization" of "information, culture, and money," called for creating a "Transparency International"-style rating system for disinformation; instituting "counter-propaganda editors" for newspapers; creating a "disinformation charter" for media and excluding "organizations that practice conscious deception"; tracking Kremlin networks and money back to pundits and think tanks; and creating public information campaigns. American and European newspapers, albeit belatedly, are now tracking down those networks and debunking propaganda. As for the rest, the censorship potential of charters, rating systems, and shunning all make me queasy.

Education (No 'Alternative Facts'), Fact Checking, Leadership

Fact-checking is essential but like whack-a-mole these days. The first line of defense has to be an informed, critical reader. Media literacy—critical thinking, the ability to recognize bias and spin, understanding the importance of breaking out of your own media bubble—should be taught in schools.

Good journalism should be recognized and encouraged as a public good. That means that democratically minded leaders need to accept scrutiny with minimally good grace (at least in public). Journalists need not only to check facts; they have to check themselves—correcting their own errors swiftly and publicly.

In Ukraine a group of reporters, journalism students, and teachers from Kyiv-Mohyla Academy run an ambitious website, Stopfake.org, that unmasks Russian-promoted fake news, in a sometimes bemused tone. In recent editions StopFake has debunked a story claiming that the city of Lviv was about to demolish the "Monument to the War Glory of the Soviet Army," and that Russian newspaper article about a Ukrainian government-run black market for organs.

The group is now raising broader public awareness with a weekly TV broadcast, podcasts, and online video digests. It is also offering training sessions to journalists in other countries. It's not clear whether StopFake has any audience in the eastern parts of the country—the main targets of Russian propaganda. Still, it is a model worth replicating and supporting in other countries. For the sake of credibility, journalism foundations should be the first funders tapped. (StopFake reports that it gets its funding from crowdsourcing and from "the international Renaissance Foundation, the Foreign Ministry of the Czech Republic, the British Embassy in Ukraine, and the Sigrid Rausing Trust.")

During the French election, Google helped underwrite a bilingual fact-checking effort that included thirty-seven news organizations. CrossCheck received some 500 stories from readers and jointly debunked sixty: Macron's campaign was not financed by the Saudis nor was Macron seen washing his hands after greeting a group of workers; Le Pen did not tweet an attack against a children's cartoon character for wearing a veil. First Draft News, the Google News Lab-financed nonprofit that organized the effort, is now reviewing what it learned, including, as First Draft's Claire Wardle told NiemanLab, whether "having organizations work together reinforces the idea that media is one big plot."[10]

Who Do You Trust?

Anyone who cares about democracy should find the results of a July 2017 Economist/YouGov poll chilling.[11] When asked if the courts should be able to "shut down media outlets for publishing or broadcasting stories that are biased or inaccurate," 28 percent of Americans (45 percent of Republicans, 25 percent of Independents, and 18 percent of Democrats) said yes, 29 percent said no, and 43 percent said they weren't sure. President Trump bears enormous responsibility for these frighteningly anti-democratic responses.

At a time when American journalism is doing some of the most extraordinary work that I have ever seen, we in the press still need to consider our own responsibility for a decline in credibility that predates Trump's election. In 1997, 53 percent of Americans polled by Gallup said they had had a "great deal" or "fair amount" of trust in the media to report the news fairly and accurately; by 2014 that number had fallen to 40 percent (it was down to 32 percent during last year's election).[12]

There are a lot of explanations. Americans, and citizens in all advanced countries, have also lost trust in churches, schools, banks, big business, the Supreme Court, and Congress. "The media" is not one entity by any means. Media and social media bubbles reinforce the perception that balance is an illusion or an outright trick—"you have your truth/bias, I have mine."

The days of Walter Cronkite are gone (and it turns out polling supports CBS's claim of his "most trusted" status). Nonpartisan news organizations, of which there are still a reassuring number, need to think seriously about what can be done to recover some of the lost ground. Reporters need to start by turning down the heat on social media. Twitter is just as much a publishing platform as a newspaper homepage or front page.

There is some (faintly) good news to be found in the polling. Gallup reported in June that 27 percent of Americans said they had "a great deal" or "quite a lot of confidence" in newspapers—up from last year's record low of 20 percent—versus 24 percent in television news and 16 percent in news from the internet.[13]

Editing the Internet?

A few days after the American elections--and long before we learned about the Russian ads, posts, and fake accounts--Mark Zuckerberg denied that fake news on Facebook played any role in skewing the results, calling it "a pretty crazy idea." Fierce public criticism, and criticism from inside Facebook, along with threats from Britain and Germany to punish internet companies for carrying hate speech or fake news have since persuaded Silicon Valley that it has no choice but to address the problem. In June 2017, the Bundestag passed a law that could fine social media companies up to €50 million if they fail to remove hate speech within twenty-four hours of it being flagged—raising legitimate concerns about censorship.

Last November, Google and Facebook announced that publishers of fake news would be barred from their advertising networks, although it turns out that it is simpler to ban sites pitching fake weight loss schemes than it is to figure out what exactly is a fake news website. Facebook has since made it easier for users to flag disputed stories and now refers frequently flagged stories to respected fact-checking organizations, including Politifact, the AP, and Factcheck.org, for review. If these sites judge the stories to be false, Facebook appends a banner and a link back to the fact-check site. Google has also added a fact-check feature and tag to some of its searches, explaining that "only publishers that are algorithmically determined to be an authoritative source of information will qualify for inclusion" in the list of its approved fact-checkers.[14] The tech companies have resisted sharing data with the fact-checkers on how the tags are affecting disputed stories' performance—whether they lessen the chance they will be clicked on or shared or are having the opposite effect.[15]

What these companies aspire to, of course, is an algorithm—rather than slow-moving humans—to edit out offensive or extremist content. But I fear allowing a machine to decide preemptively what language is merely foul and offensive versus what is foul, offensive, *and dangerous* (or at least dangerous to a company's bottom line) can too easily lead to the twenty-first century version of airbrushed Soviet photos. Who will even know when a thought or an image or a fact—or thousands of them—disappear?

Soft Power, Like We Really Mean It

On Capitol Hill a small but dedicated chorus has been calling for reinvigorating the US Cold War-era broadcasting system to push back against RT and the Kremlin's larger propaganda machine.[16] Worryingly, under a new "reform," the Voice of America (VOA) and the rest of the system are to be placed under the control of a new chief appointed by President Trump—rather than the bipartisan Broadcasting Board of Governors.[17] In June *Politico* reported that the White House was "eyeing" an ally of Steve Bannon, the president's former chief strategist and Breitbart executive chairman, for the job.

We have the best story to tell. But it is going to be a lot harder to push back against the Russian propaganda machine so long as the president of the most powerful democracy in the world is bashing the credibility of our independent media and validating so much of Vladimir Putin's anti-democratic worldview.

Harder, yes. Truth and real news are still the best defense—the only defense—against fake news, propaganda, and lies.

Carla Anne Robbins is the Marxe Faculty Director of the Master in International Affairs program and Clinical Professor of National Security Studies at Baruch College's Marxe School of Public and International Affairs and an adjunct senior fellow at the Council on Foreign Relations. An award-winning journalist and foreign policy analyst, Dr. Robbins was deputy editorial page editor at the *New York Times* and chief diplomatic correspondent at the *Wall Street Journal*. She has reported from Latin America, Europe, Russia, and the Middle East. At the *Journal* she shared in two Pulitzer Prizes—the 2000 Prize for National Reporting on the Post-Cold War defense budget and the 1999 Prize for International Reporting on the Russian financial crisis. She was also awarded the Edward Weintal Prize for Diplomatic Reporting, an Overseas Press Club Award and other prizes. Dr. Robbins is a graduate of Wellesley College, received a PhD in political science from U.C. Berkeley, and was a Nieman fellow at Harvard. She is a member of the Aspen Strategy Group.

[1] Peter Pomerantsev has written extensively about the Kremlin's new propagandists, including in his book *Nothing is True and Everything is Possible: The Surreal Heart of the New Russia* (New York: PublicAffairs, 2015).

[2] Zack Beauchamp, "Democrats Are Falling for Fake News About Russia," Vox, May 19, 2017, https://www.vox.com/world/2017/5/19/15561842/trump-russia-louise-mensch.

[3] Quoted in Peter Pomerantsev and Michael Weiss, "The Menace of Unreality: How the Kremlin Weaponizes People, Information and Money," *The Interpreter*, November 2014, http://www.interpretermag.com/wp-content/uploads/2014/11/The_Menace_of_Unreality_Final.pdf.

[4] "Counterfeit News Network," *CrossTalk*, June 30, 2017, https://www.rt.com/shows/crosstalk/394762-cnn-evidence-trump-journalism/.

[5] "'Putin killed reporters? Prove it!' – Trump to ABC show host," RT, December 21, 2015, https://www.rt.com/usa/326633-trump-putin-journalists-deaths/.

[6] Carla Anne Robbins, "The Validator-in-Chief," *The American Interest*, July 17, 2017, https://www.the-american-interest.com/2017/07/17/the-validator-in-chief/.

[7] "Trump's Tour, Geography Lessons and Who's Seth Rich," FAKEbook Live, May 25, 2017, https://www.youtube.com/watch?v=u6lQMTP4Jow.

[8] Ben Nimmo, "Hashtag Campaign #MacronLeaks," Medium, May 5, 2017, https://medium.com/dfrlab/hashtag-campaign-macronleaks-4a3fb870c4e8.

[9] Peter Pomerantsev and Michael Weiss, "The Menace of Unreality: How the Kremlin Weaponizes People, Information and Money," *The Interpreter*, November 2014, 40-43, http://www.interpretermag.com/wp-content/uploads/2014/11/The_Menace_of_Unreality_Final.pdf.

[10] Shan Wang, "The French Election Is Over. What's Next for the Google- and Facebook-Backed Fact-Checking Effort There?" NiemanLab, May 8, 2017, http://www.niemanlab.org/2017/05/the-french-election-is-over-whats-next-for-the-google-and-facebook-backed-fact-checking-effort-there/.

[11] The Economist/YouGov Poll, July 23-25, 2017, Question 88, Shutting Down the Media, https://d25d2506sfb94s.cloudfront.net/cumulus_uploads/document/u4wgpax6ng/econTabReport.pdf.

[12] "Americans' Trust in Mass Media Sinks to New Low," Gallup, September 14, 2016, http://news.gallup.com/poll/195542/americans-trust-mass-media-sinks-new-low.aspx.

[13] "In US, Confidence in Newspapers Still Low but Rising," Gallup, June 28, 2017, http://news.gallup.com/poll/212852/confidence-newspapers-low-rising.aspx.

[14] Justin Kosslyn and Cong Yu, "Fact Check Now Available in Google Search and News Around the World," The Keyword Google Blog, April 7, 2017, https://www.blog.google/products/search/fact-check-now-available-google-search-and-news-around-world/.

[15] Jason Schwartz, "Facebook Undermines Its Own Efforts to Fight Fake News," *Politico*, September 7, 2017, http://www.politico.com/story/2017/09/07/facebook-fake-news-social-media-242407.

[16] Ed Royce, "Countering Putin's Information Weapons of War," *Wall Street Journal*, April 14, 2015.

[17] Editorial Board, "A Big Change to US Broadcasting Is Coming—and It's One Putin Might Admire," *Washington Post*, December 9, 2016.

"Cyber weapons had given Putin a new tool, and new reach—a "short of war" weapon that the world has not figured out how to deter, or even how to respond to when deterrence fails."

—DAVID E. SANGER

Short of War: Cyber Conflict and the Corrosion of International Order

David E. Sanger
National Security Correspondent
The New York Times

O n Christmas week in 2016, the lights went out in Kiev.

It was not the "cyber Pearl Harbor" that American officials had warned against for so many years. The blackout was limited. But it gave a taste of what that scenario might look like. An automated "bot," installed by Russian hackers whose exact connections to the government are still murky, raced through the networks of the electric power supplier in Ukraine's capital. Workers were helpless in getting the lights back on. While the attack was not widespread, it was clearly intended as a signal to the government—one that said, "We own you"—and as a reminder to the residents of Kiev that Russia could easily turn off power to the capital of a country with which it has been in a low-level war for more than three years, mostly in the east.

Ukraine hardly needed the reminder. In 2014, President Vladimir Putin had already annexed Crimea, saying it rightfully belonged to Russia, of which it had been a part from 1783 until 1954. Then he sent equipment and troops, stripped of their normal uniforms, into the eastern part of the country and justified the action by declaring he was simply "defending the Russian-speaking population in the Donbass," the region closest to its border.

The cyber attack was simply an extension of that war, a reminder that there were ways to take the conflict to the capital and undermine the government of President Petro Poroshenko without sending a single tank into the city. Cyber weapons had given Putin a new tool, and new reach—a "short of war" weapon that the world has not figured out how to deter, or even how to respond to when deterrence fails.

Ukraine is Russia's petri dish for cyber conflict. Exactly a year before, the Russians had conducted a similar attack in a more remote region of the country. A study by American experts who flew in to analyze the attack concluded that the electric utilities recovered quickly in large part because their systems were so antiquated that they were able to turn the lights back on using big, manual switches that routed around computer controls. The American power grid, they warned, would likely not be as lucky.

Then, in June 2017, came another attack in Ukraine—this time not aimed at the power grid but at virtually every business, large and small, in the country. ATMs failed, along with the automatic radiation monitors at the old Chernobyl nuclear plant, where computers went offline. Some Ukrainian broadcasters briefly went off the air; when they came back, they could not report the news because their computer systems were seized by what appeared to be a ransomware notice. No one thought it was coincidental that the attack happened just before the holiday that marks the adoption, in 1996, of Ukraine's first constitution after its break from the Soviet Union.

And there was another feature of the attack: Russia used a hacking tool—called "Eternal Blue"—that had been stolen from the National Security Agency (NSA) sometime in the past few years. While the NSA had quietly warned Microsoft in March that a vulnerability in its old operating systems was likely to strike the world's computer networks, it had relayed nothing to the public. In fact, it had not even acknowledged to the world that the stolen code—published by a group called "The Shadow Brokers"—originated from the NSA's own software laboratories. Not surprisingly, Microsoft's attempts to patch it turned out to be insufficient. The Ukrainians, many of whom were using pirated copies of Microsoft's operating systems, never patched their systems. They were wide open to a crippling attack.

The Russians, in short, had taken a vulnerability in American-made software— stolen from the cyber arsenal of the United States—used it to build a custom-made weapon, and turned it on an adversary. They were hardly alone. They had taken a page from the playbook of the North Koreans, who had done the same thing with the same software flaw in May.

None of this surprised Dmytro Shymkiv, the former general manager of Microsoft's unit in Ukraine, who three years ago became President Poroshenko's cyber czar.

"We have a hot war in the Donbass and a cyber war in the capital," he said one evening in early July, sitting in his office in the presidential palace in Kiev. "It's happening every day. It is designed to destabilize and upend governments. And the rest of the world has barely noticed."

Certainly Americans barely noticed. They were preoccupied by a spreading investigation into the 2016 election, prompted by a very different form of cyber aggression. It was far more subtle than turning the lights out. American intelligence agencies concluded, first in October 2016 then again in early January 2017, that the Russian government had turned what began as a simple digital surveillance operation—hacking the Democratic National Committee (DNC)—into an influence campaign that took a page from the "active measures" the Soviets used so effectively in the Cold War. It had released the fruits of its intelligence gathering at key moments in the campaign. It had targeted the voter registration systems of more than twenty states, probing for vulnerabilities. The United States government had seen this coming and by the summer of 2016, the CIA had assembled evidence that Putin was directly behind it.

But President Obama said almost nothing about it in public, for fear of appearing too political. He worried that the DNC hack might prove to be just an opening shot—and that the Russians would come back on election day to attack actual vote-counting in critical states. While Obama warned Putin that this hack warranted major consequences, he took little direct action until weeks after the election was over, in his last days in office. He ejected thirty-five Russian diplomats and closed two Russian-owned facilities, the perfect nineteenth century diplomatic response to a twenty-first century challenge. There are widespread reports that he also set in motion a cyber response as a warning to the Russian leadership. If it has been executed, the evidence on the outside is sparse. Today, even some members of President Obama's administration concede the United States was slow to realize what the Russians were doing and then underreacted. Until Congress passed some mild sanctions in late July 2017, the Russian government paid no price.

The experiences over the past year in Ukraine, and beyond, raise fundamental questions. If Russia can destabilize an emerging nation like Ukraine without troops or tanks, is our traditional concept of national security outdated? If a broke and broken country like North Korea can reach for cheap, hard-to-trace cyber weapons to cripple a major American corporation, Sony Pictures Entertainment, does that mean everything we thought we understood about the traditional balance of power and deterrence must be questioned? If a technology that we convinced ourselves two decades ago would undermine the Communist Party in China, and trigger a democratic awakening in the most remote corners of the earth, is now routinely used to suppress dissent and undermine the foundations of the democratic process, do we really understand the power of what we have created?

If we cannot figure out, in real time, whether a hostile government is using our own networks to influence American elections, is the problem that we misunderstood the power of the tools we built or that we failed to imagine how other nations might turn them against us? Finally, and most importantly, are there technologies, norms, or political institutions that can deter and defend against the worst characteristics of the cyber revolution while preserving the best?

When the Aspen Strategy Group met in the summer of 2011 to consider for the first time the future of cyber conflict, its members could scarcely imagine what was to come. At that time, there was only anecdotal evidence of sustained state-against-state conflict in the digital realm. The previous summer, the first news stories had appeared citing persuasive evidence that a cyber weapon had been used against Iran's nuclear facilities and then gotten loose, spreading around the world. But the event was still wrapped in secrecy. While the United States and Israel seemed likely perpetrators, evidence was scarce.

In fact, the cyber threat was murky enough that some members of the group questioned whether we were right to focus so much time and energy on it. Compared to so many other transnational threats—pandemics, drug trafficking, human trafficking, and climate change—what made this one so dramatically different?

Six years later, doubters are now scarce. Hardly a day goes by without headlines about a major cyber attack; hardly a month goes by without evidence of a state-sponsored attack. The attack on Iran—later revealed to be part of a far broader American-Israeli program called "Olympic Games"—proved a turning point. Suddenly the prospect of using cyberspace to disable real-world systems seemed very real. The next step, automated cyber attacks that kill, cannot be that far away.

"Somebody has crossed the Rubicon," General Michael V. Hayden, the former director of the NSA and CIA, later said about the attack. "I don't want to pretend it's the same effect, but in one sense, at least, it's August 1945," when the world first saw the capabilities of a new weapon that was dropped over Hiroshima and Nagasaki.

That may have been a bit of hyperbole: as our colleague Joseph Nye has pointed out, most nuclear analogies do not transfer well to the world of cyber. While Olympic Games was a defining moment in the history of cyber conflict, in the end the United States only crashed a few hundred centrifuges at the Natanz nuclear facility and delayed the Iranians for a year or so. The cyber attack did not vaporize the place. Something similar played out after the US effort to use cyber and electronic warfare means to cripple North Korea's missile program. The effort bought some time but ultimately did not prevent the North Koreans from testing a missile in late July 2017 that could likely reach Los Angeles and beyond.

Cyber has been used as a short-of-war technology, at least so far. In the last four years of Barack Obama's presidency, and in the first year of Donald Trump's, it has become a favorite tool to intimidate, threaten, and undermine adversaries. For states that cannot take on the United States and its allies directly, it is the perfect weapon. Unlike nuclear arms, it can be used day-in and day-out. Its power can be dialed up or down, depending on the mission. Like a drone, it can be precisely calibrated to hit specific targets. And because cyber attacks have been historically hard to attribute, chances are that they can be used without fear of prompting immediate retaliation— or any retaliation at all. In the absence of any real concept of how to deter all but the most massive attacks, cyberspace has become, as Obama put it near the end of his presidency, "the wild, wild West."

He should know, because he made more use of covert cyber weapons than any American president before him. In addition to Iran and North Korea, the Islamic State became a major—and publicly announced—target of American cyber weapons. Yet, the more the US and other states used cyber techniques, the more the limitations of cyber became clear. What works to halt an adversary this week may prove useless next week, as vulnerabilities get discovered and networks get reconfigured. When the US and its allies went to wipe out the Islamic State's ability to recruit online, it discovered the videos simply reappeared. The rise of encryption made it possible for terror groups to stay a step ahead. And meanwhile, the United States discovered that cyber techniques could be used against us in ways we could scarcely have imagined in that 2011 Aspen meeting—to make Hollywood think twice about releasing a controversial movie, to embarrass a presidential candidate, to undermine confidence in the electoral system.

For that reason, it may be useful to break down the cyber attacks that have captured our attention into a few different categories, so that we can think about what kind we can live with; what kind pose a legal, political, or moral challenge; and what kind are truly a threat to American interests. Here are a few, in a less-than-comprehensive list designed to help us think about defining the challenge.

Cyber-Enabled Espionage. This describes most state-on-state cyber activity. The Chinese attack on the US Office of Personnel Management (OPM) is perhaps the most sophisticated example. The most detailed security-clearance records on more than twenty-one million Americans—their finances, medical histories, relationships (both spousal and non-spousal), their contacts—were extracted from lightly protected systems. When that information is merged with big-data techniques, it will give the Chinese the most detailed understanding of the personnel inside the US government that any foreign nation has ever had. But the US declined to name the Chinese publicly as the culprit. Meanwhile, General James Clapper, the director of national intelligence until earlier this year, conceded: "If I could have done it, I would have done it in a heartbeat."

This is a form of cyber operations that is unlikely to be regulated by political agreement. All nations spy on each other. Cyber techniques just make it possible on a grander scale, with more informative, granular results. The United States government has expressed outrage at the OPM theft but never called for agreed-upon international norms to limit such attacks—and probably never will.

Cyber-Enabled Theft. As Brad Smith of Microsoft points out, soon after Ben Franklin invented the post office, we had mail fraud. No sooner had the telegraph and telephone come along than we had wire fraud. So it should hardly have shocked us that the North Koreans figured out how to extract millions of dollars from the central bank of Bangladesh without ever breaking into its safes.

But the most vivid example of cyber-enabled theft was likely the work of Unit 61398, the People's Liberation Army unit that regularly stole intellectual property from American and European companies, often for the benefit of Chinese state-owned firms. It was in this arena that the Obama administration made its greatest progress, in an agreement with President Xi Jinping in September 2015. They reached what they called a "common understanding" that neither the US nor China would engage in state-sponsored cyber intrusions to poach intellectual property, and they would work together to seek "international rules of the road for appropriate conduct in cyberspace."

The agreement came together because there were already well-understood international rules about intellectual property theft from a pre-cyber age. Nonetheless, there was considerable skepticism two years ago that the agreement would hold. Today, there is now some evidence that the frequency and scope of Chinese intellectual-property theft has declined, even if the follow-on rules-of-the-road have been slow to develop.

Now the Chinese are becoming far more active in the diplomacy of norm-setting, and their agenda is no secret: they want rules that will limit information flows that threaten the stability of the Communist Party and that will enable Beijing to shape cyberspace to its military and messaging advantage. The country's new information security law requires data on the Chinese to be stored in China—a major step toward such control. But they are also successfully browbeating American firms, including Apple, into taking down tools that would enable the Chinese people to communicate secretly and securely.

Cyber Exploitation and Attack. This comes closest to the common definitions of cyber conflict, if not cyberwar. In these attacks, computers are used to do what previously could be accomplished only by saboteurs. The attacks on Iran's centrifuges and the "left of launch" attacks on North Korea's missiles are prime examples. But so was the North Korean attack on Sony Pictures, which destroyed 70 percent of the firm's computer systems—all in retaliation for a truly bad movie called "The Interview" that imagined the assassination of Kim Jong-un, the North Korean leader. But the list goes on: Iran's attacks on Saudi Aramco and the Russian attacks on Ukraine's power grid are other examples. While the United Nations Group of Governmental Experts has generally agreed on a set of peacetime cyber norms, including that nations should not attack each other's critical infrastructure in peacetime, nations have been deeply reluctant to discuss what that means.

The hardest questions have barely begun to be addressed. Should the act of placing "implants" in an adversary's electric grid, or gas pipeline system, or cell-phone network, be considered mere espionage? Or is that more akin to "preparing the battlefield" in case covert action, or an outright attack, is required in the future? The uncomfortable fact is that the same implant can serve all those purposes—it can be used for espionage or, with different code, for attack. So when the Chinese were discovered to have placed implants in the software system that controls many of the gas pipelines that crisscross the United States, many in the government were alarmed, fearing that Beijing was making preparations to cut off the heat in time of war. In fact, the Chinese may simply have been stealing the blueprints for computer-controlled gas pipelines. Or, they may have been doing both.

The issue is complicated by the fact that seeding foreign computer networks with American-created implants is the daily work of the NSA and United States Cyber Command, as Edward Snowden's revelations have proven. Over the past decade the United States has placed tens of thousands of such implants in computer networks around the world—as a form of defense and to lay the groundwork for offensive action, if ever so ordered by the president. It was through these implants that the US and Britain first got wind of the Russian hack into the DNC's computer systems. But such implants were also key to "Nitro Zeus," a vast American-led program to bring down Iran's infrastructure if war broke out.

Cyber-Enabled Information Warfare. A year ago, this category barely seemed worth mention. After the Russia attack, however, it is at the forefront of the American national consciousness.

There is nothing new about information warfare. Stalin used it. In the 1940s disinformation was rife, and what we today call "fake news" was often inserted into newspapers around America. But cyber technologies have put these techniques on steroids. With skillful use of Twitter and Facebook, leaked documents, fake news stories, or just plain spin can be broadcast to millions or focused on key demographic groups. Bots have automated the process, making it possible to spread a message to millions or troll someone with a different view. Russia has mastered these techniques, deploying them in Europe and the Baltics for years.

So the biggest surprise from the Russia hack is that we were surprised. A failure of imagination on the part of the FBI in 2015 meant that the evidence of Russian intelligence agencies operating inside the DNC's email system was dismissed as ordinary intelligence gathering. And by the time it became clear, in the summer of 2016, that much more was at stake—that the Russians were leaking the committee's emails, and then John Podesta's, for political effect—the Obama administration was uncertain how to respond.

Here, the scope for government action is somewhat limited. There are enormous First Amendment concerns surrounding any system in which government officials rule on what is "fake news" and what is acceptable discourse. (The risk is made plain by the fact that President Trump has already hijacked the term "fake news" to describe any story he does not like.) But Facebook and Google are already stepping into a role they resisted for years: applying editorial judgment to what gets posted in an effort to weed out news that is obviously fake, bots that seek to deceive, and trolling that violates their terms of service.

It is a start, but these efforts will likely prove insufficient. The Russian activity in the Dutch, German, and French elections demonstrate an increasingly subtle understanding of how to use social engineering techniques to manipulate voters. In short, we face at least two distinct challenges: a technical issue of staying ahead of the hackers and a political question of whether we want Facebook, Google, and Twitter deciding what constitutes legitimate political speech.

There is a parallel problem in which the government does have a legitimate role: setting standards for the integrity of the voting system. Russia's probing of the registration systems used by more than twenty states and of the software designed by contractors for voting machines should have been a major wake-up call for the US. It suggests that in the next election cycle we may not be able to declare with such authority that the vote count itself was not affected by a foreign power. But setting those standards means overcoming tremendous suspicions in some states that the federal government is attempting to take over what has been, historically, a state function.

The Long-Run Challenges

There is a growing consensus that to tame the digital beast we need three things: better defenses, stronger norms, and effective deterrence.

Defenses are a mixture of technological leaps, training to improve "digital hygiene," and the creation of resilience. Ukraine is a case study in bad hygiene; the attacks that brought its systems down in June could have easily been avoided. The improvements made in the energy sector and the financial industry in the past few years are a testament to the value of resilience: everyone needs a backup system, and then a backup to the backup.

Norms are more complicated. There is not much to be gained from trying to set norms around digital surveillance: governments spy on each other, and always will. In contrast, there is plenty of room to build on the success with China in setting norms surrounding the theft of intellectual property. Here, laws and regulations from the non-cyber world can usually be translated to the digital sphere—and significant progress has already been made. The agreements not to target the critical infrastructure of other nations in peacetime is a building-block. But one nation's "critical infrastructure" is another's legitimate target. It is worth pursuing a "Digital Geneva Convention"—modeled on the process that the Red Cross created—that would set norms of behavior without an endless negotiation among governments.

Deterrence is perhaps the most elusive problem. As Thomas P. Bossert, the president's homeland security adviser, put it recently at the Aspen Security Forum, "Right now I would say that there's not one single price that one single bad actor on the internet is paying that's high enough, both punitive or preventative." Indeed in each of the major hacks described above—from North Korea's attack on Sony to Russia's attacks on Ukraine and the United States—the penalties were barely noticeable. That has to change. The options are numerous—from deterrence-by-denial-of-success to deterrence-by-fear-of-response. As always, some of the most effective deterrents to cyber attacks lie in non-cyber responses. The Trump administration has commissioned a review of deterrence strategy; it is due later this month.

There are other major challenges as well, which eventually must also be addressed:

Overcoming the Stifling Secrecy Around Cyber. In the nuclear age everything about nuclear weapons was classified: how they were made, where they were stored, the procedures that must be cleared to authorize launch. But the United States admitted it possessed nuclear weapons, described their effects, and openly debated the strategy for using them. Thanks to that debate, the strategy changed enormously. In the 1950s General Douglas MacArthur wanted to use the weapons against the North Koreans and the Chinese. Today, there is a general understanding that the US would turn to its nuclear arsenal only as a matter of national survival.

Astoundingly, our government has refused to engage in a similar debate about the use of its cyber arsenal. In part, this is because the weapons themselves often arise from inside American intelligence agencies, and intelligence agencies are reflexively secretive. In part, it is because presidents want the option of turning to that arsenal for covert operations, which must be deniable.

But we have reached the point where secrecy is impeding our ability as a nation to decide how we want to use these enormously powerful tools. Every time the US uses a cyber weapon against another state, it creates a precedent that other nations may use—rightly or wrongly—to justify attacks on us or on our allies. Yet that tradeoff is rarely discussed.

We need some radical transparency. American citizens, and the world, need to know the rules of engagement for the use of cyber weapons. There is precedent for this: President Obama, midway through his time in office, moved unmanned aerial vehicles—"drones"—partly out of the classified world and made public the rules for employing them to minimize the harm to innocents. He never took the next step of doing the same for cyber weapons.

One place to start would be a public announcement when the NSA or other government entities lose track of cyber "vulnerabilities" they exploit to make weapons. If the United States lost track of a missile, or its key components, and it were launched back at an American city, there would be hell to pay. But when the same happened in the Wannacry case—based on an NSA-discovered vulnerability called "Eternal Blue"—there was no admission of responsibility. The NSA was hardly the only one to be blamed for the fact that a piece of its arsenal was turned into a weapon. But it had a moral obligation to help mitigate the damage. It largely failed.

Addressing Encryption. President Obama's bipartisan commission on reform of the NSA, created in the wake of the Snowden disclosures, got it right in 2014 when it said the United States should "fully support and not undermine efforts to create encryption standards" and "not in any way subvert, undermine, weaken, or make vulnerable generally available commercial software."

The evidence since—from public statements to leaks of US government practices—suggests that there is no unanimity around that recommendation. Law enforcement understandably seeks a "back door" to crack terrorists' communications or help locate a kidnap victim, but no one has yet explained how that back door—essentially a deliberately designed vulnerability—would not be exploited by nations, criminals, or ingenious teenagers. Yet without total confidence in the security of our communications, the fundamental promise of the internet and the digital age will be undermined. One only needs to look at the hesitance after last year's events to put anything sensitive into an email or text.

Moreover, American efforts to limit encryption will be exploited by the Chinese and the Russians, among others, who want to seal off any possibility that those who disagree with the government can communicate in private. There are risks, of course, to impossible-to-crack encryption. But there are also huge risks to failing to encrypt. Just ask OPM, which left the most sensitive details of the lives of almost 7 percent of the American population completely unencrypted, a gift to the Chinese government.

Getting a Handle on the "Internet of Things." Soon the dividing line between a cybersecurity problem and an everyday problem will blur to nothingness. When your car, your refrigerator, and your Alexa are all connected, the virtual and physical worlds completely meld. We are looking forward to the benefits, from driverless cars to a fridge that orders milk and eggs directly from Amazon. But we have not thought sufficiently about the fact that billions of new internet connections mean billions of new attack surfaces. The chances of repeating the OPM error, by not realizing what data we have made vulnerable, are enormous. The opportunity for malicious activity—reprogramming that car to drive into a crowd, or a nuclear plant—escalates exponentially.

We need to think about the things we never want connected to the web. Our voting machines. Our nuclear weapons. Maybe the Alexa in the living room.

If there is a lesson from the past six years, since this group last discussed cyber issues, it is this: if there is a vulnerability, someone will exploit it. We just need greater imagination, so that unlike the Ukrainian power operators or presidential candidates, we are not again taken by surprise.

David E. Sanger is National Security Correspondent for *The New York Times* and one of the newspaper's senior writers. With a team of his *Times* colleagues, he was the winner of the 2017 Pulitzer Prize in International Reporting, the third in Mr. Sanger's 35-year career at the *Times*. He is also the author of two bestsellers on foreign policy and national security: *The Inheritance: The World Obama Confronts and the Challenges to American Power* (2009) and *Confront and Conceal: Obama's Secret Wars and Surprising Use of American Power* (2012). He served as the *Times'* Tokyo Bureau Chief, Washington Economic Correspondent, White House correspondent during the Clinton and Bush Administrations and Chief Washington Correspondent. Mr. Sanger spent six years in Tokyo, writing about the emergence of Japan as a major American competitor, and then the country's humbling recession. In Washington, Mr. Sanger writes on a range of diplomatic and national security issues, and especially issues of nuclear proliferation and the rise of cyber conflict among nations. In stories in the *Times* and in *Confront and Conceal*, he revealed the story of Olympic Games, the code name for the most sophisticated cyber attack in history, the American-Israeli effort to sabotage Iran's nuclear program with the Stuxnet worm. His journalistic pursuit of the origins of Stuxnet became the subject of a major documentary, "Zero Days." A 1982 graduate of Harvard College, Mr. Sanger co-teaches "Central Challenges in American National Security, Strategy and the Press" at the Kennedy School of Government. He is a member of the Aspen Strategy Group.

"The widespread diffusion of technology in the global marketplace, while fueling astonishing economic growth, has also touched off an innovation race among advanced economies that poses a new and unprecedented threat to the primacy of the liberal world order."

—CHRISTOPHER KIRCHHOFF

An Even Flatter World: How Technology Is Remaking the World Order

Christopher Kirchhoff
Partner
Defense Innovation Unit X
US Department of Defense

The cover of Thomas Friedman's 2005 treatise on globalization, *The World Is Flat: A Brief History of the Twenty-First Century*, depicts two tall ships reaching the edge of the earth. One vessel has started tumbling off the face of the known world. The other struggles to turn back. Painted by Navy veteran Ed Miracle, the image connotes the perils of the new landscape of global and economic interdependence in which old powers must find new ways to navigate, lest they fall off the edge. Miracle titled his striking visage, "I told you so."[1]

This arresting backdrop helped propel Friedman's tome to popular acclaim. Twelve years later, "I told you so" is again relevant as a parable for how technology is disrupting the liberal world order. The "flat world" of economic interconnection Friedman described—in which the computing revolution, software, and global fiber-optic cables produced whole new flows of commerce and technology exchange—has today paved a new global reality. While Friedman focused on how Bangalore suddenly became an economic suburb of Silicon Valley, twelve years later these interconnections are flattening global power on a scale with few parallels in history.

The sum of this shift has turned the world we recently knew into something else altogether. The discontinuities are striking, with the following data points characterizing how the liberal world order's traditional sources of economic and military strength are now perversely contributing to the military, technological, and economic might of its adversaries:

- Free trade and open boarders, long assumed to draw global talent to innovation hubs within the US and EU, has now turned these hubs into export centers, leveling the global playing field for the five new technology areas that are primary enablers of future state power: machine learning/artificial intelligence, autonomy, commercial space, information technology, and biotechnology and the life sciences.

- As of 2016, Chinese firms are now investing in over 10 percent of all US venture capital deals. This means Chinese firms and state companies have likely seen 30 percent of all US venture opportunities. In today's tech economy, China is in effect able to engage in tech transfer from the epicenter of American innovation in a way that is not regulated by the Committee on Foreign Investment in the United States (CFIUS), the sole body able to block commercial acquisitions that pose a vital threat to US national security.

- As an illustration of how innovation has shifted from liberal tech centers to illiberal manufacturing centers, take autonomous aircraft. While computer scientists at MIT pioneered the first operating systems and physical prototypes for autonomous drones in the early 2000s, today 85 percent of global consumer aero vehicles, as well as their militarized versions, are manufactured in China. The Chinese firm DJI produces more than 90 percent of drones now being used by ISIS to disrupt US military operations in Raqqa and Mosul.

- Microelectronic supply chains are now so robust that all but 4 percent of the components in one of the US military's most advanced electronic warfare systems—the Aegis-class destroyer—are available today on the global market.

Each of these data points are discussed in further detail below.

The world, in short, has grown flatter still, with global flows of trade, technology, and talent leveling the playing field far beyond the landscape Thomas Friedman narrated to readers in 2005. The widespread diffusion of technology in the global marketplace, while fueling astonishing economic growth, has also touched off an innovation race among advanced economies that poses a new and unprecedented threat to the primacy of the liberal world order. Even non-state groups such as ISIS are using the global technology market to procure tactical tools—such as quadcopter drones with advanced electro-optics—that offer surprising operational competitiveness with US special forces units, who are forced to call off raids when detected in advance by drones available today on Amazon.

Changing Technology Landscape

The way innovation happens today is fueling a new reality. The global consumer market, which now generates revenues of $25 trillion annually, is an increasingly powerful determinant of geo-economic affairs. Yet despite its prominence in structuring how states interact with one another, the global technology economy is under-theorized in contemporary accounts of the liberal world order and the prospects for that order to thrive or decline in the years ahead.

Today the EU and US together comprise the single largest economy and have substantial leads in most indices of innovation. They are home to multinational firms that have enormous influence on how people buy and use technological goods around the world. Their universities continue to lead in nearly all measures of R&D productivity. Take the example of smartphones, which mediate most people's interaction with news, knowledge, and connectivity. Ninety-six percent of global operating systems on smartphones worldwide are either iOS or Android, a market-mover dynamic that effectively allows US firms to influence the global architecture on user privacy, encryption, and the market structure of telecommunications and app development—an under-appreciated lever of influence as an additional two billion people in developing nations gain access to the internet in the next five years.

In this way the consumer market is an important proxy for global power. Unlike past eras where the US defense industrial base had a virtual monopoly on advanced technology, today the commercial technology economy is many times larger than the defense sector. Both Google and Apple are each larger by market capitalization than the entire US defense industry. While in the past US defense labs and advanced technology organs such as DARPA fielded military systems that were three generations ahead of what was available on the commercial market, today the US military is often the "fast-follower," learning how to integrate innovations available on the commercial market back into military systems.

At the same time, many countries outside the liberal world order are making strides in their capacity to innovate on their own. Often, they are helped along in this pursuit by the open-tech economies of the US and EU. As previously mentioned, China is now investing in over 10 percent of US venture capital deals. China's global foreign direct investment topped $200 billion in 2016. From 2010-2016, Chinese investors participated in over 1,000 venture deals outside of China. This included thirty-nine investments in augmented and virtual reality, forty-six in financial technology, including blockchain—a potentially revolutionary encryption application—thirty-four in US start-ups at the forefront of artificial intelligence, and $342 million alone in 2016 deals with nineteen robotics companies.

The global architecture that enables investment dollars to flow into the venture ecosystem is not designed to mitigate the national security implications that stem from these investments into enabling technologies. Because the US economy is open, foreign investors are able to access the newest and most relevant technologies and thereby gain experience with them at the same rate as the US. The primary tool the government has to block or mitigate foreign investment is the CFIUS. However, since the CFIUS reviews specific deals on a case-by-case basis, and only deals that involve a controlling interest by foreign investors, the CFIUS does not effectively regulate venture investment. The other principal tool to inhibit sensitive technology transfer is export control. Much as with the CFIUS, export controls can be used to prevent the loss of known advanced technologies to known adversaries. But they are not designed to govern the control of early-stage technologies.

Commercial-Military Strategy

The technology sector and its global interdependencies thus constitute an enormous opportunity and considerable liability for advanced industrial democracies interested in furthering the liberal world order. On the one hand, centers of innovation within the liberal world order are powerful motors for economic integration and globalism (US education system, H1-B visas, Stanford). But these very clusters of innovation are also a way for illiberal adversaries to quickly level the playing field in both military and economic terms (i.e., Chinese military's use of technology to asymmetrically blunt US power projection in the South China Sea; Chinese national investment campaigns capitalizing on US discoveries in artificial intelligence, robotics, and biotech).

In a telling example, the balance of the recreational drone market has already begun to shift from the US to China. Dà-Jiāng Innovations Science and Technology Company, commonly known as DJI, controls roughly 70 percent of the worldwide recreational drone market. In the past, Chinese firms often relied on copying US products. But DJI is clearly innovating. The firm's latest drones include features based on cutting-edge computer vision technology that US competitors have not yet incorporated. DJI is also prioritizing research and development, committing 25 percent of its workforce to its R&D efforts. With the company's headquarters located in China's high-tech manufacturing hub in Shenzhen, DJI's engineers are able to quickly test and iteratively manufacture new prototypes.

A few clicks on Amazon delivers the fruit of these innovations into the hands of consumers.[2] DJI's "Phantom 4" drone comes equipped with a "1-inch 20MP CMOS sensor with gimbal-stabilized 4K60/20MP imaging," a drone camera with "redundant sensors and four directions of obstacle avoidance," "gimbal stabilization technology," and a "hover function that allows capture of smooth aerial footage."

At the same time, China is pursuing broad reforms of its military, in part to better integrate civilian technological advancements into the People's Liberation Army (PLA). Toward that end, China established the Civil-Military Integration Development Commission (CMIDC) in early 2017, which is responsible for implementing a national strategy of civil-military integration under President Xi Jinping's direction. The CMIDC is focusing on promoting dual-use technologies and improving the PLA's capacity to adopt civilian technologies. For example, a senior Chinese military official recently stated that the PLA should adopt an approach of "shared construction, shared enjoyment, and shared use" of artificial intelligence alongside the commercial sector. These moves suggest that China is positioning the PLA to rapidly integrate civilian advances in AI and other strategic technologies.

Non-state actors are also quickly adopting commercial technology, creating new and evolving threats to the US and its allies. The Islamic State of Iraq and the Levant (ISIS) has been employing small, commercially available drones in combat against coalition-backed forces in Iraq and Syria since at least 2014. The ISIS path to expanded employment of drones parallels our own development history: it has moved from using drones as reconnaissance tools to employing them as weapons. At first, ISIS used embedded cameras on drones to survey battlefields and surrounding areas. Then it used its drones as suicide technologies. In October 2016, Kurdish forces in northern Iraq were dissembling a small drone they had shot down when it exploded, killing two Kurdish fighters. Since then, ISIS has further adapted commercial drones to operate as single-mission flying bombs that drop small, grenade-sized munitions.

During some of the fiercest fighting near Mosul in February 2017, coalition officials reported encountering ten to fifteen ISIS drone attacks by per day. As fighting shifts from Mosul to Raqqa, ISIS continues to use drones to target ammunition depots and logistics hubs. Researchers in Iraq even discovered mission checklists in a captured drone workshop, suggesting that for each mission ISIS fighters are recording and reporting mission type (spy, bombing, training); location (city, province); drone components (motor, bomb ignition); and success or failure.

New Enabling Technologies

What does this mean? Technology diffusion is creating a flatter world that advantages both state and non-state actors competing with the liberal world order. Whereas a generation ago the US and EU could presume to be at the leading edge of discovery and innovation on both the commercial and military front, today the technological underpinnings of geopolitical power accrue differently. The race is more about broad classes of "enabling technologies" that open whole new fronts of economic and military competition than "point technologies" that grant asymmetric advantage. In the 1950s and 1960s, Lockheed Skunkworks gave the US the U-2 and SR-71. Yet exquisite stealth technology today, including fifth-generation fighter aircraft, can potentially be defeated by new kinds of low-cost sensing systems based on land and in space.

Artificial intelligence and machine learning is potentially the most important enabling technology today. The learning algorithms that power popular voice-assistants like Amazon's Alexa and Apple's Siri can be equally put to use mining geospatial data to identify military targets. Across many metrics, China is only slightly behind the US in the development of artificial intelligence. Estimates suggest 43 percent of the world's AI scientists reside in China. As of October 2016, China's publication of journal articles on deep learning exceeded that of the United States. American researchers still hold the most AI-related patent submissions in absolute terms, but Chinese researchers have increased their submissions by almost 200 percent over the last several years. China also has endogenous advantages that could enable it to become the world leader in AI. Refining the deep-learning algorithms underpinning AI will likely rely on vast amounts of data, which China has in abundance.

Seeking to capitalize on early gains, Chinese firms, such as Baidu and Tencent, have opened AI laboratories in Silicon Valley. Simultaneously, China's Thousand Talents Plan is attracting talented foreign researchers to work in China by offering funding and laboratory space for AI efforts. Possibly in response to these shifting incentives, talented AI executives and researchers have already jumped ship from the US for China. As one prominent example, Qi Lu—a recognized AI expert—left Microsoft for Baidu in January.

The Chinese government unveiled a detailed AI roadmap in July 2017. Under the new policy, China aspires to achieve AI parity with the US by 2020 and become the world leader in AI by 2030. The defeat of the world's top-ranked player of the board game Go by Google's AI-based program in May 2017, is widely seen as a wake-up call in China. Some have even called it China's "Sputnik moment," prompting new attention and funding for AI. Taking cues from this high-level guidance, many Chinese local governments have already begun to announce policies to incentivize further AI research, including billions of dollars in local funding for AI-related ventures, at the very moment when government investment in R&D is retrenching in both the US and Europe.

Relative Competition

The American strategist Richard Danzig notes in this volume that the survival of the liberal order will significantly depend on the relative performances of liberal and authoritarian states.[3] Since the Second World War, the core of the liberal world order—states in Western Europe and North America—have benefited from a degree of technology overmatch powered by open societies with free-market economies. This overmatch can no longer be presumed. The structure of technological discovery is evolving, with interchange between liberal and illiberal states defining a new front of global economic activity. In this new world, the very supply chains and globally distributed R&D enterprises that fuel advanced economies are also driving the militaries of the US and China toward battlefield parity at an astonishing rate.

Technology—once an unmistakable comparative advantage of the liberal world order—now almost equally empowers those who seek its undoing.

Christopher Kirchhoff is one of three partners overseeing the Pentagon's Silicon Valley Office, Defense Innovation Unit X, and its $250 million investment portfolio harnessing emerging commercial technology for national security innovation. Previously as Director for Strategic Planning at the National Security Council, he was the NSC's lead strategist on technology. Earlier he served as Special Assistant to General Martin E. Dempsey, the Chairman of the Joint Chiefs of Staff. Dr. Kirchhoff led General Dempsey's strategy unit, was his point person on the Ebola response, and was the first to inform him of Edward Snowden. Dr. Kirchhoff also served in the White House Chief of Staff's office as Senior Advisor to Presidential Counselor John Podesta and is the author of four landmark government reports: the NSC's after-action review of Ebola, the White House report on Big Data and Privacy, the Space Shuttle Columbia Accident Investigation report, and the U.S. government history *Hard Lessons: The Iraq Reconstruction Experience,* coined "the Iraq Pentagon Papers" by the *New York Times.* He has been awarded the Secretary of Defense Medal for Outstanding Public Service and the Civilian Service Medal for hazardous duty in Iraq. From 2011-2014, he was the highest ranking openly gay advisor in the U.S. military. Dr. Kirchhoff graduated with highest honors in History and Science from Harvard College and holds a doctorate in politics from Cambridge University, where he was a Gates Scholar.

---

[1] In an amusing aside, Miracle contested the publisher Farrar, Straus and Giroux's copyright for "I told you so" in the US and Britain, settling out of court for an undisclosed sum and illustrating that while the world may be getting flatter, it still contains many lawyers.

[2] https://www.amazon.com/DJI-Quadcopter-Starters-Hardshell-Backpack/dp/B01N52W70O/ref=sr_1_3?ie=UTF8&qid=1501166905&sr=8-3&keywords=dji+phantom+4+pro

[3] Richard Danzig, "An Irresistible Force Meets a Moveable Object: The Technology Tsunami and the Liberal World Order," Aspen Strategy Group, December 2017.

"Privacy is not simply a value unto itself—it is a prerequisite of freedom in the face of a totalitarian state or controlling private entity. Its erosion undermines the liberal order."

—RICHARD DANZIG

An Irresistible Force Meets a Moveable Object: The Technology Tsunami and the Liberal World Order

Richard Danzig
Senior Fellow
Johns Hopkins Applied Physics Lab

Twenty-first century technologies bring immense benefit and cannot be rolled back. But these technologies present new challenges and intensify certain problems for American democracy and the liberal world order.

I have elsewhere discouraged any pretension that we should rely on a particular prediction when we consider complex, long-run situations.[1] Technology induces conflicting currents. An assessment of the resultant from these forces can hardly be more confident than a guess about where a hurricane will make landfall. Moreover, technology is just one factor in our future and will interact with, be affected by, and itself affect other cultural, political, economic, and natural factors, producing a diversity of outcomes in different times and places.

Nonetheless, this essay argues that, even amidst many counter-currents, present technologies push in certain directions, that these directions can be described, and that an analysis that describes possible outcomes can illuminate our choices, our challenges, and our possible futures.

The invention and proliferation of the printing press and Galileo's use of the telescope undermined the church. The industrial revolution gave birth to capitalist and Marxist economies and greatly enhanced the power of the state. In our own lifetimes, birth control technologies combined with other forces have encouraged a fundamental rethinking of women's roles in society, overturning views and practices maintained for millennia. To this observer, the soundest expectation is that the present technology tsunami will have similar transformative impacts on the theory and practice of American liberal democracy and on the trajectory it has followed since the Second World War seeking to achieve a liberal world order.

That there is a technology tsunami can hardly be doubted. Digital, silicon-based information technologies dominate present discussions, but other technologies are developing as rapidly and have analogous transformative capabilities. No one can accurately predict the causes, character, and scope of the resulting revolutions, but promising and already robust technologies that may have great impact include additive manufacturing, artificial intelligence, big data analytics, "new biology" focused below the molecular level, nanotechnology and new materials, robotics and unmanned systems, quantum computing, operations in space, and systems for creating virtual realities.[2] The rate of invention, adaptation, and dissemination in all these technologies has risen, is rising, and can be expected to continue to rise.[3] This is because information and communication technology breakthroughs empower other technologies. Powerful, relatively easy-to-use devices and instruments are simplifying invention, communication, collaboration, and proliferation of ideas, tools, and products. These trends are amplified by increases in world population, the spread of technological literacy, and the expansion of capital markets.[4]

Technology often functions as an intensifier. When, for example, it makes communication and calculation faster, it serves as a means for all ends—good, ill, important, or trivial.[5] However, as the historical examples cited at the outset suggest, it also has broad effects that taken as a totality challenge the status quo in political and social institutions.

These pages sketch four ways in which I think the modern technological tsunami is likely to fundamentally challenge the liberal order.[6] I start at the level of the individual and his or her participation in democratic processes, move to terrorist groups and private corporations and then to nation-states, and conclude by highlighting rising risks of accidents and unintended emergent effects.[7]

1. Changing Conceptions of the Individual and of Individuals' Participation in Democratic Processes. Readers may object that changes in our concepts of the power and democratic participation of individuals, however important and interesting, should not be a subject of focus in a book concerned with international affairs. However, for a liberal system of thought, concepts of individuality and of individuals' participation in democratic decision-making are foundational. Technological changes will challenge these principles and to the extent the challenges force revisions in our practices and our thinking, they will reshape America's values, power, and priorities in the international order. Moreover, if—as is most likely—other countries respond to the same technology opportunities and challenges with less deference to individual rights, the resulting differences may intensify international tensions and force new security and societal decisions upon us. This section sketches some fundamental changes that I think present these challenges.

A core concept of Western individualism is that each individual is the best judge of his or her own interests. We aim to reign over ourselves—to be our own sovereigns. Moreover, we believe that free debate and free electoral processes are the best means through which individuals weigh competing priorities and find consensus around majority views. America instantiates this liberal ideal, and it is at the core of the example we offer to the world.

We have long recognized flaws in this model, but, notwithstanding its imperfections, the basic structure has stood since the beginning of our republic. Technology, the great intensifier, now is widening cracks in these foundational concepts. This is because of a triad of developments: (a) modern technologies make it almost inevitable that individuals create huge trails of data, and this data is routinely recorded; (b) when mined by sophisticated algorithms and paired with modern means of communication, this knowledge permits prediction and manipulation of individual choices; and (c) in ever-widening domains, machines are better decision-makers than humans.

It is now a familiar fact that your shopping (both online and through credit card purchases), your travels (tracked through your cell phone and car, as well as by virtue of your tickets and tolls), and your book and movie choices (including from your cable on-demand requests) are all well known. Less recognized is that with ten Facebook "likes" as inputs, an algorithm predicts a subject's other preferences better than the average work colleague, with seventy likes better than a friend, with 150 likes better than a family member, and with 300 likes better than a spouse.[8]

These algorithmic capabilities produce many consequences. In modern campaigns mass communication is dying and being replaced by targeted messages crafted to appeal to individuals' identities, psychologies, and predispositions.[9] David Reiser writes:

> Not only can machines predict what product you would prefer, but they can also predict how best to portray the product (or candidate) the machine's owner wants you to prefer, which (in conjunction with the absence of limits . on campaign financing) means that a candidate with effectively unlimited resources can effectively buy votes (not all, but all those in the persuadable category) ... on the basis of algorithms tied to past preferences. At a minimum, it fundamentally alters the electoral process in a liberal democracy from one focused on the collective evaluation of a common message (obviously, with some qualifications/tailoring) to a highly-individualized process... . If

everyone is listening to a different drummer, how do you get people marching together to face large scale problems, whether internal or national security/ foreign policy? Put differently, how much of contemporary gridlock is not just a function of structural flaws in our system of government, but also a breakdown in the primary process of uniting to address particular generally-acknowledged problems?[10]

This fragmentation and manipulation is intensified by internet technologies that permit communication immediately, at scale, anonymously, individually, and inexpensively.[11]

Elections have always, in some measure, been about technological mastery and manipulation. The printing press empowered influential pamphlets and newspapers from the revolution to our time. Franklin Roosevelt, Winston Churchill, and Adolph Hitler were masters of radio. John Kennedy owed much of his electoral success to television, Barack Obama to email and Facebook, and Donald Trump to Twitter. But as the power of technology grows, the significance of technology mastery grows concomitantly. The variables of human choices become less independent and less critical, while the variable of technological mastery becomes more dominant.

While the significance of personal decision-making erodes, our deference to machine capabilities is increasing. The more efficacious machines are in assessing inputs and predicting desires, the more we delegate to them.[12] As unsupervised machine learning grows more prevalent, machine decision-making moves beyond our comprehension. In this situation, if we are to benefit from the machine's work, it is not only its development but also its output that becomes unsupervised. For example, when a New York hospital fed clinical data to a central computing system, administrators were surprised to find that the system provided sounder than human predictions of schizophrenia in patients. Hospital administrators cannot determine the computer's basis for these judgments.[13]

Noting Facebook's predictive power and our expanded use of biometric devices to assess, report on, and control individual health, Yuval Noah Harari concludes:

> Liberalism sanctifies the narrating self, and allows it to vote in the polling stations, in the supermarket and in the marriage market. For centuries this made good sense because though the narrating self believed in all kinds of fictions and fantasies, no alternative knew me better. Yet once we have a system that really does know me better, it would be foolhardy to leave authority in the hands of the narrating self.[14]

Of course, one may object that we retain the freedom to reject the machine's outcome. But we are commonly seduced into rarely exercising that power, and even when we might want to intervene, imperatives for speed and accuracy may cause us to forgo human decision as too slow, too ill-informed, and too prone to error. If another society delegates strategic or tactical war-making capabilities to artificial intelligence agents, will our values inhibit our capabilities by our insistence on a slow and error-prone human in the loop?[15]

Beyond issues of war, I believe that the challenge to the liberal democratic model is the technocratic state. It is too sanguine and blinkered to repeat the cliché that China offers no ideology to compete with ours.[16] The PRC is groping toward an authoritarian technocratic state dedicated to serving and controlling its population by utilizing modern technologies.[17] It is not clear whether that model or the historic American model will most broadly take hold in Asia, other continents, or, for that matter, in the United States.

We can also see the turbulent effects of technology from another perspective. The liberal order is based on a consensus that individuals are free to develop and apply their minds as they judge appropriate. Our First Amendment guarantee of free speech reflects this consensus, with occasional battles at the margin, for example, over hate speech. But we are just beginning to come to grips with an issue as fundamental but much more divisive than free speech: to what extent do individuals have a right to control their own bodies? Some issues about "free bodies" are already indicative of the intensity of American conflicts in this domain: abortion, euthanasia, birth control, legalization of recreational hallucinogenic drugs. Others have been introduced in contexts that maximize consensus: medical implants and procedures to compensate for heart conditions, fertility treatments for the infertile,[18] computer-assisted prosthetic limbs and artificial voices, cochlear implants for those born with diminished hearing.

But the line between correction and improvement is difficult to discern—plastic surgery for the war wounded became cosmetic surgery for the affluent. How does liberal democracy deal with a desire to correct a fetus's genetic predisposition to incipient diabetes?[19] To autism? To improving my offspring? To select among fetuses based on their likely intelligence? To improve my intelligence as an adult?[20] On these issues there will be no ready consensus, and our struggles to resolve them, like our struggles over slavery, will determine whether we are torn apart and—if we remain united—what we mean by a democracy built upon a foundation of individual freedom.

Whatever our nineteenth century difficulties in addressing slavery as an American issue, in a twenty-first century global environment (an environment itself created by technology), we must recognize that other societies and cultures will confront these same issues and at least in some cases very probably make other decisions. How would a liberal world order address the freedom of Chinese parents and the Chinese state to select for intelligence?[21] How would the Chinese choice affect our choice? If another state enhances its soldiers' capabilities through drugs (or, as noted above, achieves greater speed or accuracy from allocating major war decisions to machines) can we ignore or reject that?[22] Can we match these changes without undermining our concepts of a liberal world order?

It is widely recognized that privacy, a core value of the Western liberal order, is eroded by a regime of information-sharing; multiple observation capabilities (cameras, geospatial identification of movement of cell phones and connected cars, credit card transactions, etc.); biometric analysis through collection of DNA and facial, iris, or heartbeat identification;[23] and data analytics. Privacy is not simply a value unto itself—it is a prerequisite of freedom in the face of a totalitarian state or controlling private entity.[24] Its erosion undermines the liberal order. And yet, as is widely recognized, technological change empowers and security challenges motivate the constriction, even essentially the elimination, of privacy.[25]

Along with security, the credibility of all modern states is determined by their ability to deliver economic growth, personal opportunity, and jobs. The Great Depression challenged democracy and spawned fascism in the decade after 1929. Conversely, from World War II to the present, the relative success of capitalism powerfully enhanced the appeal of the American system. It remains to be seen how much the future resembles the past as authoritarian states aim to win this competition. What is clear is that the ability to develop and absorb technology will be critical in any such competition.

At the same time, technology is diluting the links between growth, opportunity, and employment. Some current political debates reflect this, but the longer-term challenges are more fundamental. Economists have begun to ask whether the future of human employment is itself questionable. That circumstance seems far off, but the consensus expectation among the cognoscenti is that it will occur within the lifetimes of younger readers of this paper.[26] Even now movement in that direction is generating great tensions, within the United States and internationally, as nations compete to provide employment opportunities. If, as seems plausible, even probable, increased productivity permits increases in standards of living and support of aging populations even as employment declines, systems providing a state-assured income will expand. Domestically, this will, even more than now, have intensely debated effects that may distract us or cause us to change our conceptions of the relationship between an individual and government.

Further, what is not yet well-recognized is the close tie between work and identity. Merely compensating for lost income will not satisfy this need to work, and efforts to satisfy it (for example through systems of national service) or failures to address it may transform American democracy as well as everyday American life. Internationally, a large source of tension will likely be the ability of more developed countries to demand royalties from the machine systems and other technologies they develop.[27] Great income inequality between citizens of different countries—an unusual situation that developed over the last two centuries along with disparate industrialization and technology absorption[28]—may yet more intensely challenge the liberal world order.[29]

2. Growth of Non-State Power. It is well understood that technology has amplified the individual's and small group's power to kill.[30] This is the most dramatic manifestation of a more general phenomenon: political groups, private corporations, criminal organizations, and even individuals can now wield powers previously primarily reserved to nation-states. For example, capabilities once exclusively marshaled by an elite intelligence agency are now broadly accessible because commercial tools empower surveillance (even from space using commercial satellite data), analysis (by employing tools to interrogate "big data," reaping the bounty of information from social media, and crowdsourcing),[31] and espionage (for example, using cyber malware). Platforms for mass communication are available for attracting military recruits and civilian supporters. Commercial encryption permits protected messaging. Unmanned vehicles empower aerial and terrestrial attack, and driverless cars may well soon deliver car bombs. Digital technologies permit long-distance, mass-scale attacks.[32] The dark web facilitates transactions outside national legal systems, enforced by systems of private reputational ranking.[33] Assisting these developments, private currencies (Bitcoin, Ethereum, and scores of others) are coming into use.[34]

These changes bring private power closer to the levels of public power. Two resulting challenges are now much discussed: terrorist groups[35] and individuals and global corporations that enjoy private power beyond government control. What is not commonly observed is that these disparate abuses of private power are magnified by the same underlying force: twenty-first century technology. The modern liberal state has much more sway over private corporations than it does over terrorists, but it does not yet know how to force shared approaches to security challenges (for example, iPhone encryptions, shared user data, information on cyber attacks), and there is no American consensus about the American responsibilities of American corporations.

(When I asked him about this, a senior figure in a top thirty American corporation told me, "Our goal is to be like Switzerland: neutral and engaged with all.")[36]

The liberal state is now greatly stressed by its need to control and compete with these centers of private power. Benjamin Wittes and Gabriella Blum provide an insightful account of this situation:

> While it is not yet literally the case, every individual, every group, every company, and every state will soon have the potential to threaten the security of—and have his, her, or its security threatened by—every individual, group, company and state... . [T]he relative power of the state to that of the citizentry is reduced... . [W]e are unleashing ... enormous creative potential.... It threatens, however, to be Hobbesian as well—an environment of unaccountable freedom to do great harm.[37]

Authoritarian states are challenged by this situation, but much less so because they are not inhibited by deference to individual liberties and they commonly view corporate actors as agents of the state acting in another form. The survival of the liberal order will significantly depend not only on its ability to cope with these Hobbesian challenges, but also on whether liberal states are judged inferior to authoritarian states in this respect.

3. Growth of Foreign Power. At the end of World War II, America was in a singular position. With Europe and much of Asia in ruins, our infrastructure was intact and our producers and consumers accounted for more than half of the world's GDP. In the ensuing seven decades, the world has moved toward a more normal position, with America still economically privileged (we generate one-quarter of the world's GDP) but much less dominant. This reversion toward the norm has significant implications for America's global power, quite apart from the distribution of technological capabilities.

Of course, economic power is strongly correlated with technological capabilities. But insofar as we can assess technological capabilities as a separate variable, it seems evident that they intensified American postwar dominance. After World War II we were in a position of immense technological advantage from our wartime invention and production. Many of the world's scientists had taken refuge (and more were taking refuge) here. The US government was in the forefront of developing and more or less effectively controlling key technologies like nuclear weapons and nuclear power, missiles, computing, cryptology, digital storage, telecommunications, radar, aviation, and submarine capabilities.

The twenty-first century world is more evenly distributed.[38] In part this is because, while some technologies remain exclusively military, many critical technologies are commercial. In the decades after WWII, the US government drove research and development and dominated the market for advanced technologies. Related civilian technologies were spin-offs from military technologies.[39] When Ash Carter wrote about government and civilian R&D in 1980, his and his co-authors' principal concern was whether government R&D would crowd out civilian developments. Now American civilian R&D is two-and-a-half times government R&D, and the American government is a small participant in many markets. As a striking example, the semiconductor industry association calculates that the US government comprised 90 percent of the global semiconductor market in the early 1980s. It is now 0.5 percent of that market.[40]

The global distribution of commerce, wealth, and invention levels the playing field. The resulting national security challenge is typically put as one of superiority: As China is projected to advance to equality with our GDP a decade from now and, more notably still, to a GDP that is 50 percent larger than ours by around 2050, can we maintain technological superiority? As significant, even if we remain superior, fast followers will be much closer to us, inventing, adapting, and disseminating at a speed that shortens the first mover's advantage. Technological power, which after World War II sharply diverged, is now largely converging; hard-earned technological advantages tend only to be transitory; advantages in technology development can be negated (or amplified) by speed of dissemination and skill in adaptation. As a result, today's technologies, though often pursued under the banner of superiority, tend to be equalizers. A liberal world order, even a stronger order, can emerge from a more equal world, but we must recognize that it will be shaped less by American values and priorities and more by those of others.

4. Risk of Unintended Consequences. Ever since we harnessed the awesome technology of the atomic bomb and nuclear reactors, we have been supremely aware of the risks of accidents. But even extraordinary American efforts have not avoided harrowing nuclear incidents, some of them causing numerous casualties and requiring substantial relocations of affected populations.[41] These risks expanded as nuclear weapons were acquired by eight other nations,[42] many of which may not equally share our inclination and ability to invest in mechanisms of control and mitigation. Moreover, these risks multiply as other technologies (particularly bioengineering, cyber-attack capabilities, and artificial intelligence) proliferate to other nations. The risks of a catastrophic accident cannot confidently be calculated,[43] but it can confidently be said that they are rapidly rising. It seems more probable than not, for example, that the 1977-1978 global epidemic of H1N1 arose from human, not natural, activities.[44]

The proliferation of dangerous technologies in the hands of numerous states, groups, and even individuals, also raises the likelihood of emergent effects—unpredictable consequences from the unexpected interactions of systems whose safety and other constraints are commonly conceived to operate separately. We do not know, for example, how machine decision-making systems from one country may interact with those of another, causing (as in the World War I mobilization systems) consequences that no nation would have chosen. We do not know how cyber or biological viruses created for one purpose may affect other systems if they are released or escape into the wild.

These and many analogous possibilities warrant concern because they may be catastrophic for our lives or our environment. They are noted here, though, because of a collateral consequence: if the liberal state cannot control destructive technologies (our own and others), that failure will fuel intense demands for a more secure, and I fear authoritarian, form of governance.

Conclusion

The tectonic plates of modern technology are shifting, with results that already stress the foundations of the liberal order. Four main fault lines are evident, centering on the role of individuals, small groups and corporations, multi-state competitions, and the risks of accidents and disastrous emergent effects.

All trends produce counter-trends. Technology can be sustaining as well as subverting. The liberal order has encountered and robustly emerged from other stresses. It may survive this century's technology tsunami. The challenges, though, warrant our energetic attention. The outcome, though, is far from assured.

Richard Danzig is a Senior Advisor to the Johns Hopkins Applied Physics Laboratory, a consultant to the Intelligence Advanced Research Projects Activity (IARPA), Chair of the Advisory Panel for Idaho National Laboratories' Innovation Center, and a member of the Toyota Research Institute Advisory Board. He is also a member of the Defense Policy Board, the Homeland Security Secretary's Advisory Council, a Trustee of Reed College and of the RAND Corporation, a Director of the Center for a New American Security, and a Director of Saffron Hill Ventures (a European investment firm). In recent time he has been a director of National Semiconductor and Human Genome Sciences Corporation and has served as The Chairman of the Board of The Center for a New American Security, Vice Chair of RAND, and Chairman of the Board of the Center for Strategic and Budgetary Assessments. Dr. Danzig served as Secretary of the Navy from November 1998 to January 2001. He was the Under Secretary of the Navy between 1993 and 1997. From the spring of 2007 through the Presidential election of 2008, Dr. Danzig was a senior advisor to Senator Obama on national security issues. Dr. Danzig also served as a law clerk to US Supreme Court Justice Byron White. He was born in New York City in 1944. He received a B.A. degree from Reed College, a J.D. degree from Yale Law School, and Bachelor of Philosophy and Doctor of Philosophy degrees from Oxford University, where he was a Rhodes Scholar. He is a member of the Aspen Strategy Group.

[1] Richard Danzig, "Driving in the Dark: Ten Propositions About Prediction," Center for a New American Security, 2011, https://www.cnas.org/publications/reports/driving-in-the-dark-ten-propositions-about-prediction-and-national-security.

[2] Those interested in a current layman's overview of technologies of interest and their societal implications might consult "OECD Science, Technology and Innovation Outlook 2016" at http://www.oecd.org/sti/oecd-science-technology-and-innovation-outlook-25186167.htm. This extensive report drew its observations from six "foresight exercises" that identified "well over a hundred" technologies expected to be of significance over the next ten to twenty years. The discussion at pp. 77ff focuses on ten technologies judged to be most important.

[3] When the National Science Foundation funded an assessment of the rate of improvement across sixty-two technologies, the authors found that "[t]he historical data shows a strong tendency, across different types of technologies, toward constant exponential growth rates... ." B´ela Nagy, et al., "Statistical Basis for Predicting Technological Progress," Santa Fe Institute, July 2012, http://journals.plos.org/plosone/article?id=10.1371/journal.pone.0052669. For example, the cost of sequencing an entire human genome fell at the rate of Moore's law from 2001 to 2008. It declined much more rapidly in the years after that. The cost in January 2011 was $46,774; in October of that year it was $29,092. By January 2015 the cost was $3,970. Nine months later it was $1,245. See spreadsheet data and graphs from Kris Wetterstrand, "DNA Sequencing Costs: Data from the NHGRI Genome Sequencing Program (GSP)," National Human Genome Research Institute, www.genome.gov/sequencingcostsdata.

[4] As three particular markers of these general observations, consider that there are more than one million scientific papers published globally each year. Since World War II, the number of science papers published each year has doubled every 9.7 years. In 1989, no nation had as many as a thousand published papers with collaborators from other nations. By 2011, "every country in Europe collaborates with every other country in the region... ." For example, the United Kingdom and Germany had around 10,000 co-authored publications. By 2011, "the United States ... collaborate[d] on 3–4% of its papers with each of China (now its most frequent partner, with 19,141 papers in 2011), the United Kingdom (19,090) and Germany (16,753). These totals have all roughly doubled in the past decade." References for these points are, respectively: Lindsay McKenzie, "Want to Analyze Millions of Scientific Papers All at Once? Here's the Best Way to Do It," *Science*, July 21, 2017, http://www.sciencemag.org/news/2017/07/want-analyze-millions-scientific-papers-all-once-here-s-best-way-do-it; David Westergaard, "Text Mining of 15 Million Full-Text Scientific Articles," 2017, prepublication review version at http://www.biorxiv.org/content/biorxiv/early/2017/07/11/162099.full.pdf; Jonathan Adams, "The Rise of Research Networks," *Nature* 490 (October 2012): 335, https://www.nature.com/nature/journal/v490/n7420/pdf/490335a.pdf.

[5] As a historian observed about a critical technology that began to proliferate more than 500 years ago: "Printing presses and books from the fifteenth to the eighteenth century were shared equally between vice and virtue, the retrograde and the progressive thought of Europe... . We cannot say whom the printing press served. It enlarged and invigorated everything." Fernand Braudel, *Capitalism and Material Life*

1400-1800 (New York: HarperCollins, 1967), 298-9. Recall also, Marshall McLuhan, *Understanding Media: The Extensions of Man* (Cambridge, MA: MIT Press, 1994), 8: "Whether [electric] light is being used for brain surgery or night baseball is a matter of indifference."

[6] This is not to suggest that all technological change subverts the liberal world order. For example, global trade expands and sustains that order even as it stresses it. Cryptography protects privacy.

[7] Technology is also a cause and a potential mitigator of climate change, but this critical issue is left for other papers.

[8] Wu Youyou, et al., "Computer-Based Personality Judgments Are More Accurate Than Those Made by Humans," *PNAS* 112, no. 4, http://www.pnas.org/content/112/4/1036.full. Automated prediction of our preferences is at the core of Google's business model, drawing from the database of our searches. Other large companies use shopping patterns. Charles Duhigg, "How Companies Learn Your Secrets," *New York Times Magazine*, February 16, 2012, http://www.nytimes.com/2012/02/19/magazine/shopping-habits.html, provided an early account, noting one company's ability to discern the likelihood that a woman was pregnant from the lotions that she purchased.

[9] A candid, though self-promoting, short presentation of the use of these tools in the Ted Cruz 2016 presidential campaign may be found at https://www.youtube.com/watch?v=n8Dd5aVXLCc. (Presentation of Alex Nix, Cambridge Analytica, September 27, 2016). I note, however, that Nix's description occurs at what may be a transitory state. When others use the same tools for their own ends, the advantages he asserts may be diluted by their counter-efforts.

As with other issues commented on in this paper, the issues are complex, with many counter-currents. For instance, it is often bemoaned that technology is facilitating blogs, podcasts, tweets, websites, etc., that flood the marketplace of ideas often with false or distracting news. But it is not clear that the proliferation of news sources and voices is inimical to liberal democracy. Enshrining stable, powerful gatekeepers may be most congenial to an authoritarian state. Nostalgia may also obscure the turbulence that existed in past fights over McCarthyism, the Vietnam War, and abortion and civil rights. Furthermore, we may be reverting to a norm familiar to America's founders, whose revolutionary pamphlets and geographic and other interest groups competed in a noisy environment. That norm continued for nearly two centuries. It may be the late 20th century, when technology created a temporary oligarchy of television networks and radio stations, that was aberrational.

[10] Emails to the author, August 29 and August 30, 2017. I am also grateful to David Reiser for referring me to the talk noted in the previous reference.

[11] Cass Sunstein, *#Republic: Divided Democracy in the Age of Social Media* (Princeton, NJ: Princeton University Press, 2017), thoughtfully explores the consequences of self-segregation. Nathaniel Persily, "Can Democracy Survive the Internet?" *Journal of Democracy* 28, no. 2 (April 2017): 63-76, http://www.journalofdemocracy.org/sites/default/files/07_28.2_Persily%20%28web%29.pdf, offers a reflective assessment of the new technologies that we now see facilitating self-segregation, anonymity, manipulation from abroad, and flooding communications channels through automation (botnets, etc.). Siva Vaidhyanathan, "Facebook Wins, Democracy Loses," *New York Times*, September 8, 2017, https://www.nytimes.com/2017/09/08/opinion/facebook-wins-democracy-loses.html, provides one example of a recent development, "dark posts" on Facebook that evade requirements for attribution of electoral messages to candidates. They are "seen only by a very specific audience, obscured by the flow of posts within a Facebook news feed and ephemeral. Facebook calls its 'dark post' service 'unpublished page post ads'... . [O]ne thing is clear: Facebook has contributed to, and profited from, the erosion of democratic norms in the United States and elsewhere."

[12] Cathy O'Neil, *Weapons of Math Destruction* (New York: Crown Publishing, 2016) powerfully chronicles numerous instances of excessive deference to algorithms. Paul Robinette, et al., "Overtrust of Robots in Emergency Evacuation Scenarios," Georgia Tech Research Institute, https://www.cc.gatech.edu/~alanwags/pubs/Robinette-HRI-2016.pdf, show in a limited experiment how subjects fleeing a fire follow a robot even in the face of vivid evidence of better routes. Yuval Noah Harari, *Homo Deus: A Brief History of Tomorrow* (New York: Harper, 2015), 341-2, observes: "Once … algorithms become all-knowing oracles, they may well evolve into agents and finally into sovereigns… . Once [Microsoft's AI assistants under development] evolve from oracles to agents, they might start speaking directly with one another, on their masters' behalf."

[13] "[W]hat's puzzling is that it can also predict whether a person is prone to schizophrenia or other psychiatric disorders in the future. Joel Dudley … who leads the team, admitted that they can build such advanced AI models but they have no idea how they work. The most powerful AI machines no longer depend on commands provided by humans. Instead, they create their own algorithm based on the data and desired output given to them. In short, machines program themselves." Chris Brandt, "Deep Learning: The Most Advanced Artificial Intelligence," Mount Sinai Hospital, June 14, 2017, http://www.mountsinai.org/about-us/newsroom/in-the-news/university-herald-deep-learning-the-most-advanced-artificial-intelligence-chris-brandt. See also, Will Knight, "The Dark Secret at the Heart of AI: No one really knows how the most advanced algorithms do what they do. That could be a problem." MIT Technology Review, April 11, 2017, and Mark Wilson, "AI Is Inventing Languages Humans Can't Understand. Should We Stop It?" Co.Design, July 2017, https://www.fastcodesign.com/90132632/ai-is-inventing-its-own-perfect-languages-should-we-let-it.

[14] Yuval Noah Harari, *Homo Deus: A Brief History of Tomorrow* (New York: Harper, 2015), 338.

[15] "'Teaming military forces with autonomous systems will fundamentally alter how peace is kept and wars fought, and because potential adversaries are already heavily investing in their use, it is imperative that the United States keep pace. Military superpowers in the next century will have superior autonomous capabilities, or they will not be superpowers." Cara LaPointe and Peter L. Levin, "Automated War: How to Think About Intelligent Autonomous Systems in the Military," *Foreign Affairs*, September 2016, https://www.foreignaffairs.com/articles/2016-09-05/automated-war.

[16] Daniel A. Bell, *The China Model: Political Meritocracy and the Limits of Democracy* (Princeton, NJ: Princeton University Press, 2015), 179 and 197, argues that China offers an exportable model of meritocratic national leadership that permits experimentation at intermediate levels and democracy at lower levels. In this respect, his perspective overlaps mine. I note that he acknowledges, but does not emphasize, the authoritarian aspects of the Chinese system.

[17] China's evolving efforts at establishing a "social credit system" are suggestive of this approach. Wikipedia (https://en.wikipedia.org/wiki/Social_Credit_System) provides a reasonable summary:

> The **Social Credit System** is a proposed *Chinese government* initiative for developing a national *reputation system*. It has been reported to be intended to assign a "social credit" rating to every citizen based on government data regarding their economic and social status. In addition, it is also meant to rate businesses operating on the Chinese market.
>
> The Social Credit System is an example of China's "top-level design" approach. It is coordinated by the *Central Leading Small Group for Comprehensively Deepening Reforms*. According to the overall "Planning Outline for the Construction of a Social Credit System (2014-2020)" issued by the State Council, the Social Credit System will focus on four areas: "sincerity in government affairs" (政务诚信),

"commercial sincerity" (商务诚信), "societal sincerity" (社会诚信), and "judicial credibility" (政务诚信).... .

The Chinese government wants the basic structures of the Social Credit System to be in place by 2020. It is unclear whether the system will work as envisioned by then, but the Chinese government has fast-tracked the implementation of the Social Credit System, resulting in the publication of numerous policy documents and plans since the main plan was issued in 2014. If the Social Credit System is implemented as envisioned, it will constitute a new way of controlling both the behavior of individuals and of businesses.

As of July 2017, no comprehensive, nation-wide social credit system exists, and very little firm information is available about how this system might work in practice. There are, however, multiple pilots testing the system on a local level as well as in specific sectors of industry.

See also, Simon Denyer, "China's Plan to Organize Its Society Relies on 'Big Data' to Rate Everyone," *Washington Post*, October 22, 2016, https://www.washingtonpost.com/world/asia_pacific/chinas-plan-to-organize-its-whole-society-around-big-data-a-rating-for-everyone/2016/10/20/1cd0dd9c-9516-11e6-ae9d-0030ac1899cd_story.html, and Shazeda Ahmed, "Cashless Society, Cached Data: Security Considerations for a Chinese Social Credit System," The Citizen Lab, January 24, 2017, https://citizenlab.ca/2017/01/cashless-society-cached-data-security-considerations-chinese-social-credit-system/.

It is worth noting how aspects of the American system, including credit scores for the general population and security evaluations for those engaged by national defense and intelligence agencies, reflect analogous efforts also empowered by new tools for data mining.

[18] With remarkably little public comment, every day some 200 American babies are born after having been conceived in test tubes. (This is among a total of about 11,000 babies born in America each day). I infer this estimate (probably a modest underestimate) from a numerator of in vitro births (70,354) in 2014 as reported by the CDC at https://nccd.cdc.gov/drh_art/rdPage.aspx?rdReport=DRH_ART.ClinicInfo&ClinicId=9999&ShowNational=1 (note that multiple births from in vitro fertilization are counted as a single birth in this data). The denominator of some 3.99 million total births in that year is derived from National Vital Statistics Reports, "Births: Final Data for 2014," CDC, 2015, https://www.cdc.gov/nchs/data/nvsr/nvsr64/nvsr64_12.pdf, with slight upward adjustments to account for likely changes from that date to the present.

[19] Steve Connor, "First Human Embryos Edited in U.S.: Researchers have demonstrated they can efficiently improve the DNA of human embryos," MIT Technology Review, July 26, 2017, https://www.technologyreview.com/s/608350/first-human-embryos-edited-in-us.

[20] If in addition to participating in this summer's Aspen Strategy Group meetings, members attended the 47th Behavior Genetics Annual Meeting held around the same time, they would have gotten a glimpse of rapidly emerging "new themes that shed light on the biological underpinnings of cognitive performance." Suzanne Sniekers, et al., "Genome-Wide Association Meta-Analysis of 78,308 Individuals Identifies New Loci and Genes Influencing Human Intelligence," *Nature Genetics* 49 (2017), https://www.nature.com/ng/journal/v49/n7/full/ng.3869.html. The field is well summarized in Stephanie Pappas, "The Plot Thickens in the Gnarly Story of IQ and Genetics," Neo.Life, July 20, 2017, https://medium.com/neodotlife/intelligence-genes-eb18c5ef759c.

[21] David Cyranoski, "China's Embrace of Embryo Selection Raises Thorny Questions," *Nature*, August 16, 2017, http://www.nature.com/news/china-s-embrace-of-embryo-selection-raises-thorny-questions-1.

22468, describes cultural differences between the US and China: "In the West, PGD [pre-implantation genetic diagnosis for in vitro fertilized eggs] still raises fears about the creation of an elite genetic class, and critics talk of a slippery slope towards eugenics… . In China, however, PGD lacks such baggage. The Chinese word for eugenics, *yousheng*, is used explicitly as a positive in almost all conversations about PGD. *Yousheng* is about giving birth to children of better quality. Not smoking during pregnancy is also part of *yousheng*." The article also goes on to note, however, that "This is not to say that the Chinese haven't thought about abuses of the technology. The Chinese government was worried, as were many Western governments, that PGD would be used to select physical characteristics, such as height or intelligence. The clinics licensed to do PGD can use it only to avoid serious disease or assist infertility treatments. And sex selection through PGD is off the table."

[22] The Director of National Intelligence's "2016 Worldwide Threat Assessment of the US Intelligence Community," forthrightly stated: "Research in genome editing conducted by countries with different regulatory or ethical standards than those of Western countries probably increases the risk of the creation of potentially harmful biological agents or products. Given the broad distribution, low cost, and accelerated pace of development of this dual-use technology, its deliberate or unintentional misuse might lead to far-reaching economic and national security implications." Senate Armed Services Committee, Statement of James R. Clapper, Director of National Intelligence, February 9, 2016, 9.

[23] "Present day: facial recognition reaches 500 metres; iris recognition, 50 metres; and, heartbeat recognition, 5 metres." Canadian Security Intelligence Service, "2018 Security Outlook: Potential Risks and Threats," 2016, 76. No comment is made, however, about false-positive rates.

[24] Timothy Snyder, *On Tyranny* (Tim Duggan Books, 2017), articulates this point admirably. For those who seek a more visceral sense of the point, volume one of Vassily Aksyonov's novel, *Generations of Winter* (Vintage, 1994), vividly depicts the corrosive effects of omnipresent informants in Russia's Stalinist state.

A Pew Foundation survey reports "In the first survey in this series, Americans were asked whether or not they agree that 'it is hard to avoid surveillance cameras when I am out in public.' The vast majority – 81% – agree that surveillance cameras are hard to avoid." The survey also observes: "Beyond surveillance cameras, there are many other forms of daily data collection and use that [respondents] do not feel they can avoid. When asked how much control they feel they have over how much information is collected about them and how it is used in their everyday lives … just 9% say they feel they have 'a lot' of control over how much information is collected about them and how it is used, while 38% say they have 'some control.' Another 37% assert they have 'not much control,' and 13% feel they personally have 'no control at all' over the way their data is gathered and used." Mary Madden and Lee Rainie, "Americans' Views About Data Collection and Security," Pew Research Center, May 20, 2015, http://www.pewinternet.org/2015/05/20/americans-views-about-data-collection-and-security/.

[25] As with all trends described here, there are counter-currents. Some technologies—for example, encryption—can make privacy more robust.

[26] A recent survey elicited responses from 352 published experts on machine learning in response to questions about "when unaided machines [would be predicted to be able to] accomplish every task better and more cheaply than human workers." In response, "the aggregate forecast gave a 50% chance of [this] occurring within 45 years and a 10% chance of it occurring within 9 years." (Interestingly, "Asian respondents expect [this] in 30 years, whereas North Americans expect it in 74 years.") Even if that could be achieved, respondents anticipated a long further delay before "machines could be built to carry out [all tasks] better and more cheaply than human workers." Responses reflected only a 10 percent probability of achieving that in 20

years and a 50 percent probability that point would only be reached in 122 years. Katja Grace, et al., "When Will AI Exceed Human Performance? Evidence from AI Experts," *ArXiv*, May 2017.

[27] We see harbingers of this in the debate about pharmaceutical prices in less developed countries.

[28] "[B]efore the late 1800s, there was relatively little income disparity across countries." Keith Sill, "The Evolution of the World Income Distribution," *Business Review*, Q2 2008, https://www.philadelphiafed.org/-/media/research-and-data/publications/business-review/2008/q2/sill_evolution-of-world-income-distribution.pdf.

[29] On the other hand, increases in income and the size of the middle class in developing countries may ameliorate international tensions.

[30] Martin Shubik, "Terrorism, Technology and the Socioeconomics of Death," *Comparative Strategy*, October-December 1997, provided a first documentation.

[31] Thus, for example, Seth M. Goldstein, et al., "Assessing the Accuracy of Geopolitical Forecasts from the US Intelligence Community's Prediction Market," *PNAS*, 2017 preprint: "On unclassified questions, [crowd wisdom] platforms populated by laypeople from the general public performed as well or better than a state-of-the-art [crowd wisdom] method populated by real IC analysts. Moreover, we found no evidence that … forecasters' access to classified information conferred any advantage."

[32] "Never before could a dozen people in their pajamas meaningfully annul the monopoly on the use of force." Canadian Security Intelligence Service, "2018 Security Outlook: Potential Risks and Threats," 2016, 80.

[33] Dark web transactions are particularly resistant to government control. It should be noted though that they are small compared to offline markets for drugs and guns and that governments have not been very successful in policing those either. For good assessments, see Kristy Kruithof, et al., "The Role of the 'Dark Web' in the Trade of Illicit Drugs," RAND, 2016, https://www.rand.org/pubs/research_briefs/RB9925.html, and Giacomo Persi Paoli, et al., "Behind the Curtain: The Illicit Trade of Firearms, Explosives and Ammunition on the Dark Web," RAND, 2017, https://www.rand.org/pubs/research_reports/RR2091.html.

[34] https://coinmarketcap.com/ lists the top 100 crypoto-currencies by market capitalization. Bitcoin's capitalization is calculated at over $45 billion and Ethereum's at $21 billion. The next seven have capitalizations from $7 billion down to $651,000. A recent academic study calculates that "between 5.8 million and 11.5 million [crypto-currency] wallets are estimated to be currently 'active.'" Garrick Heilman and Michael Rauchs, "Global Cryptocurrency Benchmarking Study," The Cambridge Centre for Alternative Finance, Cambridge University, Judge Business School, 2017, 10.

[35] Global criminal groups create analogous problems. OECD, "Reviews of Risk Management: Illicit Trade: Converging Criminal Networks," 2016, 22ff, summarizes the nature and extent of these activities. Following the lead of a UN study, it estimates the size of this activity at approximately 1.5 percent of global GDP, particularly from drugs, counterfeiting, and "forced labor from private enterprise."

[36] Elite employees of global companies may share outlooks with one another more than with compatriots in their home countries, just as inhabitants of mountains, seacoasts, and islands around the Mediterranean in the late 1500s had more in common with others similarly situated than with their more proximate neighbors. Fernand Braudel observed the earlier situation in *The Mediterranean and the Mediterranean World in the Age of Philip II* (University of California Press, 1949).

[37] Benjamin Wittes and Gabriella Blum, *The Future of Violence* (Basic Books, 2015), 9. The authors also observe: "A necessary corollary of the distribution of the capacity for attack and the distribution of vulnerability … is a parallel distribution of the ability to defend… . [D]efense from harm becomes less a primary governmental function and more a collective responsibility that harnesses the private sector." See also pp. 69, 72, and 95ff. It might be added that not only is the "relative power of the state to that of the citizentry" reduced, but also there are changes to the relative power of private citizens and groups. This can have adverse effects for the liberal democratic order. For example, "[i]n the digital realm, [civil society organizations] face the same threats as the private sector and government, while equipped with far fewer resources to secure themselves." Citizen Lab, "Communities @ Risk: Targeted Digital Threats Against Civil Society," University of Toronto, 2014, https://targetedthreats.net/. "[C]ivil society is largely on its own as it goes about its work to advance human rights and other public policy goals while struggling to stay ahead of debilitating cyber threats." Ron Deibert, "Civil Society Hung Out to Dry in Global Cyber Espionage," Circle ID, March 4, 2013, http://www.circleid.com/posts/20130304_civil_society_hung_out_to_dry_in_global_cyber_espionage/.

[38] Chris Kirchhoff's paper for these sessions ("An Even Flatter World: How Technology Is Remaking the World Order") discusses the points in this and the next paragraph with broader scope and in richer detail.

[39] The internet and GPS are two striking examples.

[40] The data is reported in "Advisory Panel on Streamlining and Codifying Acquisition Regulations, Section 809 Panel Interim Report," May 2017, https://section809panel.org/wp-content/uploads/2017/05/Sec-809Panel_Interim-Report_May2017_FINAL-for-web.pdf.

[41] For example, the explosive force of a thermonuclear device tested in 1954 was three times what was predicted, with consequent exposure of fifteen inhabited Pacific islands. Thomas Kunkle and Byron Ristvet, "Castle Bravo: Fifty Years of Legend and Lore," Defense Threat Reduction Agency, January 2013, https://web.archive.org/web/20140310004623/http://blog.nuclearsecrecy.com/wp-content/uploads/2013/06/SR-12-001-CASTLE-BRAVO.pdf.

[42] Atomic Archive.com briefly chronicles thirty-two accidents involving nuclear weapons and reactors throughout the world since 1950. "Broken Arrows: Nuclear Weapons Accidents," http://www.atomicarchive.com/Almanac/Brokenarrows_static.shtml.

[43] In an ambitious effort to quantify one risk, Marc Lipsitch and Alison P. Galvani calculate that "a moderate research program of ten laboratories at US BSL3 standards for a decade would run a nearly 20% risk of resulting in at least one laboratory-acquired infection, which, in turn, may initiate a chain of transmission. The probability that a laboratory-acquired influenza infection would lead to extensive spread has been estimated to be at least 10%. Simple branching process models suggest a probability of an outbreak arising from an accidental influenza infection in the range of 5% to 60%." (Footnotes omitted.) Marc Lipsitch and Alison P. Galvani, "Ethical Alternatives to Experiments with Novel Potential Pandemic Pathogens," *PLOS Medicine* 11, no. 5 (May 2014), http://journals.plos.org/plosmedicine/article?id=10.1371/journal.pmed.1001646. The variation in these calculations underscores the limits of our understanding.

[44] Michelle Rozo and Gigi Kwik Gronvall, "The Reemergent 1977 H1N1 Strain and the Gain-of-Function Debate," *mBio* 6, no. 2 (August 2015), http://mbio.asm.org/content/6/4/e01013-15.full, credibly conclude that this epidemic was "probably not a natural event, as the genetic sequence of the virus was nearly identical to the sequences of decades-old strains." They suggest that the most plausible explanation was a live-vaccine trial escape, the next most likely was a laboratory accident, and the least likely was a deliberate release of a biological weapon.

"The only effective response to this external competition is to increase the pace of innovation by expanding support for R&D and recruiting the most talented workforce able to translate rapidly new ideas into practice."

—JOHN DEUTCH AND CONDOLEEZZA RICE

Maintaining America's Lead in Creating and Applying New Technology

John Deutch
Emeritus Institute Professor
MIT

Condoleezza Rice
Denning Professor of Global Business,
Stanford University
Stephenson Senior Fellow, Hoover Institution

At its 2017 meeting, the Aspen Strategy Group discussed the decisive impact that a growing and assertive China will have on the liberal order over the next half century. One of the issues that emerged was the rise of Chinese technical competence—and Beijing's willingness to augment these efforts with outright theft of intellectual property. That strategy is well understood and the US government has lobbied China consistently and publicly for change for more than two decades. Some argued, however, that an even more nefarious and potentially successful Chinese strategy is less obvious: imbed Chinese graduate students and scholars in American research institutions where they become a kind of "fifth column" for the transfer of ideas and intellectual property to their homeland. The picture is one of China reaping the benefits of both indigenous innovation and pilfered American breakthroughs. For American policy makers, the question is how the United States can best protect its substantial lead in technology and yet remain true to the principle of academic openness.

Most Americans understand that innovation is important for US economic growth and international competitiveness. Successful innovation, sustained over time, is the result of an educational system that stresses creativity and entrepreneurship, enjoys federal support for fundamental scientific and engineering research, and has access to a financial community that it is willing to provide risk capital for new ventures and to make investments in first-of-a-kind commercial plant and equipment. Finally, innovation rests on an intellectual property system and regulations that are fair, flexible, and responsive to changes in the application of new technology.

Effective combination of these elements implies an underlying ecosystem that encourages cooperation between government, the private sector, and many research communities. While not perfect, the United States possesses such an ecosystem, which is the envy of the entire world. Over the past two decades, the five digital US super powers—Amazon, Apple, Facebook, Google, and Microsoft—have leveraged the internet as a powerful global tool and now dominate it globally. Thousands of new, promising start-up companies, ranging from biomedicine to 3-D printing, have been launched by private equity and new government programs such as Department of Energy's ARPA-E. Foreign students and recent postgraduates come to train in US universities and to a remarkable degree these individuals seek to remain in the United States to strengthen the performance of many industries. US universities throughout the country continue to be a cornucopia of new ideas: CRISPR gene editing, quantum computing, and machine learning are just a few examples.

Not surprisingly other countries are seeking access to our secret sauce by a variety of means, fair and foul. China is the poster child for this activity. China is increasing its support for domestic R&D, emphasizing areas such as artificial intelligence where the United States has always been the leader. This is an area that is already changing commercial activity, and it has significant implications for the military sphere. Although a crude measure, China's patent production is growing substantially. China now boasts its own technology giants like Alibaba and Tencent, and Chinese firms are increasingly investing in high-technology start-up companies in Silicon Valley and elsewhere. Chinese students remain a significant presence at US universities, a trend begun during Deng Xaioping's historic 1979 visit to Washington. As China and other emerging countries mature technologically and economically, the United States should expect greater competition.

These activities are all within the bounds of legitimate competition. But China goes further. Chinese entities are involved in malicious efforts to gain access to US technology, increasingly through cyber hacking. The United States has responded, passing the Defend Trade Secrets Act of 2016. China is also known to have pressured US firms that have been encouraged to move some of their operations to China to agree to favorable IP sharing arrangements. Present and former administrations have taken steps to protect the country from these illegal efforts, as we know from our past government service.

The government should continue to press the Chinese to prevent theft of US technology, suppress the misappropriation of US intellectual property, and insist on rigorously symmetric rules for foreign investment in the emerging high-technology firms of both countries.

But judicious reports often lead to less-measured proposals that would lead the United States down a path, long discredited, of attempting to maintain US competitiveness and its lead in innovation by trying to keep others out or, for that matter, our ideas in. The only effective response to this external competition is to increase the pace of innovation by expanding support for R&D and recruiting the most talented workforce able to translate rapidly new ideas into practice.

US university research and education is especially threatened by some suggestions to slow the leakage of US technology to adversaries and competitors. Examples include pre-publication clearance of research results supported by the DoD, creating a category of sensitive but unclassified research, and restrictions on foreign graduate students joining "sensitive" research projects and on the presentation of research at international meetings. Each of these measures conflicts with the open structure of admission, research, and publication that keeps the US innovative ecosystem fresh, exciting, and agile.

There certainly will be circumstances when a university will refuse to undertake a research or education program because of uncertainty about its social or security consequences or because of conditions placed by the research sponsor on how the work is to be carried out. The institution makes its decision based on its research policy and after vigorous internal debate. But individual faculty and university administrations have limited experience determining the security risks that a proposed project might present. There is plenty of room here for misunderstanding and conflict. Universities will rightly hold to the overriding principle that no arrangement is acceptable if it restricts any member of the university community from participating in an activity where he or she meets specified academic qualifications. There can be no "nationality" test or restriction. If the federal government insists on imposing such restrictions on sponsored research, it runs the risk of weakening its link with the universities that have been so central to US innovation. We say this although we are aware that some may take advantage of the openness of our system for nefarious purposes. Yes, there will be losses, but these are minor compared to the losses that will be incurred by restricting inquiry on university campuses.

It is better for the United States to hold to the strategy that has given us the substantial technological lead that we enjoy. In that regard, the greatest danger is that the federal government may reduce its support for R&D and universities and other performers may lessen their efforts. That is a greater risk to innovation than any country—no matter how determined—could ever be. America should try not only to protect what we have created—we must strive to master the next intellectual frontier.

In other words, stay well ahead of others by doing what we do best. As former provosts of two great universities that have been a part of America's remarkable story, we are confident that the United States will maintain its technological lead for decades to come.

John Deutch is an Institute Professor at the Massachusetts Institute of Technology. Mr. Deutch has been a member of the MIT faculty since 1970, and has served as Chairman of the Department of Chemistry, Dean of Science, and Provost. Mr. Deutch has published over 160 technical publications in physical chemistry, as well as numerous publications on technology, energy, international security, and public policy issues. He served as Director of Central Intelligence from May 1995-December 1996. From 1994-1995, he served as Deputy Secretary of Defense and served as Undersecretary of Defense for Acquisition and Technology from 1993-1994. He has also served as Director of Energy Research (1977-1979), Acting Assistant Secretary for Energy Technology (1979), and Undersecretary (1979-80) in the United States Department of Energy. He is a member of the Aspen Strategy Group.

Condoleezza Rice is currently the Denning Professor in Global Business and the Economy at the Stanford Graduate School of Business; the Thomas and Barbara Stephenson Senior Fellow on Public Policy at the Hoover Institution; and a professor of Political Science at Stanford University. She's also a founding partner of RiceHadleyGates. From January 2005 to 2009, Secretary Rice served as 66th Secretary of State of the United States. Secretary Rice also served as President George W. Bush's National Security Advisor from January 2001 to 2005. She served as Stanford University's Provost from 1993-1999. From 1989 through March 1991, Secretary Rice served on President George H.W. Bush's NSC staff. She served as Director; Senior Director of Soviet and East European Affairs; and Special Assistant to the President for National Security Affairs. She's authored and coauthored numerous books, including three bestsellers, *Democracy: Stories from the Long Road to Freedom; No Higher Honor: A Memoir of My Years in Washington;* and *Extraordinary, Ordinary People: A Memoir of Family.* She currently serves on the boards of Dropbox, C3, and Makena Capital. In addition, she's vice chair of the board of governors of the Boys and Girls Clubs of America; a member of the board of the Foundation for Excellence in Education; and a trustee of the Aspen Institute. Born in Birmingham, Alabama, Secretary Rice earned her bachelor's degree in political science from the University of Denver, her master's from the University of Notre Dame, and her Ph.D. from the Graduate School of International Studies at the University of Denver. She is co-chair of the Aspen Strategy Group.

"China strategically uses aid, trade, and foreign direct investment to build goodwill, expand its political sway, and secure the natural resources it needs to grow. All are part of one, mostly coherent, national industrial policy."

—ANJA MANUEL

China's Economic March:
Will It Undermine the Liberal World Order[1]

Anja Manuel
Principal
RiceHadleyGates LLC

The Pakistani town of Gwadar was until recently filled with the dust-colored cinderblock houses of about 50,000 fishermen. Ringed by cliffs, desert, and the Arabian Sea, it was at the forgotten edge of the earth. Now it's one centerpiece of China's "Belt and Road" initiative, and the town has transformed as a result. Gwadar is experiencing a storm of construction: a brand-new container port, new hotels, and 1,800 miles of superhighway and high-speed railway to connect it to China's landlocked western provinces. China and Pakistan aspire to turn Gwadar into a new Dubai, making it a city that will ultimately house two million people.

China is quickly growing into the world's most extensive commercial empire.

It coordinates aid, government loans, foreign direct investment, and to some extent trade to help its own companies and keep its economy growing. Chinese diplomats and business leaders work hand-in-hand in an unprecedented way: investment is part of a government-encouraged industrial strategy to all at once secure natural resources, create opportunities for state-owned enterprises as China's internal boom slows, invest China's massive currency reserves, and expand its political influence. Its huge infrastructure investments are also upending the clubby world of international economic institutions like the World Bank and the International Monetary Fund. China is making its economic presence felt around the world in dramatic fashion.

Will this ambitious geo-economic strategy upend the "liberal world order"?

Other papers have outlined the history of the liberal world order and tried to define it, so here I will use a simplified definition, drawn from the Atlantic Charter of 1941[2] and the Charter of the United Nations.[3] From these documents, we can assume the liberal order has several purposes:

1. keeping the peace,[4] (including preserving each nation's sovereignty[5]);

2. spreading economic well-being[6]; and

3. preserving the global commons through high standards for the environment,[7] labor/human rights,[8] and governance.

While China's economic initiatives will likely help keep the peace, the economic impact of its vast investments so far has been mixed, and its rush into infrastructure in the developing world has had quite a negative impact on the environment, human rights, and governance.

I agree with David Shambaugh that China is "opting in" to many international institutions, trying to change them from within, and thus in some ways becoming a responsible stakeholder. Yet its biggest foreign policy initiative to date—One Belt, One Road (OBOR), which could lavish up to $1 trillion in infrastructure spending on the developing world—is a very impressive effort to redistribute soft power in the international system. It is so large that the West cannot compete. OBOR will not necessarily lead China to establish an exclusive sphere of influence over a group of "illiberal" states, but the United States and Europe must act now to co-opt and help shape this slow tidal wave, which could have the largest impact on the international system since the fall of communism.[9]

China on the March

China's march onto the world economic scene has been spectacular. By way of comparison, after World War II, the Marshall Plan provided the equivalent of $800 billion in reconstruction funds to Europe (if calculated as a percentage of today's GDP). In the decades after the war the United States was also the world's largest trading nation, and its largest bilateral lender to others.

Now it's China's turn. The scale and scope of the Belt and Road initiative is staggering. Estimates vary, but over $300 billion have already been spent,[10] and China plans to spend $1 trillion more in the next decade or so.

According to the CIA, ninety-two countries counted China as their largest exports or imports partner in 2015,[11] far more than the United States at fifty-seven.[12]

It is most astounding that—while China was the world's largest recipient of World Bank and Asian Development Bank loans in the 1980s and 1990s[13]—in recent years, China *alone* loaned more to developing countries than the World Bank, according to research by the *Financial Times*.[14]

In 2015, mainland China and Hong Kong together invested nearly $200 billion abroad. This does not yet match the United States' $300 billion, but it does make Chinese companies the second largest investor around the world.[15]

What Is OBOR?

China's authoritarian, more centralized government allows it to be strategic about spreading its economic influence. Unlike the United States and Europe, China strategically uses aid, trade, and foreign direct investment to build goodwill, expand its political sway, and secure the natural resources it needs to grow. All are part of one, mostly coherent, national industrial policy.

OBOR is the most impressive example of this. It is an umbrella initiative of current and future infrastructure projects. In the next decades, China plans to build a dizzying mesh of infrastructure around Asia and, through similar initiatives, around the world. It also has plans for greater financial integration, trade liberalization, and strengthening of people-to-people ties between China and its neighbors.[16]

The Chinese government will mobilize up to US$1 trillion of outbound state financing for this effort in the next ten years.[17] Most of this funding will come in the form of preferential loans, not grants, and Chinese state-owned enterprises will be encouraged to invest. In 2016, Chinese banks alone collectively extended more than $50 billion in loans to more than 400 projects under OBOR.[18]

At the first "OBOR Summit" in Beijing in May 2017, President Xi said nearly seventy countries and organizations are currently participating, covering more than half of the world's population and around 30 percent of the global economy. Twenty recipient nations sent their heads of state to the OBOR Summit; most of them are smaller Asian countries that are economically dependent on Beijing.

The maritime "road" includes perhaps a dozen ports from Asia to East Africa and the Mediterranean. A planned rail network will connect China with Laos and Cambodia, Malaysia, Myanmar, Singapore, Thailand, and Vietnam. To the West, new rails and roads travel through Kazakhstan, Iran, Turkey, and Russia to Europe. Because of these initiatives, you can already ship a container from China's coast through Chengdu and Xinjiang all the way to Germany by rail. Shipping time from China to Germany has been reduced by almost half, to just 16 days.[19]

Why Is China Undertaking These Hugely Expensive Projects?

Many Western analysts see a dangerous scheme to dominate the rest of the world economically. China reiterates over and over that its motives are benign, done "in the spirit of open regional cooperation," and to create an "economic cooperation architecture that benefits all."[20] "We have no intention to form a small group detrimental to stability," President Xi said at the OBOR Summit in May. "What we hope to create is a big family of harmonious co-existence."[21] The policies certainly benefit China, but seen from China's perspective, they are not necessarily menacing.

First, if China's companies need natural resources from Central Asia and export their goods to Europe, having a faster, more reliable road and rail system is helpful. Over 80 percent of Beijing's oil and many of its other natural resources pass through the narrow Malacca Strait. China worries that—if relations become hostile—the United States and its allies could blockade the strait and starve the country of resources.[22]

Second, China's large foreign currency reserves are hard to convert into renminbi because so much money flooding into China would force prices to rise.[23] China has been investing reserves mostly in US Treasury bonds, but these pay very low interest, so China may earn better returns from infrastructure projects abroad.

Finally, now that China's infrastructure has been built (or overbuilt), many state-owned enterprises have extra capacity. So the government helps them stay afloat, and saves lots of Chinese jobs, by giving Chinese companies low-interest loans to build foreign mega-projects.[24]

An important side effect is that many developing countries feel grateful and beholden to China for its generosity and are thus more likely to side with China in international disputes. The Communist Party's economic diplomacy is not meant to be malicious, but it certainly is China-centric.

OBOR IN PAKISTAN

The current centerpiece of OBOR is China's tidal wave of projects with Pakistan. Beijing announced in 2014 that it would finance an 1,800-mile super-highway, a high-speed railway, an oil-pipeline route to the inland Chinese city of Kashgar, and the expansion of a deep sea port in Gwadar.

In total, China agreed to lavish $46 billion on Pakistan alone—much more than America's yearly aid budget for the entire world. China also gives Pakistan trade preferences through a free trade agreement signed in 2006 and is Pakistan's largest trading partner, although the volume of trade with Pakistan is a drop in the bucket for Beijing.

With such Chinese largesse, it is no wonder that Pakistanis are ecstatic about the China-Pakistan Economic Corridor, as the project is called. Shiny new billboards proclaiming their enduring partnership can be seen along every highway. Almost four-fifths of Pakistanis have a positive opinion of China. In recent years, the United States has given Pakistan over $1 billion a year in aid, much of that to its security services. Pakistanis see China's engagement emotionally, as friendly assistance by a brotherly neighbor. In fact, much of this assistance is coming on commercial terms. China has been known to walk away from projects if there are safety concerns or if loans are not repaid.

Helping Pakistan in such dramatic fashion fits well into China's economic strategy. If it can create a deep sea port in the Arabian Sea and a land route to western China, Middle Eastern oil can travel this short route, instead of 6,000 miles through the Malacca Straits. Chinese companies are happy to have work to do. And the initiative has the convenient side effect of annoying India, Pakistan's archenemy and China's potential strategic rival.

How Can China Afford This?

Looking behind the impressive headline numbers, very little is actual aid. Neither side usually makes the details of the investments public.

China has a very different definition of aid than the United States and Europe, which distinguish clearly between grants that will not be paid back—aid—and other financial flows related to commerce. China's broader definition includes some grants, government loans, export credits, and preferential trade relationships.[25] Over 80 percent of China's "aid" is actually projects to develop natural resources or build infrastructure.[26] From speaking to Pakistani officials and US scholars about the $46 billion Pakistan project (see "OBOR in Pakistan" sidebar), and looking at the long list of contracts, this pattern holds. Other than small grants for feasibility studies, the Chinese government is contributing very little cash.[27] Instead, its development banks loaned money to *Chinese* firms to build a hydropower plant, develop several coal mines, and complete a pipeline to Iran, and the banks loaned money to various Pakistani entities to build all the roads and rails to connect the projects within Pakistan and to China.[28]

These loans have real collateral behind them. For example, the Chinese have the rights to operate the Gwadar port for forty years. If Pakistan can't pay, China could own many of Pakistan's coal mines, oil pipelines, and power plants.

Will OBOR Undermine the "Liberal Order"?

Now that we understand how OBOR works, and its vast scale, we can begin to analyze its potential impact on the liberal order.

First, promoting peace. If the primary purpose of the "liberal order" as envisioned after World War II is to promote peace, China's march onto the global economic scene should have a *big positive impact*. Recent research shows that countries with high levels of trade are less likely to be involved in wars with any other countries, both allies and non-allies.[29] In other words, countries that trade fight less, not just with their trading partners, but with the world in general. Some scholars believe that China's economic largesse will create a group of countries so beholden to China that they will create a "bloc" hostile to the West. But this doesn't seem to be China's goal. In its own way, China is thus helping to uphold international peace.

Yet even if there is less interstate war under a "pax-Sinica," the fact that many small "donee" states are beholden to China (as Pakistan, Kyrgyzstan, Cambodia, and many others increasingly are) will make it harder for the US and Europe to impose their will on a slew of other issues, from counter-terrorism to sanctioning countries at odds with the West.

Second, promoting prosperity and economic well-being. It is too soon to study the impact of China's programs in any detail, yet so far, its economic impact on donee countries seems mixed at best. Since OBOR began only in 2013, no long-term economic studies exist. Scholars who looked at Chinese investment from 1991 to 2010 in Africa found that Chinese foreign investment and aid *does not* appear to have a significant impact on African growth and that inexpensive Chinese imports often displace African local firms.[30] Others find that Chinese investment in Africa has negatively impacted local trade and commerce.[31] This is borne out in Pakistan, where local firms complain that they can't compete with cheap Chinese goods and worry that Chinese firms will take over good agricultural land.[32] Anecdotally, others argue that Chinese investment has helped African countries by developing human capital, providing access to technology, and creating jobs.[33]

Why is this picture so mixed? While some developing countries are happy not to endure "lectures" from Western donor governments and institutions, Chinese money comes with its own conditions, and this can limit its positive economic effect. First, China usually requires donee countries to use Chinese firms, as we saw in Pakistan. Seventy percent of China's loans are linked to involvement of a Chinese company.[34] Over the past two years, China has provided its companies with $670 billion in export financing, while America's ExIm Bank has given American exporters only about $590 billion in financing—over its entire eighty-one-year history.[35]

In Pakistan, for example, 7,000 Chinese nationals worked on the economic corridor, protected by nearly 15,000 security personnel from Pakistan to guard the Chinese.[36] This all changed recently. As Chinese wages rise, it makes more sense to use locals. A few months ago, a Chinese firm began training hundreds of Pakistani engineers to work on a power plant near Karachi, and other Chinese projects are also employing more locals.

Second, while Chinese loans used to have low interest rates around 2.5 percent, they are now creeping up to near 5 percent as China gets more savvy about political risk.[37] This will make them harder to repay. China is taking on real financial risks by exposing its government and companies to authoritarian and shaky political regimes. A large-scale default by these countries on Chinese loans, or a third-world dictator nationalizing the assets the Chinese built, would be bad for China's economy and ultimately for the world. Scholar Parag Khanna believes that Ecuador, Zambia, and some other countries already owe more to China than they can afford.[38] The Chinese have been generous in the past about loan repayments. Khanna believes China would likely soften repayment terms rather than use "gunboat diplomacy" to extract concessions,[39] but it is too soon to tell.

While the recipients of Chinese OBOR funds are happy to fix their chronic power shortages, make travel times faster, and make trade more efficient, they may be mortgaging their futures.

Third, China's largely negative influence on the "global commons." In contrast to most Western aid and loans, OBOR projects often encourage negative standards on governance, the environment, and labor/human rights, although China's record on this has improved somewhat over the past few years. The West could play a positive role here by engaging with the Asian Infrastructure Investment Bank (AIIB) and other Chinese institutions that are looking to raise their standards.

Let's begin with governance: China's massive investments go to some of the world's most unpalatable regimes. In a recent analysis, the *New York Times* argues that often, "China is going where the West is reluctant to tread."[40] It is the largest investor in many countries that others ostracize because they are run by dictators, don't respect human rights, and are corrupt—for example, Zimbabwe, North Korea, Niger, Angola, Myanmar, and other unsavories. Of course China doesn't just invest in pariah states. More than a third of China's investments actually go to developed countries.[41] But Zimbabwe and other outcasts get so little foreign investment, that even relatively small Chinese loans make it the dominant economic partner there.

When James Kynge from the *Financial Times* interviewed Ugandan President Yoweri Museveni, he explained unabashedly why Chinese investment is so attractive to questionable regimes. The Chinese don't ask too many questions, Museveni said, and they "come with a sense of solidarity and ... big money, not small money." In addition, with Chinese money for infrastructure, the Ugandans don't have to listen to endless pedantic lectures from the World Bank or Western donors. "They are jokers," Museveni said of Western critics. "You can't impose middle-class values [like clean government or gay rights] on a pre-industrial society." "The Chinese," he adds by way of contrast, "are more practical."[42] Indeed, China's white papers on aid emphasize over and over that it will not "impose any political conditions" and won't "interfere in the internal affairs of the recipient countries."

Tiny Kyrgyzstan also illustrates China's immense sway. Every road appears to be built by Chinese contractors, and many signs are in Chinese. When I asked a Kyrgyz pro-democracy advocate whether Russia or the US would win the "great game" for influence in Central Asia, he laughingly responded, "China has already won."

As Museveni implied, as part of its march onto the world economic stage, China is rewriting the rules of doing business.

China also has a troublesome record regarding worker safety and the environment. A decade ago when China first ventured abroad, these standards were often abysmal, and in some areas, Chinese firms still leave behind a mess of underpaid miners, devastated forests, and ruined rivers.[43] Yet China is slowly improving on all these measures. In 2017, the Chinese government developed and published new, more stringent guidelines for outbound investors.[44] The AIIB wants to use world-class standards, and many Chinese companies are improving as they become more international and as nonprofits and local governments push them to do so. The CEO of China's national oil company CNOOC, Li Fanrong, proudly wrote his shareholders recently that "health, safety, and environmental protection work" are a "top priority" and noted that his company's investment in Canada's tar sands achieved "record high" safety ratings.[45]

China's influence on the global commons has been detrimental so far, but it increasingly understands that it must improve.

Conclusion

If China's geo-economic push continues, it will be its largest legacy and will have the most profound impact on the world—one that does not necessarily have to undermine the liberal order. Instead of wringing our hands or opposing it, the West must look for ways to co-opt and shape this juggernaut. If the OBOR initiative is a success, asphalt will be smoother, logistics will run faster, and countries that were cut off from world markets will be able to trade more. If the research cited above holds true, that will lead to fewer interstate wars, although it will make many small countries beholden to China.

Chinese companies are likely to face some setbacks, such as nationalizations and unpaid loans, along the way. As long as these are manageable, they may have a salutary effect: both Chinese government and state-owned enterprises could be more inclined to follow Western lending standards and avoid the most corrupt regimes. US and European governments—as well as our nonprofits and corporations—can play a positive role here by engaging with the countries receiving Chinese investment, upholding our own high standards and working to strengthen international conventions on clean government, the environment, and labor standards.

Some have argued that the West should change its institutions to make real room for new players like China and India. If it is a matter of giving others a larger seat at the table, we should do so. *This does not mean, however, that we should lower these institutions' standards related to transparency, labor relations, and the environment.*

To begin, we should join the AIIB to lend support and shape its progress. If managed correctly, the AIIB is a real example of China trying to become a "responsible stakeholder" in the international system. It is voluntarily restraining its own economic clout. China could make massive infrastructure investments around the world on its own. Yet it has chosen to do much of it through the AIIB. The bank's new Chinese CEO is pushing for high transparency and environmental and other standards, and wants to cooperate with the World Bank, Asian Development Bank, and others. We should encourage initiatives like this as much as possible.

President Xi says he shares this moderate view. He emphasized in both his 2015 and 2017 visits to the United States, and at Davos, that developing countries want a more equitable international system, but they do not want to unravel the entire order. We should hold him to it.

Anja Manuel is Co-Founder and Principal along with former Secretary of State Condoleezza Rice, former National Security Advisor Stephen Hadley and former Secretary of Defense Robert Gates in RiceHadleyGates LLC, a strategic consulting firm that helps US companies navigate international markets. She also lectures at Stanford University. Ms. Manuel is the author of *This Brave New World: India, China and the United States*, published by Simon and Schuster in May 2016. From 2005-2007, she served as an official at the US Department of State, responsible for South Asia Policy. She serves on the corporate boards of OSG Inc. and Ripple Inc., and on a number of nonprofit boards and advisory boards. She is a graduate of Harvard Law School and Stanford University.

[1] Other papers for this conference are looking at China's impact on international institutions and its trade diplomacy, so I am focusing here explicitly on its vast geo-economic strategy.

[2] The Atlantic Charter of August 14, 1941, signed by Franklin D. Roosevelt and Winston Churchill, https://digital.library.unt.edu/ark:/67531/metadc581/.

[3] The Charter of the United Nations was signed on June 26, 1945, in San Francisco, at the conclusion of the United Nations Conference on International Organization, and came into force on October 24, 1945.

[4] The Atlantic Charter called for peace and security. In later documents, mostly drafted by Western democracies, this took on the additional meaning that scholar John Ikenberry explains is a liberal order in the sense of being "rules-based," in contrast with one that is Westphalian or "organized into rival blocs or exclusive regional spheres." G. John Ikenberry, *Liberal Leviathan* (Princeton, NJ: Princeton University Press, 2012), xii. China of course subscribes to the Westphalian idea that sovereignty of individual states is the bedrock principle.

[5] "The Organization is based on the principle of the sovereign equality of all its Members." UN Charter Article 2, Clause 1.

[6] Both the Atlantic and UN Charter desired to bring about collaboration in the economic field to secure, for all, improved labor standards and economic advancement. http://www.un.org/en/sections/history-united-nations-charter/1941-atlantic-charter/.

[7] United Nations Conference on the Human Environment, Stockholm, Sweden, June 5-16, 1972, http://www.un-documents.net/aconf48-14r1.pdf.

[8] " …Encouraging respect for human rights and for fundamental freedoms for all…" UN Charter, Art. 1, Para. 3.

[9] Of course, China's own internal economic challenges could circumscribe its ability to keep investing abroad in this way: if China's SOE's do collapse and lay off workers, or China runs down its currency reserves, we may see much less of this investment in a few years. The future of China's economy is not necessarily linear.

[10] http://docs.aiddata.org/ad4/pdfs/WPS46_Aid_China_and_Growth.pdf

[11] *The World Fact Book*, CIA, 2015, https://www.cia.gov/library/publications/the-world-factbook/. The Chinese government claims that it was the largest trading partner of 130 countries around the world in 2013. Zhou Mingwei, "Promoting China-Japan Relations Through Culture," China.org.cn, June 18, 2014, http://www.china.org.cn/opinion/2014-06/18/content_32690843.htm.

[12] According to CIA World Fact Book data for 2015, 59 countries count China as their largest import trade partner, 33 countries count China as their largest exports partner, 21 countries count the US as their largest imports partner, 36 countries count the US as their largest exports partner. *The World Fact Book*, CIA, 2015, https://www.cia.gov/library/publications/the-world-factbook/.

[13] See David Shambaugh's chapter, "China and the Liberal World Order," in this book.

[14] Jamil Anderlini, Geoff Dyer, and Henny Sender, "China's Lending Hits New Heights," *The Financial Times*, January 18, 2011. In the 1980s and '90s, China became the largest recipient of World Bank loans and projects. By the end of 2009, the World Bank had cumulatively committed a total of $46.06 billion in loans, involving 309 projects, to China. From 1986-2007 China received $19.25 billion in loans and grants from the Asian Development Bank (ADB). More recent data is hard to come by, but in 2016, the World Bank Group supplied $61 billion in loans, grants, equity investments, and guarantees supporting countries and private businesses in fiscal year 2016 (July 1, 2015-June 30, 2016). Chinese banks alone extended $50 billion in just loans last year (2016) to more than 400 projects under One Belt, One Road. This does not count any Chinese government grants or direct equity investments, so it's fair to assume that in total, it is still more than the World Bank. Chuin-Wei Yap, "Chinese Banks Ramp Up Overseas Loans," *Wall Street Journal*, April 9, 2016, https://www.wsj.com/articles/chinese-banks-ramp-up-overseas-loans-1491649206.

[15] http://unctad.org/en/Pages/DIAE/World%20Investment%20Report/Country-Fact-Sheets.aspx.

[16] Scott Kennedy and David Parker, "Building China's 'One Belt, One Road,'" Center for Strategic & International Studies, September 10, 2015; Charles Hutzler, "China Lays Out Path to Silk Road," *Wall Street Journal*, March 28, 2015, http://blogs.wsj.com/chinarealtime/2015/03/28/china-lays-out-path-to-one-belt-one-road/.

[17] *China's New Silk Route*, PWC Growth Markets Centre, February 2016, https://www.pwc.com/gx/en/growth-markets-center/assets/pdf/china-new-silk-route.pdf. The government has created specific vehicles to help allocate this money to appropriate projects and initiatives. These include, among others, the New Silk Road Fund (NSRF) with $40 billion and the Asian Infrastructure Investment Bank (AIIB) with $100 billion in initial capital. Also, the government is directing large sums of its foreign exchange reserves and several of its largest state-owned banks, such as the China Development Bank and the Export-Import Bank of China, to the initiatives. The New Development Bank, launched by China, India, Russia, and South Africa, will kick in $10 billion. See PWC report, and also François Godement and Agatha Kratz, eds, *"One Belt, One Road": China's Great Leap Outward*, European Council on Foreign Relations, June 2015, http://www.ecfr.eu/page/-/China_analysis_belt_road.pdf.

[18] Chuin-Wei Yap, "Chinese Banks Ramp Up Overseas Loans," *Wall Street Journal*, April 9, 2017, https://www.wsj.com/articles/chinese-banks-ramp-up-overseas-loans-1491649206.

[19] Steve LeVine, "China Is Building Biggest Commercial-Military Empire in History," Reuters, June 9, 2015, http://qz.com/415649/china-is-building-the-most-extensive-global-commercial-military-empire-in-history/; "West China's International Railway Development." Maxxelli Consulting, February 2015, http://www.maxxelli-consulting.com/west-chinas-international-railway-development/.

[20] Tian Shaohui, "Vision and Actions on Jointly Building Belt and Road," Xinhua, March 28, 2015, http://news.xinhuanet.com/english/china/2015-03/28/c_134105858.htm.

[21] "Full Text of President Xi's speech at opening of Belt and Road forum," Xinhua, May 14, 2017, http://news.xinhuanet.com/english/2017-05/14/c_136282982.htm.

[22] "Annual Report to Congress: Military and Security Developments Involving the People's Republic of China 2015, " Department of Defense, April 2015, http://www.defense.gov/Portals/1/Documents/pubs/2015_China_Military_Power_Report.pdf.

[23] Qiao Yu, *Relocating China's Foreign Reserves*, Brookings, November 21, 2013, http://www.brookings.edu/research/papers/2013/11/21-relocating-foreign-reserves.

[24] Finally, cultural factors are important. Chinese companies are new to overseas investment, often acting just like they would at home: in China there is no real sanctity of contract, so companies often buy the land, the transportation links, and whatever else is necessary to get the oil out of the ground or the project completed. When they go abroad, they do the same.

[25] Paul Callan, Jasmin Blak, and Andria Thomas, "Breaking Down China's Foreign Aid and Investment," The Dalberg Group, April 12, 2013. See also Charles Wolf, Xiao Wang, and Eric Warner, China's Foreign Aid and Government-Sponsored Investment Activities, RAND Corporation, 2013, http://www.rand.org/content/dam/rand/pubs/research_reports/RR100/RR118/RAND_RR118.pdf.

[26] Charles Wolf, Xiao Wang, and Eric Warner, *China's Foreign Aid and Government-Sponsored Investment Activities*, RAND Corporation, 2013, http://www.rand.org/content/dam/rand/pubs/research_reports/RR100/RR118/RAND_RR118.pdf.

[27] Andrew Small, author interview, August 14, 2015; Awais Khan, CEO of U.S.-Pakistan Foundation, author interview, September 2, 2015. See also, Andrew Small, *The China-Pakistan Axis: Asia's New Geopolitics* (Chicago: C. Hurst & Co. Publishers, 2015). See also, "Agreements Signed Between Pakistan and China." *Express Tribune*, April 26, 2015, http://tribune.com.pk/story/876286/agreements-signed-between-pakistan-and-china/.

[28] The Chinese Railways Ministry is paying a small amount to do a feasibility study to build the rail line. After that, the free money mostly ends. The China Development Bank is loaning some money to Chinese enterprises. The "Silk Road Fund," which China capitalized with $40 billion, made its first signature investment in Pakistan. It is loaning almost $2 billion to finance a hydropower plant at close to market-rate returns. In one controversial project, the Chinese have agreed to fund a natural gas pipeline from Iran to energy-starved Pakistan, in anticipation that sanctions on Iran will soon be lifted. Chinese state-owned enterprises investing in Pakistan are being announced as part of an overall "aid" package. Shanghai Electric, for example, will develop several coal mines.

[29] Matthew O. Jackson and Stephen Nei, "Networks of Military Alliances, Wars, and International Trade," *Proceedings of the National Academy of Sciences* 112, no. 50 (2015), http://www.pnas.org/content/112/50/15277.

[30] Mattias Busse, Ceren Erdogan, and Henning Mühlen, "China's Impact on Africa – The Role of Trade, FDI and Aid," *Kyklos 69*, No. 2: 228-62.

[31] Kinfu Adisu, Thomas Sharkey, and Sam Okoroafo, "The Impact of Chinese Investment in Africa," *International Journal of Business and Management* 5, No. 9 (September 2010), http://www.ccsenet.org/journal/index.php/ijbm/article/viewFile/7301/5671.

[32] "China Makes Pakistan an Offer It Cannot Refuse," *Economist*, July 2017, https://www.economist.com/news/special-report/21725101-leg-up-all-weather-friend-china-makes-pakistan-offer-it-cannot-refuse.

[33] http://www.ippanigeria.org/articles/China%20-Africa%20relation_Workingpaper_final.pdf

[34] Grisons Peak is the research firm. See coverage in James Kynge, "Chinese Overseas Lending Dominated By One Belt, One Road Strategy," *Financial Times*, June 18, 2015, http://www.ft.com/intl/cms/s/3/e9dcd674-15d8-11e5-be54-00144feabdc0.html#axzz3hCVi6p4C.

[35] *Report to the U.S. Congress on Global Export Credit Competition*, Export-Import Bank of the United States, June 2015, http://www.exim.gov/sites/default/files/reports/EXIM%202014CompetReport_0611.pdf. This reports also explains that China gives lenient interest rates and long repayment terms to countries that buy big Chinese projects, such as hydropower or water treatment plants. The US and European countries have rules preventing them from making many economically unsound loans to countries that then won't be able to repay. Developed countries have also placed voluntary limits on benefits they can give to emerging economies in loans given to buy Western products. China and Russia aren't governed by these rules and thus are able to offer more lenient financing that is more attractive than US/developed country terms. In 2014 only 34 percent of the world's export credits came from countries that abide by these international rules, compared to 100 percent in 1999. China was the source of more than half of that unregulated credit.

[36] John Calabrese, "The China-Pakistan Economic Corridor (CPEC): Underway and Under Threat," Middle East Institute, December 20, 2016, http://www.mei.edu/content/map/china-pakistan-economic-corridor-cpec-underway-and-under-threat; Rajeev Deshpande, "15K Pakistanis Guarding 7K Chinese Working on China-Pakistan Economic Corridor," *The Times of India*, September 12, 2016, http://timesofindia.indiatimes.com/world/pakistan/15K-Pakistanis-guarding-7K-Chinese-working-on-China-Pakistan-Economic-Corridor/articleshow/54283602.cms. See also Kadira Pethiyagoda, "What's Driving China's New Silk Road, and How Should the West Respond?" Brookings, May 17, 2017, https://www.brookings.edu/blog/order-from-chaos/2017/05/17/whats-driving-chinas-new-silk-road-and-how-should-the-west-respond/; Christine R. Guluzian, "Making Inroads: China's New Silk Road Initiative," *Cato Journal* 37, No. 1 (Winter 2017), https://object.cato.org/sites/cato.org/files/serials/files/cato-journal/2017/2/cj-v37n1-10.pdf.

[37] James Kynge, author interview, June 19, 2015; James Kynge, "Chinese Overseas Lending Dominated By One Belt, One Road Strategy," *Financial Times*, June 18, 2015, http://www.ft.com/intl/cms/s/3/e9dcd674-15d8-11e5-be54-00144feabdc0.html#axzz3hCVi6p4C. This earlier book on China's aid to Africa describes China's interest-free loans: David Shinn and Joshua Eisenman, *China and Africa: A Century of Engagement* (Philadelphia: University of Pennsylvania Press, 2012).

[38] Parag Khanna, Senior Research Fellow at the Centre on Asia and Globalisation at the Lee Kuan Yew School of Public Policy at the National University of Singapore, author interview, August 27, 2015.

[39] Parag Khanna, Senior Research Fellow at the Centre on Asia and Globalization at the Lee Kuan Yew School of Public Policy at the National University of Singapore, author interview, August 27, 2015.

[40] Gregor Aisch, Josh Keller, and Rebecca Lai, "The World According to China," *The New York Times*, July 24, 2015, http://www.nytimes.com/interactive/2015/07/23/business/international/100000003776021.mobile.html?_r=0.

[41] Author calculation based on data from 2009 to 2015 from the China Global Investment Tracker compiled by the American Enterprise Institute and The Heritage Foundation.

[42] James Kynge, "Uganda Turns East: Chinese Money Will Build Infrastructure Says Museveni," *Financial Times*, October 21, 2014, http://www.ft.com/intl/cms/s/0/ab12d8da-5936-11e4-9546 00144feab7de.html?siteedition=intl#axzz3hnKQEkzd; James Kynge, author interview, June 20, 2015.

[43] For details on the negative environmental and labor impact of Chinese foreign investments see, for example, Rebecca Ray, Kevin Gallagher, Andres Lopez, and Cynthia Sanborn, *China in Latin America*, Boston University, April 2015, http://www.bu.edu/pardeeschool/files/2014/12/Working-Group-Final-Report.pdf.

[44] The Chinese government recently issued specific guidelines on environmental protection in mining and forestry that touch on impact assessments, resettlement, public participation, and legal compliance. Yet many of the standards applying to Chinese overseas projects are basic, and in some cases voluntary. They are a relatively recent creation and will take time to become established, understood, and implemented. *Safeguarding People and the Environment in Chinese Investments*, Inclusive Development International, 2017, http://www.inclusivedevelopment.net/wp-content/uploads/2017/03/Safeguarding-People-and-the-Environment-in-Chinese-Investments.pdf. See also "Notification of the Ministry of Commerce and the Ministry of Environmental Protection on Issuing the Guidelines for Environmental Protection in Foreign Investment and Cooperation," Ministry of Commerce People's Republic of China, March 1, 2013, http://english.mofcom.gov.cn/article/policyrelease/bbb/201303/20130300043226.shtml. (Note that these MofCom standards are nonbinding overseas, so enforcement is left to weak host governments.)

[45] Euan Rocha, "CNOOC Closes $15.1 Billion Acquisition of Canada's Nexen," Reuters, February 25, 2013, http://www.reuters.com/article/2013/02/25/us-nexen-cnooc-idUSBRE91O1A420130225. China's state-owned oil company, CNOOC, has its largest investment in the world in Canada's tar sands, partly because it likes Canada's rule of law and high labor and environmental standards. CNOOC board member, author interview, June 2015.

"While China chafes at the notions that the international order is Western in origin and thus should be guided by Western liberal principles in perpetuity, it in fact adheres to and upholds the majority of these principles, largely accepts the LWO institutional architecture, and increasingly embraces its own role in sustaining the system."

—DAVID SHAMBAUGH

China and the Liberal World Order

David Shambaugh
Gaston Sigur Professor of Asian Studies, Political Science & International Affairs
George Washington University

In order to adequately address the issue of China's position in, and approach to, the liberal world order (LWO) it is critical at the outset to define and disentangle the various elements of the LWO.

The LWO is one of those phenomena that means very different things to different people and for which selective interpretation is commonplace. Many in the US and West associate it with the post-World War II San Francisco and Bretton Woods institutional systems, undergirded by the "universal" principles of openness, democracy, human rights, and collective action.

By contrast, the Chinese emphasize the institutional "order" but distinctly do not endorse many of the liberal normative underpinnings of that order. In all my years of reading Chinese writings on international affairs and interacting with Chinese policy elites, I have never once encountered the use of the term "liberal world order." The Chinese normally use the terms "international order" (*guoji zhixu*, 国际秩序) or "international structure" (*guoji tixi*, 国际体系), and when they refer to globalization it is usually limited only to "economic globalization" (经济全球化).

As "liberalism" (自由主义) is a very negative political term in Chinese Communist lexicon—epitomized by frequent campaigns against "bourgeois liberalism"—Chinese officials and scholars would never characterize the existing world order as "liberal." To do so would countenance their acceptance of an order constructed on (Western) liberal principles. While Chinese leaders regularly assert that China will never adopt the Western political system, the government holds the view that the international system has multiple origins, multiple components, and is an ever-evolving process that should involve multiple participants from all over of the world. China is therefore primarily concerned with diversifying the *representativeness* of participation in international institutions,[1] and has long been critical of the "hegemony" exercised by Western states in the postwar system.[2] Beijing is secondarily interested in selectively undermining some liberal principles—such as freedom of expression and information, universal social and political rights, decision-making transparency, aid conditionality, *habeas corpus* and rights of the accused, and other procedures that mandate accountability for official malfeasance—while not mounting a full frontal assault on the postwar liberal system.

While China chafes at the notions that the international order is Western in origin and thus should be guided by Western liberal principles in perpetuity, it in fact adheres to and upholds the majority of these principles, largely accepts the LWO institutional architecture, and increasingly embraces its own role in sustaining the system. It is fair to say that today—and particularly since Xi Jinping came to power in 2012—China has increasingly become the "responsible [international] stakeholder" that Robert Zoellick famously envisioned in 2005.[3] China under Xi has undertaken a marked, notable, and commendable increase in its involvement in, and contributions to, global governance (hereafter GG).

Why is this the case? Why, after years of free-riding, has Beijing stepped up its involvement in global governance? The explanation brings us back to the origins and basic elements of the LWO.

Here, Princeton Professor G. John Ikenberry's writings are very helpful in understanding what actually constitutes the LWO and why China is comfortable with it in the main.[4] Ikenberry usefully reminds us, first of all, that the LWO does not simply date to the post-WWII era, but that it has its origins in the Westphalian system of 1648 which accepts the *sovereignty* of all states as its bedrock foundational principle. China readily and adamantly accepts this core element of the LWO— for China there is no more important principle in international affairs than state sovereignty. China's embrace of this core principle grows directly out of its own modern history of sovereign dismemberment by Western imperial powers and Japan. Thus, Beijing views *every single issue* in international affairs—whether it is governing cyberspace, protecting human rights, managing humanitarian crises, addressing security challenges, or other issues—through the imperative to uphold state sovereignty as *the* basis of international relations. And Beijing only participates in international organizations in which state sovereignty is the criterion of membership. There is, however, an increasing contradiction and tension between China's emphasis on sovereignty and the reality that in today's world many (most) issues transcend national boundaries and state control.

Relatedly, the principles of self-determination and nondiscrimination are embedded in the primacy of state sovereignty. Ikenberry also reminds us that the

LWO is also premised on the norms of openness and inclusiveness, as well as laws and rules as made, interpreted, and enforced by international bodies—constituted by *sovereign states*. So, in these basic senses, China is very comfortable with—and supportive of—the LWO, and China (Imperial, Republican, and Communist) has thus been supportive of—and a party to—the panoply of international institutions that date to the late nineteenth century that seek to regulate interstate behavior based on immutable state sovereignty.

As the world entered the twentieth century, however, international order began to take on a less sovereign-based and more universalist orientation. The United States in particular began to champion the principles of open and free trade (John Hay's "Open Door Notes" of 1899-1900), democratic political principles (Woodrow Wilson's 14 Points), freedom of the seas and arms control (Washington Naval Conference of 1922), multilateral diplomatic governance, collective security, and conflict prevention (League of Nations). While the League failed, these multilateral liberal principles endured and became embedded in the post-WW II San Francisco and Bretton Woods systems. The Republic of China was very much a part of this post-WW II architecture, but following the Chinese Communists' seizure of power in 1949, the PRC began a protracted and ambivalent relationship with the postwar LWO.

China's Evolving Path to Global Governance

Since coming into being, the PRC's approach to the LWO and GG has evolved over time: from being an opponent and critic during the 1950s-1970s → a generally passive position during the 1980s-1990s when it sought membership in international institutions and to learn the "rules of the road," which it obeyed to a large extent → a more selective and activist position in international institutions during the early-2000s in which Beijing became more confident and contributed more tangibly → a new moderately revisionist posture since 2011 that seeks to selectively alter the "balance of influence" *within* existing institutions while simultaneously trying to establish *alternative* institutions and norms and redistribute power and resources within the international system from North to South and from West to East.

While the world has generally witnessed China evolving from passive actor to selective activist, many observers now see China becoming a more proactive player in international institutions, which reflects both its growing power and confidence. This recent tendency should not be overstated, however, as China still remains very reluctant to become engaged on some issues and still displays a distinct "selective multilateralist" posture. China continues to display and practice a distinct "transactional" style of diplomacy—which carefully weighs national costs and benefits for any commitment of resources, rather than comprehensively contributing to collective global "public goods." Until very recently, China did not understand the concept of public goods and suspiciously viewed Western calls for China to increase its contributions commensurate with its increasing capabilities. Chinese President Xi Jinping himself deserves credit for this change in China's global governance diplomacy. In both his speech to the 2017 World Economic Forum in Davos and his Report to the 19th National Congress of the Chinese Communist Party, Xi made abundantly clear that China under his leadership would assume an ever-increasing role and responsibility in global governance. There are thus encouraging reasons to believe that China is avoiding what Joseph Nye has described as the "Kindleberger Trap."[5]

While assiduously and tenaciously guarding its own corner to protect its own national interests in the international institutional arena, China has also long articulated a foreign policy agenda that favors multipolarization (as distinct from multilateralism), equality (termed "democratization") in international relations, and empowerment of developing nations. This has hardly been a hidden agenda. Now, with Beijing's own growing international influence, along with the reality of other rising powers and the general fluidity of the international system, the world is beginning to witness China's attempt to redistribute power and influence in the system.

Five Phases of Evolution

It is useful to have some sense of how China has evolved to this point. In my view, China's government has passed through five distinct phases in its approach to global governance and involvement in international institutions.

First, from its inception in 1949 through its admission to the United Nations in 1971 and until the late-1970s, China was a *system challenger*. Prior to its admission to the UN China was excluded from the Western-constructed international system and thus was a fierce critic of it. Its Marxist-Leninist-Maoist ideology also had much to do with its critical and combative posture. This outlook became a deeply embedded element in its international identity at the time. Even after China's admission to the UN and continuing throughout most of the 1970s, Beijing continued to challenge the existing order and the institutions that had excluded its participation over the previous two decades. Beijing regularly denounced the international system as unequal and unfair, limited its involvement to selective UN-affiliated bodies, often refused to participate in UN voting (in protest), and advocated reform of the system to increase the role and voice of developing countries while criticizing the Soviet Union at the same time.

With Deng Xiaoping's and other reformist leaders' full ascension to power in 1978, China's stance in the UN and international bodies shifted to a second phase: *system student*. During this prolonged period China sought to learn how the system worked and how its institutions operated.[6] This indicated a shift from Beijing's advocacy of changing the international system to upholding it. In terms of its participation in international organizations, China remained passive but studious. From 1977 to 1984 it only joined eight more IGOs (although its participation in NGOs jumped from 71 in 1977 to 355 in 1984). Importantly, this included the three main Bretton Woods institutions—the World Bank, International Monetary Fund, and General Agreement on Tariffs and Trade[7]—as well as the Asian Development Bank (ADB).

This apprentice-like period led to a lengthy third phase from 1985-2000 when China's approach can be described as *system exploiter*. During this time, China further integrated into the international institutional order and learned very well how to benefit from it by extracting resources from the system. For example, China became the largest recipient of World Bank loans and projects. By the end of 2009 the World Bank had cumulatively committed a total of $46.06 billion in loans, involving 309 projects, to China.[8] From 1986-2007 China received $19.25 billion in loans and grants from the ADB.[9] Beijing had learned to milk a wide variety of other multilateral agencies for aid, loans, and investment—surpassing all other nations in the world. These IGOs played a significant role in several dimensions of China's modernization during this phase.

While Beijing learned how to "play the system," its presence and voice in international institutions and organizations also increased. Numerically, China progressively joined an increasing number of IGOs (51 by 1996) and NGOs (1,079 by 1996), representing the country's increased integration into the system. In addition to joining more institutions, during the 1990s China also acceded to a large number of international treaties and conventions. By signing these treaties and joining these regimes, China took tangible steps indicating it was a "status quo" and system-maintaining power.

Diplomatically, during this third period, Chinese leaders and officials increasingly began to address more international gatherings to discuss issues on the global governance agenda. In these speeches, China was unfailingly supportive of multilateral efforts to address global issues, but it also continued to emphasize state sovereignty, greater multipolarity, and a redistribution of power from North to South; in addition, it was often critical of the United States. Thus, on one hand, China sought to act as a status-quo system-supporting power by working *through* international organizations—but on the other hand, it continued to evince discomfort with the way the system was configured.

Thus, during this third period of international institutional interaction, we see a China that was technically more integrated in terms of its growing membership and participation in international and regional bodies, legally and normatively more integrated through its growing accession and adherence to international treaties and accepted practices, a major beneficiary of the resources international institutions had to offer, increasingly more proactive in international institutions, but still extremely uncomfortable with the Western structural and normative biases in the system.

This ambivalence continued into the fourth phase: *system supporter*. This phase of China's evolving relationship with international institutions and global governance existed from 2000 through roughly 2011. The fourth phase is characterized by expanded membership and deepening participation in international institutions. China had become a member of more than 130 IGOs and 24 UN specialized agencies, and signatory to more than 300 multilateral treaties.[10] By this time it was evident that China was fully integrated into the international institutional architecture. It had become a full "member of the club." It remained outside of very few major IGOs—only the Organization for Economic Co-operation and Development (OECD) and the International Energy Agency.

As it integrated, Beijing's confidence grew and its participation became more self-assured. Chinese diplomats assigned to IGOs received high marks for their knowledge, preparedness, and sophistication. They mastered the technical details and operating procedures of institutions, and became increasingly active in setting and shaping agendas. It was during this period that China also became more tangibly and *proactively involved* in a range of GG activities: particularly in peacekeeping, disaster relief, development assistance, climate change, public health and pandemics, antipiracy, counter-terrorism, energy security, and other transnational security cooperation. During this phase, China ceased to be a free (or partial) rider and began to become a "responsible international stakeholder" and shoulder a greater share of responsibility proportionate to its capabilities. Thus, during the first decade of this century there was increasing optimism about China becoming a status-quo power, partner of the West, and more equal contributor to the world community.

Since around 2012 we have seen China enter a fifth phase in its relationship with GG institutions: *system stakeholder and revisionist*. This has been manifest in two principal forms.

First, we have witnessed China under Xi Jinping continually expand its involvement in GG institutions and issues. In addition to the issue areas noted above, China has become deeply involved in international economic governance within the G-20 framework; it played an instrumental role in global climate change negotiations that resulted in the 2015 Paris Climate Change Agreement (COP-21); it expanded its financial contributions to the United Nations and other regional development banks in Asia, Africa, and Latin America; it increased both its financial and human contributions to UN peacekeeping operations (PKO); and antipiracy operations in the Gulf of Aden; and it deepened its involvement in other areas.

But, secondly, China has become increasingly proactive in pushing for change within some IGOs—to reflect Beijing's long-stated commitment to enhance the influence of developing countries. This included trying to change the membership as well as the procedures of some organizations. Some observers labeled Beijing's strategy as one of "hollowing out from within,"[11] although actual evidence of such behavior is difficult to identify. This has resulted in China's establishment of a broad range of regional groupings and two new institutions: the (BRICS) New Development Bank (organized by China together with Brazil, Russia, India, and South Africa) and the Asian Infrastructure Investment Bank (AIIB). These new institutional initiatives supplement other regional bodies China has previously created around the world—such as the Shanghai Cooperation Organization (SCO), the Forum on China-Africa Cooperation (FOCAC), the China-Arab States Cooperation Forum, the China-Community of Latin American and Caribbean States Forum, and the China-Central and Eastern Europe Leaders Meeting.

Taken together, I would describe these groupings and institutions as the wellsprings of a *parallel alternative institutional architecture* to the postwar LWO. How far those institutions will go, and whether they will challenge the underlying norms and principles of the postwar LWO remains to be seen, but an alternative structure is gradually taking shape. The inclusion of OECD member states in institutions such as the AIIB offers an encouraging check on this institution becoming an *illiberal* institution that skirts well-developed official development assistance (ODA) standards, but it very much remains a work in progress.

China and the Future of the Liberal World Order and Global Governance

Since the PRC came into existence, it has thus passed through these five phases in its evolving approach to international organizations and GG. It is important to bear this historical evolution in mind when contemplating the future. While China's ambivalence has been apparent throughout, it is also clear that China has become a "good global citizen" in almost all areas of GG (in many cases halting its previously noncompliant behavior). We have witnessed a much more proactive China in the GG arena during Xi Jinping's tenure.

Yet, China's ambivalence and discomfort with the LWO continues to remain apparent. While China definitely is a status-quo power insofar as it seeks to *uphold* and even strengthen the core institutions and rules of the LWO, it is *simultaneously* a dissatisfied and (quasi) revisionist power insofar as it seeks to (1) selectively opt out of participating in certain aspects,[12] while (2) spearheading *new* institutions.

On some issues—such as global trade and investment—China has cast itself as the primary *upholder* of economic globalization and open and inclusive institutional arrangements (as evidenced in President Xi Jinping's widely covered speech to the 2017 World Economic Forum in Davos[13]). The best example may be free trade agreements (FTAs).[14] China has also been very constructively involved in G-20 global economic governance. On other issues China clearly disagrees with the underlying norms of the LWO, yet still works through existing institutions to *undermine* some liberal norms while upholding others—the United Nations Human Rights Council (UNHRC) is an illustration. China could have refused to participate in the UNHRC given international criticism of its own human rights record, but instead Beijing decided to actively participate in the Council (along with other authoritarian states) in order to shape its agenda and tactics. Yet on other issues, such as the challenge to China's territorial claims in the South China Sea heard by the Permanent Court of Arbitration (PCA) in The Hague in 2016, China refused to even participate and has rejected its ruling out-of-hand.

Looking to the future, I believe that the trends witnessed over the past few years will continue:

1. China will continue to contribute more and more tangible financial and human resources to GG activities and will continue to be a status quo power and upholder of the LWO in the main. Beijing has gained increasing confidence, as well as experience in, working with other actors within multilateral frameworks. It also better appreciates (although not yet completely) the

downside, in terms of its international reputation and soft power, of *not* contributing at a reasonably high level, commensurate with China's global standing and resources. It also has a leader (Xi Jinping) who believes in China being a major world power that contributes significantly to global public goods. This is all good.

2. China will continue to be one of the greatest supporters of the United Nations in the world (although Beijing hypocritically blocks the expansion of Security Council permanent membership). To the extent that there will be UN reform, expect China to be centrally involved in the process.

3. China will remain ambivalent about some of the underlying liberal premises of GG. This will lead China to simply ignore or not comply with some elements (e.g., human rights, ODA, responsibility to protect, collective security).

4. China will remain committed to its longstanding desire to "democratize" GG institutions and substantially empower other developing countries' voices and participation. This will become manifest both *within* existing institutions as well as by establishing new alternative institutions. Beijing has the financial wherewithal to fund many new institutions that will increasingly operate *in parallel* to the existing Western-constructed GG system. In this regard, China *is a revisionist* power and it *will* present a *challenge* to the existing LWO system.

5. China's alterations to the existing LWO are coming "around the edges" and are not (at least yet) a frontal *illiberal* challenge to the LWO as some had previously envisioned.[15] It is not (yet) establishing exclusive blocs of states, separate spheres of influence, or mercantilist networks. The question remains, however, should Beijing begin to move in these directions, would others *follow* its lead? And will Beijing's enormous financial promises actually materialize on projects like "One Belt, One Road"? If others do not follow China's lead and if its promised resources do not materialize, or if China stumbles in trying to set up and make these institutions functional, then what impact will it have on China's credibility and image as a global power?

6. Finally, should other nations—notably Russia—seek to undermine and overturn the LWO, what will Beijing do? Will China collaborate in such a revisionist undertaking? I doubt it. This could become an element of friction between Moscow and Beijing. Conversely, as President Trump leads the United States to relatively withdraw from the LWO and previous commitments such as the Paris Climate Accord and Trans-Pacific Partnership (TPP), will

Beijing step into the void, along with others, to uphold the core elements of the LWO and postwar liberal institutional architecture?[16] We are already beginning to see this with China's cooperation with Germany and other G-7 and G-20 members. This is an encouraging indication that China has become a responsible international stakeholder and can be expected to do more to uphold the LWO than to tear it down in the coming years.

David Shambaugh is an internationally recognized authority and award-winning author on contemporary China and the international relations of Asia. He currently is the Gaston Sigur Professor of Asian Studies, Political Science & International Affairs, and the founding Director of the China Policy Program in the Elliott School of International Affairs at George Washington University. From 1996-2015 he was also a Nonresident Senior Fellow in the Foreign Policy Studies Program at The Brookings Institution. Professor Shambaugh was previously Lecturer, Senior Lecturer, and Reader in Chinese Politics at the University of London's School of Oriental & African Studies (SOAS), 1986-1996, where he also served as Editor of *The China Quarterly* (1991-1996). He has served on the Board of Directors of the National Committee on U.S.-China Relations, and is a life member of the Council on Foreign Relations, U.S. Asia-Pacific Council, and other public policy and scholarly organizations. He has been selected for numerous awards and grants, is an active public intellectual and frequent commentator in the international media, serves on numerous editorial boards, and has been a consultant to governments, research institutions, foundations, universities, corporations, banks, and investment funds. As an author, Professor Shambaugh has published more than 30 books, including most recently *China's Future* and *The China Reader: Rising Power* (both 2016). Both *China's Future* and *China Goes Global* were selected by *The Economist* among "Best Books of the Year." His next book (2018) will be *Where Great Powers Meet: America & China in Southeast Asia.*

---

[1] This is what the PRC means by its desire for the "democratization of international relations."

[2] This includes what Beijing perceives to be the "hegemony of Western media." See David Shambaugh, "China's Soft Power Push," *Foreign Affairs* 94, No. 4 (July/August 2015).

[3] Deputy Secretary of State Robert B. Zoellick, "Whiter China: From Membership to Responsibility," (speech, New York, NY, September 21, 2005), https://2001-2009.state.gov/s/d/former/zoellick/rem/53682.htm.

[4] See, in particular, G. John Ikenberry, "The Rise of China, the United States, and the Future of the Liberal International Order," in David Shambaugh (ed.), *Tangled Titans: The United States & China* (Lanham, MD: Rowman & Littlefield, 2012). See also, G. John Ikenberry, *Liberal Leviathan: The Origins, Crisis, and Transformation of the American World Order* (Princeton: Princeton University Press, 2011).

[5] Joseph S. Nye, "The Kindleberger Trap," Project Syndicate, January 9, 2017.

[6] See, for example, Elizabeth C. Economy and Michel C. Oksenberg (eds.), *China Joins the World: Progress and Prospects* (New York, Council on Foreign Relations, 1998); and Samuel S. Kim, *China, the United Nations, and World Order* (Princeton: Princeton University Press, 1979).

[7] See Harold K. Jacobson and Michel Oksenberg (eds.), *China's Participation in the IMF, World Bank, and GATT: Toward a Global Economic Order* (Ann Arbor: University of Michigan Press, 1990).

[8] Ministry of Foreign Affairs, *China's Foreign Affairs 2010* (Beijing: Shijie zhishi chubanshe, 2010), 338.

[9] Tsinghua University Department of International Relations and Economic Diplomacy Research Center, *Zhongguo Jingji Waijiao* 2009 [China's Economic Diplomacy in 2009] (Beijing: Shijie zhishi chubanshe, 2009), 33.

[10] "Guoji Diwei" [International Position], *Renmin Ribao* [People's Daily], September 23, 2009.

[11] See Gregory Chin and Ramesh Thakur, "Will China Change the Rules of Global Order?" *The Washington Quarterly* 33, No. 4 (October 2010): 119-138.

[12] Richard Haass once described this as an *"a la carte* approach" to multilateralism.

[13] Xi Jinping, "Jointly Shoulder Responsibility of Our Times, Promote Global Growth" (speech, Davos, Switzerland, January 17, 2017), CGTN America, https://america.cgtn.com/2017/01/17/full-text-of-xi-jinping-keynote-at-the-world-economic-forum.

[14] China's Ministry of Commerce (MOFCOM) currently lists 14 FTAs in place (13 bilateral plus 1 multilateral with the 10 members of ASEAN), 12 under active negotiation, 11 under discussion, and 1 Preferential Trade Agreement in place. China has also proposed a full Asia-Pacific FTA (APFTA) while being a major proponent of the Regional Comprehensive Economic Partnership (RCEP) proposed by ASEAN. Source: http://fta.mofcom.gov.cn/english/.

[15] See, for example, Elizabeth C. Economy, "The Game Changer: Coping with China's Foreign Policy Revolution," *Foreign Affairs* 89, No. 6 (November/December 2010).

[16] See David Shambaugh, "China Rethinks Its Global Role in the Age of Trump," *Bloomberg View*, June 13, 2017, https://www.bloomberg.com/view/articles/2017-06-13/china-rethinks-its-global-role-in-the-age-of-trump.

"It should be unacceptable to NATO members, especially the United States, that the EDA (European Defense Agency) exhibits greater transparency than NATO."

—JOHN DOWDY

More Tooth, Less Tail:
Getting Beyond NATO's 2 Percent Rule

John Dowdy
Senior Partner
McKinsey & Company

As a presidential candidate, Donald Trump suggested that the North Atlantic Treaty Organization (NATO) was "obsolete,"[1] casting doubt on America's commitment to the collective defense of Europe. On the eve of accepting the Republican nomination for president, he went so far as to suggest that the United States would only come to the defense of its NATO allies if they had "fulfilled their [financial] obligations to us."[2] This called into question America's commitment to one of NATO's core tenets, collective defense, enshrined in Article 5 of the founding treaty. Shortly after taking office, President Trump revised his view on NATO's relevance, saying that NATO is no longer obsolete. And just before the July 2017 meeting of the G-20, he offered a more vigorous expression of support for Article 5, saying, "The United States has demonstrated with its actions, not just words, that it stands firmly behind Article 5."[3]

The question of obsolescence seems to have been settled. But the debate on burden-sharing continues unabated. In his roundabout way, President Trump has done a notable job of raising the issue of the adequacy of European NATO's defense spending. Criticism has focused almost entirely on the level of investment by member countries—whether they are meeting the 2 percent commitment—with far less attention paid to their actual ability to defend themselves, and their allies. All things considered, the 2 percent rule is a poor way to measure burden-sharing. It came about in part as a convenience, as this was the level of NATO Europe's spending in 2002, when the target was first agreed upon. It is one of the few things that NATO reports externally. It is useful, if a little crude, but it has a few methodological flaws and only takes us so far. Even the wider concept of burden-sharing, the desire for members to "pay their fair share," is inherently flawed, since it focuses on inputs rather than outputs.

What is needed is a more explicit focus on the capabilities NATO can deploy in the conduct of its core tasks of collective defense, crisis management, and cooperative security, and new metrics to assess these. A much more robust discussion is possible, even with the fairly limited data publicly available today. This paper is my attempt to contribute to that discussion.

Disproportionate Spending? The 2 Percent Obsession

President Trump argues that "NATO is unfair economically to us, to the United States. Because it really helps them more so than the United States, and we pay a disproportionate share."[4] His message has been echoed by senior administration officials. Secretary of Defense James Mattis, in his first meeting with NATO defense ministers in February 2017, warned that the United States could "moderate its commitment" to the alliance if allies did not get serious about meeting the 2 percent goal. "No longer can the American taxpayer carry a disproportionate share of the defense of Western values."[5]

A perception of unequal burdens is not a new issue. It is as old as the alliance itself. President Trump is far from alone in calling for NATO members to meet the 2 percent target. A wide array of American officials has pressured our NATO allies to live up to their commitment, not just in this administration but in the prior ones as well.

President Obama complained of "free riders."[6] Former Defense Secretary Robert M. Gates used no less colorful language in his valedictory speech in Brussels, warning of a "dim if not dismal future" for the alliance, pointing to the "very real possibility of collective military irrelevance" and issuing the prescient warning that Americans were beginning to grow tired of expending precious resources defending nations "unwilling to devote the necessary resources . . . to be serious and capable partners in their own defense."[7]

The historical roots of the issue run even deeper. Indeed, complaints date back almost to the foundation of the alliance in 1949. In 1953, Secretary of State John Foster Dulles threatened "an agonizing reappraisal" of the US commitment to European security if its allies did not step up.[8] If nothing else, the 2 percent rule has provided a yardstick to measure the gap that has provoked all the complaints (see Exhibit 1). From 1985-1989, NATO Europe spent an average of 3.1 percent of GDP on defense. With the fall of the Berlin Wall in 1989, Western European countries no longer felt an imminent threat from the Warsaw Pact countries and elected to take a "peace dividend." Spending fell to 2.5 percent in 1990-1994, 2.0 percent in 1995-1999, and 1.9 percent in 2000-2004. Five years later, the average fell yet again, to 1.7 percent. A low point of 1.43 percent (1.40 percent including Canada) was reached in 2015.

Only five member states (Estonia, Greece, Poland, the United Kingdom, and the US) hit the 2 percent benchmark in 2016, and only three of those—the United States, Britain, and Poland—also met NATO's target of spending 20 percent of their annual defense expenditure on equipment. In 2016, the United States well exceeded the target, spending 3.6 percent of GDP on defense, contributing fully 68 percent of NATO's combined defense expenditure despite representing only 46 percent of the alliance's combined GDP.

EXHIBIT I

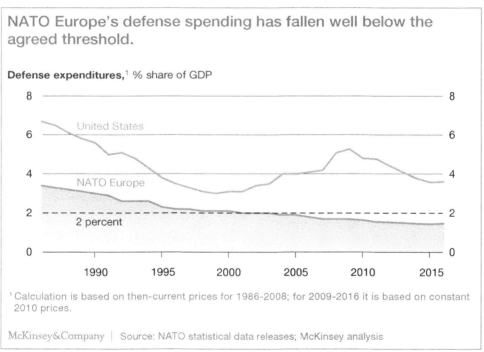

NATO Europe's defense spending has fallen well below the agreed threshold.

Defense expenditures,[1] % share of GDP

[1] Calculation is based on then-current prices for 1986-2008; for 2009-2016 it is based on constant 2010 prices.

McKinsey&Company | Source: NATO statistical data releases; McKinsey analysis

Some Progress, but to What End?

The 2 percent figure dates to the 2002 Prague summit, when it was established as a non-binding target; it was reiterated in Riga in 2006. At the NATO 2014 summit in Wales, all states not meeting the target pledged to do so within the next decade (and states above 2 percent agreed to maintain that level). In the three years since the Wales summit, spending has started to move in the right direction, increasing by 1.8 percent in 2015, 3.3 percent in 2016, and a projected 4.3 percent this year.

Some might argue that the president's "very strong and frank discussions"[9] have begun to pay dividends. It is, however, equally plausible that governments have begun to slowly increase spending not just because of US comments but also because they are reassessing their presumption that Western Europe is safe from outside threats. Several former NATO officials have commented on the rising number of geopolitical challenges.[10]

And in any event, the recent increases have raised the overall figure only slightly, to 1.47 percent of GDP—an indicator of how much further the European allies must go to recover lost ground. To get to 2 percent, spending will need to increase by another $107 billion annually ($28 billion in Germany, $17 billion in Italy, $15 billion in Spain, $12 billion in Canada, $5 billion in France, and smaller sums elsewhere).

Some question whether 2 percent is still the right target. It would seem so, as the present level of spending is not producing the desired results. Shortfalls in NATO's fighting power were most graphically illustrated in Libya in 2011. After taking command of the air war there, the alliance ran short of munitions after just eleven weeks, drawing a harsh rebuke from Defense Secretary Robert Gates, who pointed to shortages not just in "boots on the ground, but in crucial support assets such as helicopters, transport aircraft, maintenance, intelligence, surveillance and reconnaissance, and much more."[11]

Flawed but Indispensable

Many allies question the relevance of the 2 percent target on methodological grounds, citing different methodologies used to calculate national defense spending or calling for related spending to be included. There is no shared understanding of what makes up defense spending. In its definition of "military expenditure," NATO includes defense ministry budgets, expenditure for peacekeeping and humanitarian operations, and research and development costs. Significantly, it also includes pensions. For many states, military pensions represent a substantial proportion of their defense budget (in 2016, 33 percent of Belgium's defense budget was spent on pensions, as was 24 percent of France's and 17 percent of Germany's). The trouble is that while pensions contribute to the 2 percent target, they do not contribute to a state's fighting power.[12]

Others, notably Germany, make the case that non-military contributions to security, such as development aid, or even non-monetary contributions such as overflight rights or basing, should be taken into account. In March 2017, German

Foreign Minister Sigmar Gabriel said that the 2 percent target was neither "reachable nor desirable" for Germany, and that "it is better to talk about better spending instead of more spending."[13] Wolfgang Ischinger, chairman of the Munich Security Conference, suggests a broader 3 percent target for crisis prevention, development assistance, and defense.[14]

Finally, some argue that the United States' status as a global power means that its defense spending is not directly comparable to that of other NATO members. Of nearly 200,000 US forces deployed overseas, just over 99,000 of them are deployed in Europe, suggesting that roughly half of US deployed forces (and by extension roughly half its spending) are dedicated to non-European missions.[15] By that measure, the US contribution to NATO would not seem nearly so disproportionate.

For all of those problems, the 2 percent metric retains its appeal. It is simple, straightforward, and (relatively) easy to measure. Jan Techau, director of Carnegie Europe, argues that the 2 percent target is "flawed but indispensable" as a measure of "who is and who is not politically committed to NATO's core task: European Security."[16]

Current Metrics Inadequate

In addition to defense spending as a percent of GDP, and the percent of that spending dedicated to major equipment purchases, NATO has set a number of other targets for defense output. At the Riga summit in 2006, it introduced a target that NATO land forces be at least 40 percent deployable and 8 percent deployable on a sustained basis (raised to 50 percent and 10 percent in 2008).[17] In 2011, NATO went further, developing a more detailed set of output metrics—nine in all, focused on deployability, sustainability, and numbers of deployed air, land, and maritime forces.

NATO member states' performance on these metrics remains classified, with the notable exception of Denmark.[18] However, some of these same figures are publicly reported by the European Defense Agency (EDA) (twenty-two members are common to NATO and the EDA). The latest official figures from the EDA show that only 29 percent of EDA member forces are deployable, and less than 6 percent of them on a sustainable basis,[19] with unofficial figures suggesting that fewer than 3 percent of European troops are deployable due to a lack of interoperability and equipment shortages.[20]

Yet even these numbers, while more revealing than the blunt instrument of the 2 percent rule, do not provide a full picture of NATO's health. The current set of metrics is inadequate to determine whether alliance members are spending enough and on the right things, and generating real combat power as a result. While measuring such attributes is of course more difficult, and the data harder to obtain, the fact remains that there is enough information in the public domain for a robust discussion.

Expect What You Inspect

"There is too much focus on the 'input' (how much the member states spend) and too little focus on the 'output' (how much they get out of it)," says Magnus Petersson, the head of the Centre for Transatlantic Studies at the Norwegian Institute for Defence Studies. The Center for a New American Security argues that what matters is not just how much a nation spends on defense, but what it spends it on, and—critically—its willingness to use it.[21] Jan Techau, former director of Carnegie Europe, says it all: "Spending at 2 percent says very little about a country's actual military capabilities; its readiness, deployability, and sustainability levels; and the quality of the force that it can field. It also is mum about a country's willingness to deploy forces and take risks once those forces are deployed. It does not assess whether a country spends its limited resources wisely."[22]

The 1949 Strategic Concept called for this level of rigor: "A successful defense of the North Atlantic Treaty nations through maximum efficiency of their armed forces, with the minimum necessary expenditures of manpower, money and materials, is the goal of defense planning."[23] NATO recognized the need again in a recent paper: "Currently, each Member Nation manages its defense budgets in support of the Alliance independently, without fully leveraging successful resource management practices and lessons learned. This study highlights the need for NATO to adopt an analytical framework that provides Alliance Nations a common foundation to achieve effective and efficient defense resource management. The aim is for countries to adopt resource management practices to maintain the future credibility and effectiveness of the Alliance."[24] NATO Secretary General Jens Stoltenberg has recently suggested that member states publish plans detailing three elements: cash, capabilities, and commitments.[25]

In the following, I propose a framework to meet the needs that NATO and others have identified.

1. Spend Enough

NATO must measure and report total defense spending.

It is inarguable that there can be no output without investment. Ambassador Doug Lute, former US representative to NATO, makes this case: "there's a correlated effect, empirically, between input measures and output measures. . . . You've got to pay more to get more."[26] It is important to start with a pure measure of military spending—expenditure that directly contributes to the military output of a nation—what one might call a "real" 2 percent. The NATO definition allows for the inclusion of items such as military and civilian pensions, spending by other government agencies on defense (for example, intelligence services), and military aid. This prompted the UK, in 2015, to add some £2.2 billion to its reported NATO figure by adding civilian and military pensions, contributions to UN peacekeeping missions, and a large portion of the Ministry of Defence's income from other countries' defense ministries, to its reported figure.[27] Although these inclusions were seen as legitimate, it seems likely that they do not contribute to the UK's fighting power and should be removed from the NATO definition for all nations.

2. Spend It on the Right Things

NATO should measure and report what the money is spent on.

Measures of defense spending should be the beginning of a discussion on burden-sharing, not the end. Many forces do not allocate defense spending in a manner that maximizes fighting power. In its own NATO 2020 report, the alliance observes that "European Defense spending has been consumed disproportionately by personnel and operational costs."[28] In fact, more than 50 percent of European spending goes to salaries and pensions. Roughly speaking, an optimal mix is no more than 40 percent on personnel and a quarter on major equipment. Yet NATO Europe forces only spend 15.2 percent of their budgets on equipment, versus a much healthier 25 percent in the United States (and 24.5 percent in France and 22.6 percent in the UK).[29]

The net result is that the US spends fully $127,000 on each soldier's equipment, while NATO European members spend only one-fifth that amount, $25,200 per soldier (see Exhibit 2). So in addition to the question discussed above about the deployability of Europe's forces, their actual fighting power if deployed is also in question. The discrepancy in the level of investment on research and development of future weapon systems is equally pronounced: $43,500 per soldier in the US versus less than $9,400 for NATO Europe. (These are 2014 figures; the US figure also includes expenses for testing and evaluation.)

EXHIBIT 2

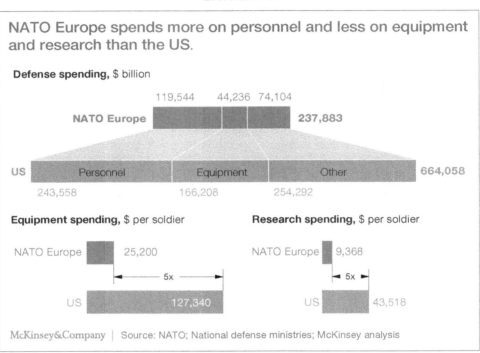

NATO Europe spends more on personnel and less on equipment and research than the US.

Defense spending, $ billion

NATO Europe: 119,544 44,236 74,104   237,883

US: Personnel 243,558   Equipment 166,208   Other 254,292   664,058

Equipment spending, $ per soldier

NATO Europe: 25,200
US: 127,340
5x

Research spending, $ per soldier

NATO Europe: 9,368
US: 43,518
5x

McKinsey&Company | Source: NATO; National defense ministries; McKinsey analysis

In addition to committing to spend 2 percent of GDP on defense, NATO members have committed to spending 20 percent of their annual defense expenditure on equipment and are reporting progress against this target. Although this is an admirable start, NATO should be measuring spending at a more granular level: military pay, civilian pay, major equipment acquisition, research and development, operations and maintenance, and infrastructure. And it must announce the results, even if that causes discomfort in some defense ministries.

3. Spend It Well

NATO should measure efficiency and effectiveness in each of these three categories.

Personnel: A big part of the problem of spending too much on personnel is the way many forces waste precious resources, maintaining Cold War bureaucracies rather than prioritizing frontline forces. The people and infrastructure supporting the fighting force (the tail) has failed to shrink as fast as the fighting force itself (the tooth), resulting in an ever deteriorating tooth-to-tail ratio (see Exhibit 3). The force is at the same time too large, with too many non-deployable forces, and too small, with too few deployable fighting forces.

Equipment: Compounding the problem of too few euros going to equipment, the purchasing power of European governments is dissipated by an inefficient industry structure. Alexander Mattelaer at the Institute for European Studies argues: "the present degree of fragmentation in the European defense markets and organizational structures virtually guarantees a poor return on investment."[30] McKinsey's analysis shows 178 different weapon systems in service in Europe, versus thirty in the US.[31]

EXHIBIT 3

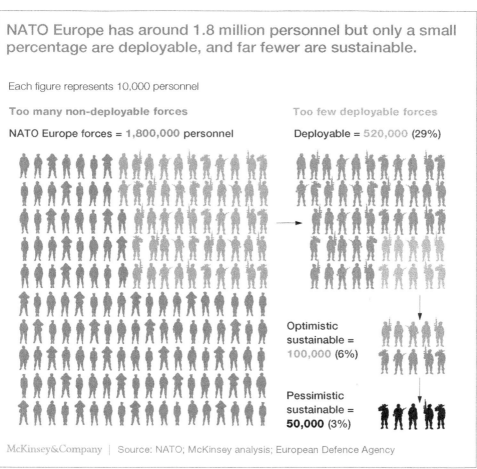

NATO Europe has around 1.8 million personnel but only a small percentage are deployable, and far fewer are sustainable.

Each figure represents 10,000 personnel

Too many non-deployable forces

Too few deployable forces

NATO Europe forces = 1,800,000 personnel

Deployable = 520,000 (29%)

Optimistic sustainable = 100,000 (6%)

Pessimistic sustainable = 50,000 (3%)

McKinsey&Company | Source: NATO; McKinsey analysis; European Defence Agency

Operations and Maintenance: Many forces have failed to spend enough to maintain what equipment they do have, and their overall maintenance productivity is low. In 2014, German Defense Minister Ursula von der Leyen revealed major deficiencies in the operational capability of important German weapons systems. For example, only forty-two of 109 Eurofighters, thirty-eight of eighty-nine Tornado fighters, and four of twenty-two Sea Lynx helicopters were ready for service, mostly due to a lack of spare parts.[32] Much new spending, in Germany at least, will have to go towards repairs of existing equipment that is no longer deployable due to cuts in spending on maintenance since 2010.[33]

Experience suggests that overall maintenance productivity is low. In areas where allies operate common equipment, NATO should compile and share operational benchmarks—cost per flying hour or track mile, for example. The top dozen air platforms (fighter jets, transport aircraft, and helicopters) are on average operated by five countries in Europe. Each platform has on average four deep maintenance sites, suggesting a great degree of duplication and overlap.[34]

4. Measure the Outputs

NATO should measure capabilities and continue to measure the readiness, deployability, and sustainability of forces (and its will to use them).

Capabilities. During the Cold War, each NATO member had a commitment to a "self-defense plan" that specified a required force structure, a certain readiness level, and a deployability level for their forces. Following the fall of the Soviet Union, those self-defense plans were shelved. Two critical and necessary steps to reform the notion of burden-sharing would be for NATO to craft an integrated defense plan, and for nations to commit to making force structure contributions to that plan, which they agree to fund.

Readiness, Deployability, and Sustainability. As noted, NATO requires members to measure the deployability of their forces and the ability to sustain them in the field, as agreed upon at the Riga summit. It should take the next step and ask nations to publish the figures. There is no reason why the EDA should provide greater transparency than NATO.

Deployed on NATO Missions. Finally, it would be useful to measure actual contributions to NATO missions as a measure of commitment to the alliance. Which nations are punching above their weight? Purely investment-related metrics have been a notoriously poor guide to predicting actual contributions to NATO missions.

Denmark and a few other nations do not meet the 2 percent target, but when it comes to capabilities and contributions, they manage to outperform most other allies.[35]

The US Is Not Immune

The challenge of productivity is equally important to the US defense industry and the Department of Defense (DoD). A recent study by the Defense Business Board found that more than 20 percent of the DoD's nearly $600 billion annual budget was dedicated to six back-office business processes (facilities management, HR, finance, logistics, acquisitions, and health management).[36] This spending represents a combination of outsourced goods/services, active-duty military, and civilian personnel. In total, over one million people work across these six processes, nearly equivalent to the one million or so active-duty military personnel working in mission-facing roles.

The report went on to identify over $125 billion in savings potential over a five-year period, which could be used as "warfighter currency" to fund fifty Army Brigades, ten Navy Carrier Strike Group deployments, or eighty-three Air Force F-35 fighter wings. Although this may seem like an ambitious target, it represents an annual productivity gain of just 7 percent per year, which private sector companies commonly achieve in order to renew, modernize, and strengthen their business. In summary, the DoD has significant opportunity to improve its own tooth-to-tail ratio, focusing on achieving productivity gains in the back-office core business processes and support functions, and reinvesting the savings to fund mission needs.

A Path Forward

NATO should seek to become the leading proponent of transparency in defense by launching a drive to improve the efficiency and effectiveness of its members. It should be unacceptable to NATO members, especially the United States, that the EDA exhibits greater transparency than NATO. To keep metrics simple, the public focus should be on inputs (spending) and outputs (capabilities measured in deployable, ready, sustainable forces). Productivity metrics—the efficiency and effectiveness with which inputs are converted to outputs—should be provided for the benefit of member nations. Burden-sharing can then appropriately focus not simply on what countries spend, but on the forces they provide to ensure the security of Europe and the North Atlantic, as the treaty originally intended.

"We must be careful not to reduce the NATO alliance or the notion of burden-sharing to simply '2 percent.' Our allies don't just need to spend more. They need to spend better."

—Senator John McCain,
Chairman of the US Senate Armed Services Committee[37]

John Dowdy is a Senior Partner in the London office of McKinsey & Company. He led the Firm's global Defense and Security practice from 2010-2016. Mr. Dowdy has conducted more than 100 projects on defense and security issues in eight different countries over his 27 year McKinsey career. He has worked extensively in countries including the US, the UK, Denmark, Australia, Japan and Canada. Over the past decade, he has been involved in projects improving the efficiency and effectiveness of Air, Land and Maritime forces, headquarters organization, defense supply chain and logistics processes, and counter terrorism, among others. Mr. Dowdy leads McKinsey's research on best practices in defense. He led McKinsey's benchmarking on the efficiency and effectiveness of 33 defense forces around the world. He is a fellow at the Royal United Services Institute (RUSI), where he serves as a member of the Board of Trustees. Mr. Dowdy holds an MBA with high distinction from Harvard Business School, where he graduated as a George F. Baker scholar, and a B.S. in Electrical Engineering and Computer Science with honors from the University of California at Berkeley. He is a private pilot.

[1] Mark Makela, "Transcript: Donald Trump Expounds on His Foreign Policy Views," *New York Times,* March 26, 2016, https://www.nytimes.com/2016/03/27/us/politics/donald-trump-transcript.html.

[2] Maggie Haberman and David E. Sanger, "Donald Trump Sets Conditions for Defending NATO Allies Against Attack," *New York Times,* July 20, 2016, https://www.nytimes.com/2016/07/21/us/politics/donald-trump-issues.html.

[3] Matthew Day and James Rothwell, "Donald Trump Says West Must Show 'the will to survive' in Face of Threats from Russia and North Korea," *Telegraph,* July 6, 2017, http://www.telegraph.co.uk/news/2017/07/06/donald-trump-meets-polish-president-warsaw-ahead-g20-summit/.

[4] Mark Makela, "Transcript: Donald Trump Expounds on His Foreign Policy Views," *New York Times,* March 26, 2016, https://www.nytimes.com/2016/03/27/us/politics/donald-trump-transcript.html.

[5] Michael Birnbaum and Dan Lamothe, "Defense Secretary Mattis Issues New Ultimatum to NATO Allies on Defense Spending," *Washington Post,* February 15, 2017, https://www.washingtonpost.com/news/checkpoint/wp/2017/02/15/mattis-trumps-defense-secretary-issues-ultimatum-to-nato-allies-on-defense-spending/?utm_term=.6401a731b8ed.

[6] Jeffrey Goldberg, "The Obama Doctrine," *Atlantic,* April 2016, https://www.theatlantic.com/magazine/archive/2016/04/the-obama-doctrine/471525/.

[7] Robert M. Gates, "Future of NATO" (speech, Brussels, Belgium, June 10, 2011), US Department of Defense, http://archive.defense.gov/Transcripts/Transcript.aspx?TranscriptID=4839.

[8] Brian R. Duchin, "The 'Agonizing Reappraisal': Eisenhower, Dulles, and the European Defense Community," *Diplomatic History* 16, no. 2 (April 1992): 201-22.

[9] Donald Trump, "Remarks by President Trump in Joint Address to Congress" (speech, Washington, DC, February 28 2017), White House Office of the Press Secretary, https://www.whitehouse.gov/the-press-office/2017/02/28/remarks-president-trump-joint-address-congress.

[10] Fabrice Pothier and Alexander Vershbow, *NATO and Trump: The Case for a New Transatlantic Bargain,* Atlantic Council, June 2017, http://www.atlanticcouncil.org/publications/issue-briefs/nato-and-trump; Kelly Russo, *Putin, Not Trump, Has Led NATO Members to Increase Defense Spending,* Atlantic Council, May 25, 2017, http://www.atlanticcouncil.org/blogs/new-atlanticist/putin-not-trump-has-led-nato-members-to-increase-defense-spending.

[11] Robert M. Gates, "Remarks by the Secretary at the Security and Defense Agenda" (speech, Brussels, Belgium, June 10, 2011), US Department of Defense, http://archive.defense.gov/Transcripts/Transcript.aspx?TranscriptID=4839.

[12] Lucie Béraud-Sudreau and Bastian Giegerich, "Counting to Two: Analysing the NATO Defence-Spending Target," Military Balance Blog, February 14, 2017, https://www.iiss.org/en/militarybalanceblog/blogsections/2017-edcc/february-7849/counting-to-two-67c0.

[13] Robert-Jan Bartunek and Lesley Wroughton, "Germany Balks at Tillerson Call for More European NATO Spending," Thompson Reuters, March 31, 2017, http://www.reuters.com/article/us-nato/germany-balks-at-tillerson-call-for-more-european-nato-spending-idUSKBN1720WV.

[14] Wolfgang Ischinger, "More EU Foreign and Security Policy," Munich Security Conference, February 17, 2017, https://www.securityconference.de/en/news/article/more-eu-foreign-and-security-policy/.

[15] Location country report, counts of active duty and reserve service members and APF civilians by location country, personnel category, service, and component as of December 31, 2016. Defense Manpower Data Center, February 27, 2017, dmdc.osd.mil.

[16] Jan Techau, *The Politics of 2 Percent: NATO and the Security Vacuum in Europe*, Carnegie Europe, September 2, 2015, http://carnegieeurope.eu/2015/09/02/politics-of-2-percent-nato-and-security-vacuum-in-europe-pub-61139.

[17] *NATO 2020: Assured Security; Dynamic Engagement*, North Atlantic Treaty Organization, May 17, 2010, http://www.nato.int/cps/en/natohq/topics_85961.htm.

[18] Input / output metrics – National fact sheet – Denmark, Forsvarsministeriet (Danish Ministry of Defense), 2014–15, http://www.fmn.dk/temaer/nato/Documents/Input-Output-Metrics-2014-2015.PDF.

[19] *Defence Data 2014*, European Defence Agency, 2016, https://www.eda.europa.eu/docs/default-source/documents/eda-defencedata-2014-final.

[20] *Defending Europe: The Case for Greater EU Cooperation on Security and Defence*, European Commission, May 24, 2017, https://ec.europa.eu/commission/sites/beta-political/files/defending-europe-factsheet_en.pdf.

[21] Rachel Rizzo and Jim Townsend, "NATO Allies Should Not Be Judged on Defense Spending Alone," *National Interest*, May 23, 2017, http://nationalinterest.org/feature/nato-allies-should-not-be-judged-defense-spending-alone-20809.

[22] Jan Techau, *The Politics of 2 Percent: NATO and the Security Vacuum in Europe*, Carnegie Europe, September 2, 2015, http://carnegieeurope.eu/2015/09/02/politics-of-2-percent-nato-and-security-vacuum-in-europe-pub-61139.

[23] *The Strategic Concept for Defense of the North Atlantic Area*, North Atlantic Treaty Organization, DC 6/1, December 1, 1949, http://www.nato.int/docu/stratdoc/eng/a491201a.pdf.

[24] *Future Defence Budget Constraints: Challenges and Opportunities*, North Atlantic Treaty Organization, December 2016, sto.nato.int.

[25] Jens Stoltenberg, "Doorstep statement" (speech, Brussels, Belgium, March 31, 2017), North Atlantic Treaty Organization, http://www.nato.int/cps/en/natohq/opinions_142787.htm?selectedLocale=en.

[26] Malcolm Chalmers, et al., "The cost of European security" (statement by Doug Lute on the panel at the Carnegie Endowment for International Peace), September 17, 2015, Carnegie Europe, carnegieeurope.eu.

[27] *Shifting the Goalposts? Defence Expenditure and the 2% Pledge: Government Response to the Committee's Second Report of Session 2015–16*, House of Commons Defence Committee, June 28, 2016, https://www.parliament.uk/business/committees/committees-a-z/commons-select/defence-committee/inquiries/parliament-2015/defence-expenditure-and-the-2-per-cent-pledge/.

[28] *NATO 2020: Assured Security; Dynamic Engagement*, North Atlantic Treaty Organization, May 17, 2010, http://www.nato.int/cps/en/natohq/topics_85961.htm.

[29] *Defence Expenditure of NATO Countries (2009-2016)*, North Atlantic Treaty Organization, March 13, 2017, http://www.nato.int/cps/en/natohq/news_142152.htm.

[30] Alexander Mattelaer, "US Leadership and NATO: Revisiting the Principles of NATO Burden-Sharing," *Parameters* 46, no. 1 (Spring 2016), https://ssi.armywarcollege.edu/pubs/parameters/issues/Spring_2016/6_Mattelaer.pdf.

[31] *Munich Security Report 2017*, Munich Security Conference, 2017, https://www.securityconference.de/en/discussion/munich-security-report/.

[32] Spiegel Staff, "Germany's Disarmed Forces: Ramshackle Military at Odds with Global Aspirations," Spiegel Online, September 30, 2014, http://www.spiegel.de/international/germany/ramshackle-army-at-odds-with-berlin-s-global-aspirations-a-994607.html.

[33] Hans Kundnani, "Merkel and Whose Army?," *Foreign Policy*, December 13, 2016, http://foreignpolicy.com/2016/12/13/merkel-and-whose-army-germany-military-nato/.

[34] *The Future of European Defence: Tackling the Productivity Challenge*, McKinsey & Company, May 2013, http://www.mckinsey.com/industries/aerospace-and-defense/our-insights/the-future-of-european-defence-tackling-the-productivity-challenge.

[35] Alexander Mattelaer, "US Leadership and NATO: Revisiting the Principles of NATO Burden-Sharing," *Parameters* 46, no. 1 (Spring 2016), https://ssi.armywarcollege.edu/pubs/parameters/issues/Spring_2016/6_Mattelaer.pdf.

[36] *Transforming Department of Defense's Core Business Processes for Revolutionary Change*, Defense Business Board, 2015, http://www.dtic.mil/dtic/tr/fulltext/u2/a618526.pdf.

[37] John McCain, "Opening Statement by SASC Chairman John McCain at Hearing on Posture of U.S. European Command," March 23, 2017, https://www.mccain.senate.gov/public/index.cfm/floor-statements?ID=CFFF0DDE-A2F8-43EE-BE92-4B60EE0C42B1.

"*The threat posed by these newer capabilities, coupled with its employment of its military forces under the guise of local insurrectionists, has made Russia a far more complex, even if less potent, threat than the Soviet Union ever was.*"

—DOV S. ZAKHEIM

NATO and Its Authoritarian Member States

Dov S. Zakheim*
Senior Advisor
CSIS

N ATO today faces a challenge unlike that which it confronted during the Cold War. During the four decades between its creation and the collapse of the USSR, NATO remained unified in the face of the Soviet threat even when some of its members completely discarded the democratic norms that supposedly bound the alliance together under the terms of Article 2 of the North Atlantic Treaty. Article 2 states:

> The Parties will contribute toward the further development of peaceful and friendly international relations by strengthening their free institutions, by bringing about a better understanding of the principles upon which these institutions are founded, and by promoting conditions of stability and well-being. They will seek to eliminate conflict in their international economic policies and will encourage economic collaboration between any or all of them.

Indeed, Portugal was a founding member of NATO, although it had been a right-wing dictatorship under António Salazar since 1933 and had remained neutral during World War II.

Beginning in 1960, Turkey, another neutral country in World War II, suffered from several military-led coups, yet it too remained a key member of NATO. The Eisenhower administration was aware that growing instability in Turkey might lead to a coup; it did not seem particularly perturbed when the Turkish military overthrew the Menderes government in May 1960. Washington's highest priority was to maintain NATO solidarity; it was especially important to ensure that Turkey, one of only two NATO members to share a boundary with the USSR (Norway's border with Russia was only a third as long) remained in the alliance.[1]

* The author wishes to thank Secretary Madeleine Albright for her comments on an earlier draft of this paper.

For similar reasons, the Nixon administration did little to protest the Turkish military's imposition of "guided democracy" in 1971 after overthrowing the government of Suleyman Demirel. Nor did the Carter administration exert any particular pressure on the military junta that removed another government led by Demirel, installing General Kenan Evren in 1980. America's NATO allies were not indifferent to any of the three coups, but none advocated for the expulsion of Turkey from the alliance.

Washington's attitude to the far more ruthless Greek military putsch of 1967 was even more benign; the Johnson administration actually supported the overthrow of the democratically elected government in Athens, although the junta arrested government and opposition leaders, suspended the constitution, trampled on human rights, exiled the king, and created a dictatorship that lasted nearly a decade. Greece had been a major focal point of the earliest US-Soviet confrontation in the aftermath of World War II, and it continued to be seen as a bulwark against communism. As had been the case with Turkey in 1960, none of the allies moved to expel Greece from NATO.

In all of these instances, what mattered was the anti-communism of the governments in question; the nature of their governance was a nicety that commanded little attention.

Once again, NATO faces a challenge from the East, but it is very different in nature and kind. Whereas the Soviet threat was both military and ideological, the current Russian threat involves as many, if not more, nonmilitary tools, which it has employed to undermine NATO's cohesion and its member governments. Some of these tools, such as bribing foreign politicians or spreading propaganda—now termed "fake news"—were long part of the Soviet toolkit. Russia has added to its kit by drawing upon technological advances over the past quarter century. It has added cyber warfare and exploitation of social networks to its vehicles for undermining NATO and the West.

The threat posed by these newer capabilities, coupled with its employment of its military forces under the guise of local insurrectionists, has made Russia a far more complex, even if less potent, threat than the Soviet Union ever was. Moreover, the fact that most of the USSR's former Warsaw Pact allies and three of its former republics are now NATO members has added to Moscow's incentives for, at a minimum, re-creating its former sphere of influence.

Even as Russia has expanded its nonmilitary means for undermining NATO, and has embarked on an ambitious military modernization program, NATO, for its part, faces a new set of internal challenges that are different in nature from those that forced it to accommodate the Portuguese, Greek, and Turkish dictatorships during the Cold War. Whereas all members of the alliance were united in their opposition to Soviet communist expansionism, and therefore could be relied on to invoke Article 5 if one or more of them were attacked, it is questionable whether the same degree of unanimity can be found today among NATO's far larger group of member countries. At least three NATO members—Hungary, Turkey, and Poland—have been moving ever closer toward the kind of authoritarianism that distinguished Portugal (until 1974), Greece under the colonels, and Turkey during its periods of military rule.

Equally ominously, Hungary and Turkey have adopted a far more benign view of Russia and its motives. They cannot be counted upon to invoke Article 5 should a NATO state be attacked. Indeed, one or both of them could actively work to prevent the adoption of a unified NATO response to such an attack, since NATO requires the unanimous consent of all its members, or at least the abstention of those who oppose action, before it can respond as a single alliance entity.

Hungary is the NATO ally that is perhaps the most willing to cozy up to Vladimir Putin's Russia. Hungary's prime minister, Viktor Orban, was initially an anti-communist dissident. As a student leader, he gained a national reputation in 1989 when he demanded at the reburial of the leaders of the 1956 revolution that all Soviet troops leave Hungary. He became leader of the Fidesz party when Hungary broke away from the Soviet bloc and gradually moved the party toward the conservative end of the political spectrum. Elected prime minister in 1998 at the head of a conservative majority, he lost the following two elections to the Socialists, only to be returned to office in 2010 again at the head of a conservative majority. Since then Orban has become increasingly authoritarian, tolerating a return to the xenophobic and anti-Semitic instincts that colored Hungarian policy during the 1930s and 1940s, and taking concrete measures to prevent Muslim immigrants from entering his country.

In an earlier time, Orban's domestic policies might well have been tolerated by his NATO allies, had Hungary been a member of the alliance rather than of the Warsaw Pact. But Orban has also been far more approving of Vladimir Putin than most other leaders of NATO and, for that matter, the European Union, of which Hungary is also a member. Speaking at a joint press conference with Putin during the latter's visit to Budapest in February 2017, Orban stated that it was an "honor" to have the Russian president visit Hungary and that "[i]n the Western half of the continent, anti-Russian politics have come into fashion." The two countries agreed to a "foreign affairs consultation plan" as well as student exchanges. Orban announced a plan to renovate

Russian Orthodox churches in Hungary, and he and Putin signed an agreement in which Russia will supply Hungary with natural gas until 2021, and another on nuclear cooperation. The two men agreed to continue their annual "home and home" meetings, and Orban summed up the Putin visit by stating that they had "saved and protected everything we could in Russian-Hungarian relations."

None of this bodes well for Hungarian cooperation within NATO at times of crisis. Orban's Hungary could resist any effort to implement Article 5 or, indeed, to permit NATO's integrated military command to undertake preparations in anticipation of a joint military operation. Yet Orban is not alone either in moving toward authoritarianism or in embracing Putin's Russia. If anything, Turkey's Recep Tayyib Erdogan has in effect established himself as Turkey's dictator, attempting to have the courts beholden to him and dominating a supine legislature. Like Orban, Erdogan began his political career as something of a reformer, at least in the economic realm, even as he advocated for secular Turkey's transition to a more traditional Islamic state.

Prior to the aborted military coup against Erdogan in July 2016, his government had arrested scores of journalists, purged hundreds from the army and the civil service, tolerated riots against Turkey's small Jewish community, supported the Muslim Brotherhood, and renewed military operations against the Kurds. Using the failed military coup as an excuse, Erdogan has moved even further to consolidate his power through the passage of a new constitution that places virtually unchallengeable authority in his hands. At the same time, he has stepped up arrests of journalists, civilian government employees, and members of the military, and he has also prompted the arrest of Kurdish opposition leaders. In all, tens of thousands of journalists, judges, police, members of the military, and other Turkish citizens have been jailed since the coup. Erdogan has also used the coup as justification for shutting down many of Turkey's leading opposition newspapers and television channels.

In addition, Erdogan has engaged in a war of words with German Chancellor Angela Merkel; increasingly, friction between Germany and Turkey has gone beyond mere verbiage. Germany, which has long been critical of Erdogan's human rights abuses, infuriated Erdogan by preventing his ministers from campaigning among German Turks for support for the April 2016 referendum that granted more powers to the president. The Bundestag also angered Erdogan by recognizing the Armenian genocide, which Turkey has consistently denied having occurred. Erdogan retaliated by banning German legislators from visiting German troops stationed in Turkey.

When Turkey arrested the German head of Amnesty International's Turkish office and a second German citizen in July 2017 on charges of terrorism, Merkel threatened to block the 3 billion in EU aid payments that were promised in exchange for Ankara's help in blocking the European migration of Syrian and other Middle Eastern refugees. In addition, Germany issued a travel advisory to tourists planning to visit Turkey that said German citizens were no longer safe in Turkey. Berlin also warned German investors against doing business there and announced that it was reconsidering export credit guarantees for trade with Turkey. Merkel's government also ordered a complete embargo on arms sales to Turkey. Finally, Germany announced that it would transfer to Jordan all its forces at Incirlik Air Base. These forces were contributing to the operations against ISIS that Turkey finally agreed to join in 2014. There is widespread agreement that relations between the two countries are the lowest since World War II.

As the withdrawal of German forces from Incirlik makes clear, Turkey is at odds not only with Germany, but also with NATO, the EU, and the United States for reasons that go beyond domestic human rights abuses and go to the heart of Turkey's perception of its role in the Middle East. Having reached out to Bashar al Assad for years, Erdogan is now determined to see his overthrow. Turkey has supported some of the more extreme Islamist elements in the Syrian opposition, such as Jabhat al-Nusra, while at the same time bitterly opposing any support for Syrian Kurdish operations against Assad's forces. For years there was a considerable body of evidence that Turkey was coordinating closely with ISIS, especially when the latter operated against the Syrian Kurds. Turkey also let hundreds of ISIS fighters cross its border into Syria, much to the consternation of the United States, until it finally promised to seal the border. Turkey has taken some steps in that regard, but the border remains porous.

Washington has provided both military support to Kurdish operations and, since Donald Trump entered the White House, materiel support to the YPG, the Syrian Kurdish militia. Trump's decision appears to have taken Erdogan by surprise and certainly angered the Turkish president, since Trump had consistently voiced his admiration for authoritarian strongmen and had only words of praise for Erdogan. As a result of their working at cross purposes, tensions between Ankara and Washington have continued to mount. That thuggish members of Turkey's security detail beat Americans in downtown Washington during Erdogan's visit did little to reduce tensions between the two governments. Erdogan's response has been to accuse the United States of supporting Kurdish terrorist organizations; he has called for a review of Turkey's alliance with NATO.

Erdogan's obsession with the Syrian Kurds, whom he accuses of supporting the outlawed Kurdish PKK organization, has only intensified since the Kurds proclaimed their semi-independent region of Rojava. It has also led him to order his forces into Iraq. There are about 2,000 Turkish troops in northern Iraq, including about 500 Turkish troops in the Bashiqa camp, that ostensibly are there to train local fighters against ISIS. In fact, those forces may well be the vanguard of a Turkish intervention should Ankara perceive that the Kurdish regional government will take any real steps towards independence. It is noteworthy that Iraq's Prime Minister Haider al-Abadi has repeatedly called upon Turkey to withdraw its forces, and Washington has supported Baghdad's demand. Turkey has ignored Baghdad's entreaties.

Like Orban, Erdogan has moved Turkey closer to Russia, closer in fact, than it has been in decades, if not centuries. Despite the confrontation between the two countries when a Turkish F-16 fighter shot down a Russian SU-24M Fencer all-weather bomber over the Turkish border on November 24, 2015, relations have become even warmer than they were before the incident took place. Since then the two countries have expanded their regional and security cooperation, even though they support opposite sides in the Syrian civil war. For example, it appears that Turkey actually will complete the purchase of Russian S-400 air defense missile systems, making it the only NATO country to employ Russian systems for its defenses. Since it is unlikely that the export version of the system would pose a threat to Russia itself, one wonders against whose air attacks the Turks would actually operate the system.

Turkey joined Russia, and Iran, in formulating the basis for the Astana agreements of May 2017. These agreements have resulted in the creation of four de-escalation zones in Syria, including the most recent in Idlib. Neither the United States nor any other NATO country was invited to play an active role in the Astana talks.

Finally, Turkey and Russia continue to maintain their symbiotic energy relationship. Turkey imports 60 percent of its natural gas from Russia. While Russia benefits from the revenues that these exports generate, Turkey is clearly more dependent on this energy supply arrangement. To the extent that this situation could change, that would be due to the opening of the TurkStream pipeline in 2019 that would make the two countries partners in the supply of natural gas to Europe; in other words, the prospects are good for even closer economic cooperation between the two countries.

And then there is Poland. Poland was in the forefront of new NATO members that had made tremendous strides both politically and economically for more than a decade after leaving the Soviet bloc. Under the domination of the Kazcynski twins and their ultra-conservative Law and Justice Party, however, the country is relapsing into the authoritarianism that marked its governance during the interwar period. Under the leadership of Lech Kaczynski, Poland's president from 2005 until his death in an airline crash in 2010, and of his brother Jaroslaw, prime minister in 2005-2006 and again since 2010, the government has taken an increasingly anti-EU stance, restricted the activities of democracy-promoting nongovernmental organizations, tolerated an upsurge in anti-Semitism, arrested opposition leaders on trumped-up corruption charges, and attempted to bring the court system under its control.

Poles harbor no great love for Russia, which participated in each of the three eighteenth century partitions of their country, colluded with the Nazi invasion of 1939, and sliced off some 77,000 square miles of eastern Polish territory that remained within the Soviet Union after World War II. Poland remains deeply suspicious of Russia, particularly since its annexation of Crimea and its ongoing military buildup in Kaliningrad. Nevertheless, like Turkey and Hungary, Poland's lurch toward authoritarianism clearly violates Article 2 of the NATO Treaty, which, as noted,explicitly states: "The Parties will contribute toward the further development of peaceful and friendly international relations by strengthening their free institutions, by bringing about a better understanding of the principles upon which these institutions are founded, and by promoting conditions of stability and well-being."

The government has taken an increasingly anti-European stance as well. In particular, it has refused to entertain any changes in EU directives regarding the movement of labor inside the EU, thereby creating tremendous friction among the EU's member governments. In so doing, it has also violated another part of Article 2, which calls on its NATO members to "seek to eliminate conflict in their international economic policies and ... encourage economic collaboration between any or all of them." Poland's anti-European, anti-democratic behavior prompted France's newly elected president, Emmanuel Macron, to condemn it in the harshest of terms. In addition to arguing that Poland's labor policy is in effect "social dumping," Macron asserted that "Europe is a region created on the basis of ... a relationship with democracy and public freedoms with which Poland is today in conflict."

Erdogan insists that his ever closer ties with Russia do not prejudice Turkey's NATO commitments. Orban says the same. Yet both—and Poland—already are in violation of their NATO commitments under Article 2, while Hungary and Turkey are cozying up to Russia despite its aggressiveness toward its immediate neighbors. It is therefore highly questionable whether NATO should continue to tolerate their retreat from democracy, as well as Turkish and Hungarian attitudes toward Russia, which differ sharply from those of the rest of the alliance.

The case for maintaining NATO unity is as strong as ever, but the circumstances that bind NATO have changed markedly. The Soviet military threat to Europe during the Cold War provided the justification for NATO to wink at its members' authoritarian behavior. Today's Russian threat is different, more subversive than military in nature. Given the change in circumstances, it is arguable that NATO members that undermine their countries' democratic norms are actually fostering Russian subversion. For that reason, NATO should seriously consider curtailing the membership of those states that do not comply with its norms.

NATO has never expelled a member, even when Turkey invaded Cyprus, a sovereign country, in 1974. Nor has it ever suspended a country's membership. France chose to leave the integrated military command in 1966 and remained outside it until 2009. Spain also chose to remain outside NATO's integrated military command from 1982, when it joined NATO, until 1996. But no country has left the command, much less the alliance, involuntarily.

The time has come for NATO to act, however. While there have been some calls in Europe for expelling Turkey (though not Hungary or Poland), NATO could take some steps short of expulsion. NATO could move to suspend Hungary and Turkey's membership in the integrated military command. Or it could suspend their membership entirely. Both steps would enable NATO to act in unison in the event of a crisis, especially one involving a confrontation with Russia.

Poland presents a special challenge, because suspension could be seen in the Kremlin as an invitation to act against NATO's Baltic members, while assuming that Poland would choose to sit on the sidelines. On the other hand, given Poland's unease with Moscow's aggressive behavior, even the threat of suspension, such as that which the EU recently issued, could push the Polish government to reverse its authoritarian impulses—as has already been the case with President Andrzej Duda's veto of two of the Sejm's proposed laws to restrict the independence of Poland's court system.

NATO has always claimed that it stands for democracy and freedom of the individual, as well as for the defense of its member states. The leaders of Hungary, Turkey, and Poland, each in his own way, are undermining the values for which NATO—and for that matter the EU—stands. With Russia once again seeking to undermine not only NATO's cohesion but its very purpose through everything from bribing politicians to "fake news" to cyber warfare, there is a need for the alliance, led by the United States, to take drastic action. Such action may have been unheard of in the past, but it is more than ever necessary today if NATO is to maintain its credibility not only as a guarantor of security but also as a bastion of democracy and freedom for all who live within the boundaries of its member states.

Dov S. Zakheim is Senior Advisor at the Center for Strategic and International Studies and Senior Fellow at CNA Corp. Previously he was Senior Vice President of Booz Allen Hamilton, where he led support of US Combatant Commanders. From 2001 to 2004, Dr. Zakheim served as Under Secretary of Defense (Comptroller) and Chief Financial Officer for the Department of Defense. From 2002 to 2004 he was also DOD's coordinator of civilian programs in Afghanistan. He was a senior advisor to George W. Bush during the 2000 presidential campaign and to Mitt Romney in the 2012 campaign. From 1985 to 1987, Dr. Zakheim was Deputy Under Secretary of Defense for Planning and Resources. He is currently a member of the Defense Business Board and the Chief of Naval Operations Executive Panel and serves on several corporate and nonprofit boards. He has chaired the National Intelligence Council's International Business Practices Advisory Panel and served on the Military Compensation and Retirement Modernization Commission. He frequently testifies before Congress as an expert witness. Dr. Zakheim is Vice Chairman of both the Foreign Policy Research Institute and the Center for the National Interest, and has been an Adjunct Senior Fellow at the Council on Foreign Relations and an Adjunct Professor at several universities. He received a B.A. summa cum laude from Columbia University and a D. Phil. from St. Antony's College, University of Oxford. He is a Fellow of the Royal Swedish Academy of Military Sciences and a member of the Aspen Strategy Group.

[1] Christopher Gunn, "The 1960 Coup in Turkey: A U.S. Intelligence Failure or a Successful Intervention?" *Journal of Cold War Studies* 17, no. 2 (Spring 2015), 103.

"Going forward, the United States will need to invest in improving its ability to defend against and counter Russian intervention in US domestic politics while also developing a more effective cost-imposition strategy to deter Russian meddling."

—MICHÈLE A. FLOURNOY

Russia's Campaign Against American Democracy: Toward a Strategy for Defending Against, Countering, and Ultimately Deterring Future Attacks

Michèle A. Flournoy
Co-founder and CEO
Center for a New American Security

During the 2016 US presidential election, the Russian Federation launched a substantial, multifaceted campaign to influence the outcome of the election and cast doubt on the legitimacy of American democracy. While several countries in Europe had experienced similar Russian-sponsored campaigns in the past, Moscow's extensive use of cyber hacking, fake news, disinformation, and cultivation of individuals involved in the Trump campaign was unprecedented in the US context. Although the full extent of Russian meddling is still being investigated, Russian objectives and intent are fairly clear: support the election of a candidate that President Putin judged would be easier to deal with, discredit democracy more broadly by sowing doubt and dissention about the US election, and create more room for maneuver for Russia to reclaim its status as a great power on the world stage and ultimately re-create a Russian sphere of influence in its near abroad.

While some may be tempted to think that Russia's meddling in the American political system was a one-off campaign that is now receding in our rearview mirror, there is every indication that Russia will continue to use its information warfare toolkit to sow discord in the United States in the future. The lack of a strong US response to Russia's 2016 campaign has enabled President Putin to achieve a great deal of success with minimal costs. In short, his strategy appears to have worked, so why not continue to pursue it? Going forward, the United States will need to invest in improving its ability to defend against and counter Russian intervention in US domestic politics while also developing a more effective cost-imposition strategy to deter Russian meddling in the 2018 and 2020 election cycles, and beyond.

This paper first describes the key elements of the Russian campaign to influence the 2016 elections in the United States as well as some of its precedents in Europe—the what. It then attempts to discern Russian objectives based on President Putin's broader approach to the West over the last decade—the why. Lastly, it offers a preliminary set of recommendations to strengthen the US ability to defend against, counter, and ultimately deter Russian meddling in US democratic processes in the future.

The Anatomy of the Russian Campaign

In some respects, the Russian information warfare experienced by the United States in the 2016 election cycle was nothing new. Over the last decade, the use of cyber hacking, disinformation, fake news, and intelligence operations to recruit or compromise influential individuals has become standard fare in Moscow's efforts to influence the politics and election outcomes in a variety of countries, especially in Europe.[1] President Putin appears to have taken a page—actually, many pages— from his old KGB playbook on how to undermine the effectiveness and legitimacy of democracies. Recall that in 2007, Russia launched DDoS (denial of service) attacks on election systems and hacked the websites of political parties in Estonia and Georgia. Fast forward a decade and, according to the unclassified report released by the Director of National Intelligence, we saw Putin directing a widespread, multidimensional campaign "to undermine public faith in the US democratic process, denigrate Secretary Clinton, and harm her electability and potential presidency."[2]

The Russian campaign included several elements. First, it directed the hacking of emails of the Democratic National Committee and Clinton campaign staffers and then provided these emails to WikiLeaks to be leaked publicly. The theft and release of these emails shaped mainstream and social media coverage of the election in a way that clearly helped candidate Trump. Second, it sponsored a propaganda campaign that included the generation and dissemination of fake news stories (the most infamous of which led to an attack at a pizza restaurant in Washington, DC), including the extensive use of both paid creators of fake content and "troll farms" and botnets to spread and amplify the false information across social media platforms. In addition, Russian hackers penetrated and probed key elements of our election infrastructure. Under the direction of the Russian General Staff Main Intelligence Directorate, a team of Russian hackers tasked with cyber espionage against US and foreign elections targeted parts of the system directly connected to voter registration, including a private sector manufacturer of devices that maintain and verify voter rolls. All in all, Russian hackers hit various systems in thirty-nine states, including incursions into voter databases, software to be used by poll workers on Election Day, and campaign finance databases.[3] Lastly, Moscow undertook a sustained effort to engage, influence, and co-opt individuals in and around the Trump campaign. The full extent of this intelligence operation is being investigated by the House and Senate Intelligence Committees and former FBI Director Robert Mueller.

Having paid a remarkably small price for this campaign and having achieved a level of success that likely exceeded his wildest dreams, President Putin then trained his sights on the French presidential election, directing a group tied to Russian military intelligence called APT 28 (more commonly known as Fancy Bear) to hack emails from Emmanuel Macron's campaign and leak them just days before the vote in an effort to increase support for his preferred candidate, Marine Le Pen.

Given this pattern of behavior and the lack of an effective US response to date, there is no reason to believe that Moscow will refrain from meddling in the 2018 midterm elections and the 2020 presidential election in the United States.

Russian Objectives: Why This Campaign?

The objectives behind the 2016 Russian information campaign appear rather straightforward: prevent the election of a candidate (Hillary Clinton) that President Putin believed had instigated pro-democracy protests in Russia and would be a tougher interlocutor in the White House, discredit democracy as a system of government by undermining the US election's integrity and legitimacy, and create more room for maneuver for Russia to reassert itself as a great power on the international stage and ultimately reestablish a Russian sphere of influence on its periphery.

These objectives reflect President Putin's evolving calculus over the last two decades. For starters, Putin and many other Russians have expressed a deep and growing sense of grievance about how Russia was treated after the end of the Cold War. The initial period of high hopes for closer economic and political ties with Europe has given way to feelings of betrayal, disillusionment, and anger. The internal chaos of the 1990s, the demise of the Warsaw Pact and Russia's loss of influence over Central and Eastern European states and two million square miles of territory, the violent protests that erupted in Russian cities, the enlargement of the NATO alliance and the European Union right up to Russia's borders, and the West's general lack of respect for Russia as a great power—all these factors, and more, deepened a shared sense of grievance and set the stage for Putin to claim the mantle of the strongman who would defend Russia against a hostile West and restore Russia to its rightful place in the world.

Over this same period, Russia's economy has fallen far short of expectations. Only a small fraction of Russian society has enjoyed the benefits of Russia's economic growth. While Russia's economy is now ranked twelfth in the world, wealth is highly concentrated in the hands of a few. According to a recent Credit Suisse report, "the top decile of wealth holders owns 85% of all household wealth in Russia. This is significantly higher than any other major economic power: the corresponding figure is 75% for the USA, for example, and 64% for China."[4] Indeed, there are 111 billionaires in Russia who together own 19 percent of all household wealth.[5] And Transparency International's 2014 Corruption Perceptions Index ranks Russia 136 out of 175 countries—with a corruption score of 27 (0 being highly corrupt and 100 being clean).[6] Putin's oligarchic, authoritarian Russia has become the textbook definition of a kleptocracy.

Moreover, Russia has failed to diversify and privatize its economy. Russia's economy remains highly dependent on hydrocarbons, with oil and natural gas revenues accounting for more than 40 percent of federal budget revenues.[7] In addition, approximately 70 percent of its exports are hydrocarbons.[8] As for privatization, in October 2016, the Russian government and state-owned enterprises (SOEs) accounted for 70 percent of Russia's economy. In fact, the number of government-owned "unitary enterprises" has tripled in the past three years, exceeding 24,000 as of 2016, according to the State Department's Office of Investment Affairs Investment Climate Statement.[9]

For average Russians, this has meant falling far behind their European neighbors in both wealth and health. In 2014, Russia's median wealth was $2,360 per adult compared to $140,638 in France and $130,590 in the UK.[10] In addition, life expectancy for Russian males is just under 66 years old—about 10 years younger than their counterparts in Europe on average.[11]

In light of these trends, Putin has sought to direct an understandable sense of grievance among the Russian people outward. Despite his poor domestic performance, he has sought to consolidate power by tapping into this sense of grievance and blaming the West—particularly the United States—for Russia's ills. He has also sought to tighten his grip on power by building up his national security and intelligence apparatus; assassinating, imprisoning, or persecuting political rivals; muzzling independent media; and discrediting champions of democratic reform. It is in this fraught, cutthroat domestic political context that Putin decided that meddling in the US presidential election was an opportunity too good to pass up.

Unfortunately, Putin managed to achieve many of his campaign's objectives with little cost. In the wake of the hacking scandal in the United States, then-President Barack Obama sanctioned a number of Russian intelligence officials, expelled thirty-five Russian "diplomats" suspected of being spies, and shut down two suspected Russian intelligence collection facilities in the United States. These actions were widely viewed as inadequate given the magnitude and gravity of Russia's actions. More recently, Congress has passed a bill that would impose additional sanctions on Russia. But these actions alone are unlikely to sufficiently deter Putin from continuing to try to subvert American democracy in the future. Nor are they likely to dissuade other countries that may be taking notes and considering similar actions against the United States in the future.

How Should the United States Respond?

Perhaps the most disturbing and dangerous aspect of the Trump administration's response to Russian information operations to date is that it has focused primarily on denying and disputing the facts rather than accepting the high-confidence judgments of the intelligence community and undertaking a concerted government-wide effort to improve the US ability to deter and defend against such attacks in the future.

Assuming Moscow will continue to employ a similar toolkit heading into the 2018 and 2020 election cycles, the United States needs to do two things urgently: First, improve our capabilities to defend against and counter key elements of the ongoing Russian campaign. Second, develop a cost-imposition strategy designed to deter President Putin from interfering in US democratic processes in the future. The recommendations below provide a starting point for developing both a "layered defense" and a cost-imposition strategy in several key areas.

It is important to emphasize up front that the federal government alone cannot tackle this set of challenges. Private sector companies will be critical partners in key areas, as will state and local governments. In addition, the United States would benefit greatly from sharing lessons learned and best practices with European nations that have faced or likely will face similar campaigns orchestrated by Moscow.

Countering and Deterring Russian Cyber Activities

The first and most obvious step is for the United States to strengthen its cybersecurity surrounding all election-related systems and processes to reduce the risk of successful Russian-sponsored hacking. For starters, candidates, campaigns, and political parties should take the steps necessary to make themselves harder to hack. This should include everything from adopting cyber hygiene best practices (e.g., multi-factor authentication, different passwords for different accounts, taking care about what is written in email) to avoiding the use of insecure technologies when more secure, encrypted alternatives are available. Parties who intend to participate in the 2018 and 2020 elections should begin now to develop new IT platforms, strategies, and practices with greater security built in from the start, rather than wait until they discover they have been targeted.

In addition, state and local governments should prioritize assessing key elements of their voting infrastructure and remediating vulnerabilities to remote access, computer-based threats to the integrity and availability of data. This should include improving the cybersecurity and audit trail of a highly decentralized, distributed, and diverse set of voting systems. The challenge is that voter processes and voting technologies differ from state to state, and often from county to county. While this can certainly complicate Russian targeting, it also complicates our own efforts to strengthen these systems. What's more, there is no single entity with the responsibility or the authority to safeguard the nation's voting system. (This is beyond the Federal Election Commission's writ.)

One idea is to purchase and deploy voting machines that generate a verifiable paper audit trail.[12] As a second line of defense, state authorities should also strengthen their post-election audit capabilities, applying statistically rigorous methods to improve confidence in the reported results.[13] The problem is, critical steps like these will cost money that many states lack.

The federal government, therefore, has a critical role to play in providing assistance to the states to strengthen the integrity and security of their voting systems. First, the Department of Homeland Security, working with the Federal Election Commission and state and local governments, should take the lead in setting broad standards for localities to secure their voting polls and processes. Congress, for its part, should create a federal grants program to assist states in meeting these standards and improving the security of their voting systems. This will be no small challenge, but the effort is essential as even modest irregularities in future elections could crater public confidence in our democracy and create disproportionate harm.

In addition to hardening its cyber defenses, the United States needs to develop a strategy to impose sufficient costs on Moscow to make the Kremlin think twice about undertaking cyber attacks in the first place. Such a strategy could include several lines of effort.

To the greatest extent possible, the US government should publicly disclose the nature and extent of Russian cyber activities targeting our election systems, media, and social media. While there are legitimate concerns about protecting the sources and methods of our intelligence community, there are compelling reasons to "out" the Russians for these activities when they occur. The public has a right to know about foreign interference in our democratic system, and naming and shaming Moscow will complicate Putin's efforts to regain legitimacy and respect on the world stage.

In addition, the United States needs to develop a clear strategy and robust set of options for responding to significant cyber intrusions. No such strategy exists today and, as we saw during the Obama administration's deliberations about how to respond to Russia's hacking, the lack of a strategic framework and well-developed response options contributed to the lack of a timely and effective US response. The US government needs to undertake a deliberate planning effort similar to how the military prepares contingency plans for various possible conflict scenarios. This should include both symmetric (cyber) and asymmetric (non-cyber) responses. This planning effort would inevitably raise fundamental policy questions that would spur the development of a broader strategy. For example, should the United States undertake a retaliatory cyber attack on Russia? What would such an attack target, and with what scope and duration? Thinking more asymmetrically, should the United States threaten to disclose evidence of the extent of Mr. Putin's illicit financial gains while in office? Should Washington increase sanctions and link all sanctions relief to cessation of any further Russian cyber meddling in our democratic processes? Again, the purpose would be to identify a set of actions that the United States would be willing to consider to dramatically increase the costs of any future cyber intrusions, thereby deterring a repeat of the Russian campaign in the next election.

Working with Congress and the European Union, the administration should also develop a broader set of sanctions that could be used to impose greater costs on Russia should it intervene in future elections. As Eddie Fishman argues, US officials should begin working with their European counterparts now to develop a range of punitive options, including new sanctions that could be deployed quickly if Russia interferes in an election on either side of the Atlantic.[14] The United States and its NATO allies should also make clear to Russia that an attack on one member's democratic processes and institutions is an attack on all, and that the transatlantic community will respond with tough measures in concert.[15]

Countering Russian-Sponsored Fake News and Disinformation

In many ways, countering Russian disinformation and fake news may be the most difficult area, given the United States' fundamental commitment to free speech, a strong and independent media, and a free and an open internet. Any success in reducing the amount and efficacy of fake news and disinformation will require a closer public-private partnership between elements of the US government and both the tech and media industries.

In a recent paper on information operations, Facebook executives offered a useful framework that disaggregates three major features of online information operations:

1. *targeted data collection* to steal and often expose non-public information that can provide unique opportunities for shaping public discourse (such as information gathering/reconnaissance, cyber operations against organizations or individuals, spear phishing or account takeover, and data theft),

2. *content creation*, both false or real (such as seeding stories to the press, meme and story generation, and fake account/persona creation), and

3. *false amplification*, which involves coordinated activity by inauthentic accounts with the intent of promoting or denigrating a specific cause or issue, sowing distrust in political institutions, and spreading confusion and tension (such as creating fake accounts, often using "bots"; spreading memes and content; creation of astroturfing groups; and comment spam).[16]

Facebook, Google, and other tech companies have pledged to take steps to counter these kinds of activities, including notifying users who have been or may be targeted; working with candidates, campaigns, and political parties to improve the security of their online networks and social media; improving efforts to identify and remove fake accounts; and strengthening their ability to distinguish content generated by human beings from content generated by bots. To borrow a phrase recently coined by Alphabet's Eric Schmidt, "We should protect free speech for humans, not for bots." Several companies are also adapting algorithms and changing practices to tag and deprioritize suspect content. While the tech companies rightly have the lead here, the US government should do everything it can to support these efforts, including sharing information on malicious actors and their activities online. How much the tech companies will ultimately invest in these efforts remains to be seen and will depend on both how they see the business case for doing so and the reputational risk associated with not sufficiently acting.

In addition, leaders of the media industry should convene to discuss the norms that should govern reporting in an era of fake news. Too often, a fake news story that has germinated in the dark corners of the internet, where propagandists, extremists, and conspiracy theorists congregate, only gets traction when the mainstream media picks it up without adequately investigating its sources and veracity. This gives the story much wider dissemination and legitimacy than it otherwise would have achieved. The mainstream media needs to hold itself to a higher standard if it is to maintain the trust and confidence of the American people. Traditional media outlets need to become more vigilant about where the news they report or repeat originates, especially when the content is suspect.

For its part, the US government should strengthen its own mechanisms for countering Russian propaganda and disinformation, including creating an interagency task force to assess and respond to Russian information operations. Here, there is a useful historical precedent: in the 1980s, the United States responded to Soviet propaganda by establishing a small, interagency committee called the Active Measures Working Group (AMWG) comprised of experts from the State Department, the Department of Defense, the intelligence community, and the technology community. The AMWG collected data, painted an accurate picture of the extent and nature of disinformation efforts, assessed their impact, and devised ways to counter their effectiveness. One of the group's most effective tactics was exposing the perpetrators, their methods, and the scope of their actions. Such naming and shaming could be coupled with imposing financial and/or travel sanctions on the individuals and entities involved. While digital disinformation may be harder to detect and counter than broadcasts and leaflet drops once were, some of the AMWG's experience and tactics may be instructive.[17]

Countering Russian Efforts to Recruit or Compromise Political Influencers

The last aspect of Moscow's information operations is as old as the hills, a tactic that has been used as long as espionage has been practiced—seeking to recruit or compromise influential individuals in the target country. In this case, Russia appears to have focused on engaging individuals in and around the Trump campaign. According to multiple news reports, at least ten associates of Donald Trump had possible or known ties or contact with Russian officials or intermediaries.[18] Whether Russia was seeking agents and allies or something more innocuous, these relationships and contacts are now the subject of investigations by both the House and Senate Intelligence Committees and Special Counsel Robert Mueller. Assuming this will not be the last time that Russia seeks to gain influence or leverage over Americans involved in our political process, the US intelligence and law enforcement communities should offer to work with political campaigns to increase their counterintelligence awareness. They should also be prepared to increase their surveillance and counterintelligence efforts during election cycles in order to better monitor and report contacts between any possible agents of a non-allied foreign government and American political candidates and campaigns.

Strengthening Partnerships to Combat the Threat

In addition to enhancing its collaboration and information-sharing with key private sector players, like the tech and media industries, the US government should give particular priority to sharing threat information, lessons learned, and best practices with other countries whose democratic institutions are targeted by Russia. The transatlantic community will be far more effective in defending against and deterring future Russian information operations if its members can compare notes on what they have experienced, share insights on what countermeasures have worked or not, and position themselves to respond to any future attacks with strong, coordinated actions.

In conclusion, the measures recommended here to strengthen our ability to defend against, counter, and hopefully deter future Russian (or other) attacks on our political processes should be considered just the beginning of a conversation that is critical to preserving one of the things we hold most dear: our democracy. We need a comprehensive, forward-looking plan of action, now.

Michèle Flournoy is co-founder and CEO of the Center for a New American Security and co-founder of WestExec Advisors. Ms. Flournoy served as the Under Secretary of Defense for Policy from 2009 to 2012. Prior to confirmation, Ms. Flournoy co-led President Obama's transition team at DoD. Previously, she was senior adviser at the Center for Strategic and International Studies for several years and, prior to that, a distinguished research professor at the Institute for National Strategic Studies at the National Defense University (NDU). In the mid-1990s, she served as Principal Deputy Assistant Secretary of Defense for Strategy and Threat Reduction and Deputy Assistant Secretary of Defense for Strategy. Ms. Flournoy is a former member of the President's Intelligence Advisory Board and the CIA Director's External Advisory Board, and is currently a member of the Defense Policy Board, the Council on Foreign Relations, and the Aspen Strategy Group, and is a Senior Fellow at Harvard's Belfer Center for Science and International Affairs. She also serves on the boards of CSRA, Amida Technology Solutions, The Mission Continues, Spirit of America, and CARE. Ms. Flournoy earned a bachelor's degree from Harvard University and a master's degree in international relations from Balliol College, Oxford University, where she was a Newton-Tatum scholar.

[1] For an excellent analysis of Russian interference in Europe, see Heather A. Conley, et al., *The Kremlin Playbook: Understanding Russian Influence in Central and Eastern Europe*, CSIS, October 2016.

[2] *Background to "Assessing Russian Activities and Intentions in Recent US Elections:" The Analytic Process and Cyber Incident Attribution*, United States Office of the Director of National Intelligence, January 6, 2017.

[3] Michael Riley and Jordan Robertson, "Russian Cyber Hacks on US Electoral System Far Wider Than Previously Known." *Bloomberg*, June 13, 2017, https://www.bloomberg.com/news/articles/2017-06-13/russian-breach-of-39-states-threatens-future-u-s-elections.

[4] *Global Wealth Report 2014*, Credit Suisse, October 2014, https://publications.credit-suisse.com/tasks/render/file/?fileID=60931FDE-A2D2-F568-B041B58C5EA591A4.

[5] *Global Wealth Report 2014*, Credit Suisse, October 2014, https://publications.credit-suisse.com/tasks/render/file/?fileID=60931FDE-A2D2-F568-B041B58C5EA591A4.

[6] *Corruptions Perception Index 2014*, Transparency International, https://www.transparency.org/cpi2014/infographic.

[7] US *Russia Country Report*, US Energy Information Administration, October 26, 2016, https://www.eia.gov/beta/international/analysis.cfm?iso=RUS.

[8] William T. Wilson, "Russia's Economy: What Do the Numbers Tell Us?" Heritage Foundation Commentary, November 17, 2015, http://www.heritage.org/europe/commentary/russias-economy-what-do-the-numbers-tell-us.

[9] State Department's Office of Investment Affairs Investment Climate Statement, "Russia's State Owned Enterprises," July 17, 2017, https://www.export.gov/article?id=Russia-State-Owned-Enterprises.

[10] *Global Wealth Report 2014*, Credit Suisse, October 2014, https://publications.credit-suisse.com/tasks/render/file/?fileID=60931FDE-A2D2-F568-B041B58C5EA591A4.

[11] Russian Federation Country Page, World Bank, http://data.worldbank.org/indicator/SP.DYN.LE00.MA.IN?locations=RU&view=map.

[12] Ben Buchanan and Michael Sulmeyer, *Hacking Chads: The Motivations, Threats, and Effects of Electoral Insecurity*, Harvard Kennedy School, Belfer Center for Science and International Affairs, October 2016, http://www.belfercenter.org/sites/default/files/files/publication/hacking-chads.pdf.

[13] Ben Buchanan and Michael Sulmeyer, *Hacking Chads: The Motivations, Threats, and Effects of Electoral Insecurity*, Harvard Kennedy School, Belfer Center for Science and International Affairs, October 2016, http://www.belfercenter.org/sites/default/files/files/publication/hacking-chads.pdf.

[14] Edward Fishman and Mark Simakovsky, "The Do-No-Harm Principle of Kremlin Relations," *Foreign Policy*, July 6, 2017, http://foreignpolicy.com/2017/07/06/the-do-no-harm-principle-of-kremlin-relations/.

[15] Edward Fishman and Mark Simakovsky, "The Do-No-Harm Principle of Kremlin Relations," *Foreign Policy*, July 6, 2017, http://foreignpolicy.com/2017/07/06/the-do-no-harm-principle-of-kremlin-relations/.

[16] Jen Weedon, William Nuland, and Alex Stamos, *Information Operations and Facebook*, Facebook, April 27, 2017, https://fbnewsroomus.files.wordpress.com/2017/04/facebook-and-information-oprations-v1.pdf.

[17] Madeline Christian, "Countering Disinformation Online Will Require Long-term Engagement from the Feds," *The Hill*, June 12, 2017, https://origin-nyi.thehill.com/blogs/pundits-blog/technology/337439-countering-disinformation-online-will-require-long-term.

[18] Philip Bump, "The Web of Relationships Between Team Trump and Russia," *The Washington Post*, March 3, 2017, https://www.washingtonpost.com/news/politics/wp/2017/03/03/the-web-of-relationships-between-team-trump-and-russia/?utm_term=.b8d6f22ed894.

"There will always be an "international system" of some kind — some set of rules or structure or framework within which states and other international actors interact with one another. The question is which values and principles will serve as the foundation for that structure, how formal or informal it will be, and whether it will produce peace, security, and prosperity or conflict, insecurity, and impoverishment."

—STEPHEN HADLEY

Modernizing the International System:
What Needs To Change?

Stephen Hadley
Principal
RiceHadleyGates

Much has been written about the need to revise and adapt the current international system to reflect the changed world of today. Less has been written about what a revised and adapted international system would actually look like. This chapter is an initial attempt to bridge that gap. The ideas presented here are offered not as firm recommendations for how the international system should be modified, but in the spirit of jumpstarting debate and discussion on this issue.

What Is the "International System"?

There is a lot of discussion and commentary about the threat to the "global order." But as Henry Kissinger and Joe Nye have pointed out, there in fact has never been a "global order." There has been since the end of World War II a set of alliances created and underwritten largely by American diplomatic, military, and economic power that has produced a fairly remarkable period of relative stability, prosperity, and peace. But the "order" provided by this system of alliances was never really "global"; it never included China, the Soviet Union (and now Russia), and several other key international actors.

Over time a plethora of international arrangements developed on top of or in parallel with this system of alliances. If there is an overarching framework to this structure, it is probably the United Nations—its charter and supporting institutions—which generally enjoys global support. But underneath this overarching framework is a network of principles, rules, practices, institutions, agreements, conventions, and other arrangements that help to structure the security, economic, political, social, and cultural relations among nations. These arrangements have overlapping and non-overlapping memberships—involving some nations, but not others; supported by many parties, but not all.

Increasingly, as Anne-Marie Slaughter has written, this web of relationships has come to include non-governmental entities—companies, charitable organizations, philanthropic groups, scientific bodies, civil society, and stakeholders of every sort. The multi-stakeholder group exercising authority over ICANN's maintenance of internet names and addresses is one of the most advanced and sophisticated arrangements of this sort.

As with the US alliance system, this web of relationships has largely been created and sustained by American leadership with the support of Western European and other democratic states, and it reflects a shared commitment to the principles of political democracy and free market economics. But forces have arisen that threaten to disrupt if not destroy key elements of the current international system. At the same time, many Americans seem less willing to bear the burden of leading and supporting that system. This raises the question: Can the international system survive—and, if so, how?

What Are the Challenges to the International System?

The world has entered a new era. Much has changed since the events of World War II and the end of the Cold War—events in which the current international system was forged. In the last several decades, the world has seen:

- The dramatic economic rise first of the European Union (EU), Japan, and South Korea, then China and India, and now emerging nations in Southeast Asia, Latin America, and even Africa, which has both shifted the center of gravity of global economic power and made it more diffuse.

- The return of great power competition as Russia and to some degree China increasingly confront the United States and act in ways that seek to undermine America's power and influence in the world.

- The emergence of authoritarian state capitalism (practiced increasingly by China, Russia, Turkey, Egypt, and a number of Central and Eastern European states) as an alternative to the model of political democracy and free market economics that seemed to emerge as the global norm after the end of the Cold War.

- Russia's increasing adoption of a "containment strategy" towards the United States and other liberal democracies that, as Madeleine Albright has pointed out, seeks to exploit the current dislocations within democratic American societies, undermine the appeal of democratic ideals, and separate the United States from its closest allies.

- As shown in recent polling and election results, the loss of confidence in democratic governance on the part of many citizens living in established democratic states as those states struggle to produce sustained, inclusive economic growth and a hopeful vision for their people.

- Globalization that has provided real economic growth and societal benefit but has also left many citizens untouched if not disadvantaged, provoking a sense of powerlessness, disaffection, and despair, and providing fertile ground for the proponents of economic nationalism and social exclusiveness.

- Technology that is revolutionizing life in the twenty-first century and empowering individual citizens in positive ways but is also disorienting many citizens, undermining their faith in institutions, and providing new tools for authoritarians who style themselves as the alternative to social chaos.

- The emergence of global, transnational challenges—including financial instability, environmental degradation, terrorism, human trafficking, proliferation of weapons of mass destruction, fragile states—that no nation can manage alone but that every nation needs to see addressed if they are to realize their own national aspirations.

- Increasing volatility and crisis—states riven by violence and conflict, failing and failed states, humanitarian disasters, defiance of the international community, challenges in what was thought to be a stable Europe—all cascading together on a scale that the world has rarely seen.

- The emergence of non-state actors as major international players— some generally positive (like international corporations, civil society, and philanthropic organizations) but some completely malign (like organized crime, narco-traffickers, and terrorist groups).

- The disaffection of many Americans with the burdens of international leadership at the same time that many nations actually want the opportunity to do more—and not just big states like China, but also smaller states in the developing world.

- The calling into question of many of the institutions and arrangements of the international system by some members of the Trump administration and its supporters.

The international system has begun to adapt to these changes, but has not gone far enough, fast enough. What is required is a more systematic and intentional effort to revise, adapt, and revitalize the international system.

Can the International System Be Saved?

There will always be an "international system" of some kind—some set of rules or structure or framework within which states and other international actors interact with one another. The question is which values and principles will serve as the foundation for that structure, how formal or informal it will be, and will it produce peace, security, and prosperity or conflict, insecurity, and impoverishment.

The international system created since the end of World War II has a pretty good record in this regard. It avoided another world war, produced global economic growth that lifted hundreds of millions of people out of poverty, and furthered the advance (at least until recently) of freedom, democracy, rule of law, and human rights.

For this progress to continue, the international system must be revised and adapted to meet current challenges. Failure to do so runs the risk that the current system will be overwhelmed by these challenges and circumvented by states increasingly operating outside its institutions. The result would be a world of increased entropy, disorder, and disruption. Cooperation would increasingly give way to competition, win-win solutions to zero-sum thinking, and public goods to private advantage. Getting things done at the global level would be more and more difficult. And the risk of confrontation and armed conflict would likely increase.

One can see all of these trends in the world today, and just at the time when the world confronts critical problems that can only effectively be addressed by joint, coordinated action among governments, constructive non-state actors, and ordinary citizens based on principles of mutual benefit, mutual responsibility, and a sense of the common good.

Failure to adapt the international system is also likely to accelerate a global trend toward authoritarianism and away from political democracy and free market economics. To the extent that authoritarian states feel excluded from the current international system, they will be motivated to create alternatives based on anti-democratic, non-market principles. The result could be an "authoritarian ecosystem" that not only supports existing authoritarian states but also attracts and encourages leaders of other states to adopt a more authoritarian/state control model. This authoritarian ecosystem is also likely to become a safe haven in which states under international sanctions (like North Korea and Iran) and nefarious non-state actors (like organized crime and traffickers of various sorts) find refuge from the writ and rules of the rest of the world community.

The global community needs a revised, adapted, and revitalized international system that encourages and facilitates a safer, more secure, and more prosperous world in which freedom and free markets can flourish.

American leadership will be essential. There is really no alternative. The EU is too consumed with its own internal problems and in trying to define the future of Europe. China at present has neither the diplomatic, economic, or military assets, nor the international community's trust and confidence to lead the effort. The same is true of Russia. India will be a critical player in this effort but cannot really lead it.

The United States no longer has the predominance it enjoyed in the 1940s and 1950s when the current international system was born. But America's "decline" is only relative. Other countries have been able to grow their economies and provide a better life for their people precisely because of the success of the international system that America helped create.

The United States is still by almost any measure the most powerful nation in the world today. It has the political, economic, diplomatic, and military heft required to lead the effort to revise, adapt, and revitalize the international system. But such an effort will require the understanding and support of the American people. In this respect the future of the international system will depend heavily on the future of American politics. The American people will have to be persuaded that a revised, adapted, and revitalized international system is essential for their future security, prosperity, and way of life.

How Should America Lead?

If America wants to create a revised, adapted, and revitalized international system that enjoys wide support within the international community—and in which others both assume more responsibility and carry more of the burden—then it will have to give others the opportunity to participate in setting the rules, running the institutions, and establishing new arrangements. Otherwise they will not participate. America might lead, but others will not follow.

To renovate the international system, America must lead a process that:

- Involves not just America's friends and allies but other major players—India, China, and Russia—as well as the rest of the international community. Only this kind of process will generate the global consensus required to sustain a renovated international order.

- Involves companies, charitable organizations, scientific bodies, civil society, and other nongovernmental entities, for they will be crucial actors in the emerging international order.

- Overcomes the "not invented here" syndrome and embraces sensible ideas and innovations from other sources, while reaffirming the foundational principles of political democracy and free market economics.

The United States missed an opportunity to demonstrate this kind of leadership when it refused to participate in the Asian Infrastructure Investment Bank (AIIB) proposed by China. It must not miss a similar opportunity in its response to China's One Belt, One Road (OBOR) initiative.

In sum, the United States will need to resist its natural tendency to impose and dictate. Instead, it must see its role more as catalyst, facilitator, and enabler— empowering governments, constructive non-state actors, and individual citizens to common action—while still holding fast to its principles.

What Should Be the Strategy?

Experts have pointed out that major redesign of international institutions usually follows cataclysmic events. The present international system was itself a product of the global devastation caused by World War II. The system evolved and changed following the end of the Cold War. The rise of global terrorism after the 9/11 attacks on the United States provoked another period of adaptation and institution building.

Why should the world wait for another cataclysmic event when it is already clear that the international system needs to change, and when the nature of at least some of the required changes is already apparent? Wouldn't it be wiser to act now to renovate the international system in hopes of averting a future cataclysmic event—or at least making the international system more resilient when and if such an event occurs?

Some at the ASG August sessions rightly argued that the strategy for revising the international system ought to focus on increasing the forces of community and cooperation while reducing and managing the forces of competition, so that confrontation and conflict can be avoided.

One participant pointed out that within the broad range of serious global challenges that can only be addressed successfully by collaborative international action, the need to manage the impact of technological change is particularly urgent. Change will continue to be rapid and disruptive, particularly in fields such as biotechnology, geo-technology, artificial intelligence, robotics, renewable energy, and cyber. Building patterns, institutions, and arrangements of cooperation in these areas—particularly if China and Russia can be involved—may help mitigate competitive pressures in other areas and make it easier to manage difficult geo-political issues like Iran, North Korea, Syria, and the South China Sea.

What Might a Revised, Adapted, and Revitalized International System Look Like?

A revised and adapted international system is likely to be even more diffuse in its structure and more proliferated in its arrangements than the current system, with even less agreement on core principles. The United Nations and its charter will undoubtedly survive as an overall framework because all nations are represented and participate in it—even China and Russia, the greatest critics of the current international system. But the global consensus that appeared to exist at the end of the Cold War in support of the so-called "Western values" of political democracy and free-market economics has eroded.

After the end of the Cold War, even China and Russia paid lip service to these principles. But at least by the second decade of the twenty-first century, both had dropped much of the pretense. Each increasingly asserted its own national "exceptionalism" with distinctive values, principles, and culture. In different ways they have adopted the basic formula of authoritarian state capitalism—less political freedom, fewer checks on governmental authority, and more state control over the economy—and have begun to promote this alternative model both at home and abroad.

Given this ideological struggle between free market democracies and authoritarian state capitalists, just how much consensus can be generated behind any revised, adapted, and revitalized international system? China, Russia, India, and most of the nations of Southeast Asia, Africa, and Latin America had little role in the formation of the post-World War II international system. But they will have to be full participants in any effort to revise and adapt that system. If they are not, Russia in particular will try to undermine the effort, and China has the economic wherewithal to create alternative institutions to compete with it that other nations would likely feel some pressure to join.

1. Beginning the process

An open discussion about how to revise, adapt, and revitalize the current international system will undoubtedly give rise to a substantial list of grievances against that system. Leaders of a number of countries (including of the United States) are likely to want to eliminate a number of elements of the current system. These could include, for example, eliminating the veto power of the five permanent members of the UN Security Council; eliminating the American alliance system (eliminating NATO, in the case of Russia, and eliminating the defense agreements with Japan and South Korea, in the case of China); and eliminating a wide array of international organizations and institutions (from the UN Human Rights Council to the International Criminal Court to the World Trade Organization).

The grievances against the current international system are not just the grievances of governments. Many angry citizens—especially in the United States and Europe— feel victimized by globalization, threatened by immigration, abandoned by their governments, and betrayed by their national elites. Any effort to revise and adapt the international system must address these grievances and make the international system more responsive to those who have been aggrieved.

But starting with a list of institutions, agreements, and arrangements identified for elimination is looking through the wrong end of the telescope. The international system cannot be fixed so easily. The substantial global consensus that used to support the international system needs to be rebuilt—and from the bottom up. Basic principles need to be identified upon which this global consensus can be restored and upon which a revised, adapted, and revitalized international system can be based.

2. Identifying the basic principles of a renovated international system

a. Reestablish the principles of "World Order 1.0"

The architects of the current international system were motivated to avoid the kind of global armed conflict that they had witnessed in World War II. This worthy goal is still a top priority today. So perhaps we begin the renovation of the international system by identifying and seeking commitment to those basic principles designed to minimize conflict among states.

In his book *A World in Disarray*, Richard Haass identifies these principles as "World Order 1.0." The principles include: recognition of the sovereignty of the nation state, respect for existing territorial borders, no use of force to change those borders; no stationing of foreign forces on a state's territory without its consent, and no state to allow its territory to be used to attack another state. These principles are enshrined in documents like the UN Charter, the Organization for Security Cooperation in Europe (OSCE) (with its "Helsinki Principles"), and the Charter of Paris (adopted to establish a post-Cold War order in Europe).

It is precisely these principles that Russia violated with its invasion first of Georgia in 2008 and of Ukraine in 2014, and that China has largely ignored in its activities in the East China and South China Seas. Reinvigorating these principles will probably require a settlement of the Ukraine conflict on terms consistent with them and adoption of these principles in a code of conduct for the South China Sea/East China Sea disputes (like that which has been discussed within ASEAN). The goal should then be to reestablish a global consensus behind these principles—codifying the commitments by Russia and China but on a universal basis.

One vehicle for doing so would be a "global convention on the prevention of violent conflict among states" adopted under the auspices of the United Nations as an elaboration of the principles of the UN charter. However, such a UN-focused approach may be too much for some countries (even for the United States). An alternative approach would be to incorporate these principles in separate security frameworks for Europe and Asia (a subject discussed later in this chapter). In Europe such a security framework would in effect reflect a return to and revitalization of the Charter of Paris.

To achieve this result, the United States and its European and Asian allies would likely have to address grievances felt by Russia and, to a lesser extent, China (as well as some other countries) over what these states regard as military actions undertaken in violation of those principles in Afghanistan, Iraq, and Libya. Addressing these grievances would require a candid discussion of the framework and principles under which military interventions can properly be undertaken, consistent with a nation's right of self-defense under the UN Charter. This would be a difficult conversation and one for which the United States in particular may have no appetite. But the subject probably cannot be ignored if the principles of World Order 1.0 are to be reestablished.

b. Strengthen the consensus against terrorism and the proliferation of weapons of mass destruction

A series of UN Security Council resolutions on both the general issue and on particular cases has gone a long way toward establishing as a global norm both that terrorism is not justified by any cause and that nations must not be allowed to acquire weapons of mass destruction (whether nuclear, chemical, or biological). These two principles are now widely supported even by China and Russia and by all but a handful of renegade states. Further efforts should be made both to universalize these principles and to codify them in regional security architectures.

Such efforts will not be without difficulties. The label of "terrorism" is freely applied by some authoritarian states to activities that most democratic states would classify as legitimate political activity and peaceful dissent. Going forward, the definition of "terrorism" will continue to be a critical point of discussion and negotiation.

c. Start the conversation on "World Order 2.0"

Under Richard Haass's construct, "World Order 1.0" is based on the notion of "sovereignty," while "World Order 2.0" is based on the notion of "sovereign obligation." "Sovereign obligation" means holding states responsible for what happens within their borders if it spills over to adversely affect others outside their borders. The emergence of this concept parallels the rise of global challenges (such as environmental degradation, health pandemics, financial meltdowns, and refugee flows) that do not respect national borders. The failure of any state to manage these challenges on its territory will directly affect its neighbors.

The concept of "sovereign obligation" admittedly raises a whole host of problematic issues:

- What exactly is the obligation of the offending state to its neighbors?
- Who is to enforce that obligation and how?
- Under what circumstances would intervention be justified to halt the harmful activity that is spilling over into neighboring states?
- What if internal political oppression is the cause?
- Who would intervene and under what authority?
- Does the neighboring state have a right of "self help" or "self defense"?

Difficult though these issues may be, they need to be addressed because the global challenges that have brought the concept of "sovereign obligation" to the fore are not going away. Discussion of these issues is a natural follow-on to the discussion of the framework and principles for military intervention that, as previously discussed, will have to be addressed in reestablishing World Order 1.0.

d. Reinvigorate the community of democracies and boldly make the case for freedom

It goes without saying that the United States and other democratic states must press to include the principles of individual liberty, political democracy, respect for human rights, the rule of law, free markets, and open economies among the basic principles of any revised, adapted, and revitalized international system. Russia, China, and other authoritarian states may resist this effort and seek to exclude some or all of these principles. Alternatively, they may follow the precedent of the Soviet Union in accepting the Helsinki Principles—signing on to the words, while draining them of much of their meaning by their actions. It is worth recalling that in the Cold War period, socialist and communist states frequently included the words "people's" or "democratic" in their names, although they were far from bastions of human freedom and human dignity. Yet their embrace of these terms and of documents like Helsinki provided platforms from which both internal and external advocates could pressure these societies in the direction of freedom, democracy, and respect for human rights and the rule of law.

The world's democratic states must join together and defend political democracy and free market economics as the core of any revised and adapted international system. They should argue that it is democratic states that are most likely to support in practice the principles of World Order 1.0. An international system based on political democracy and free markets is more likely to see disputes among nations resolved peacefully, without disruptive confrontation or armed conflict.

If they are to make this case successfully, the democratic states must dramatically increase their efforts on behalf of freedom's cause. So far they are largely missing in action. They are still too much in denial about the ideological campaign being waged by Russia, China, and other authoritarian states to discredit democratic principles at home and abroad. The democratic states need to develop a new and more comprehensive set of tools to make the case that societies based on individual liberty, human rights, rule of law, democratic politics, and free market economics both better meet the aspirations of their people and provide them with a more secure and prosperous future.

It is equally important that democratic states demonstrate the benefit of these principles in their own societies. The "democracy" brand is tarnished in the world today and badly needs a refresh. Democratic states need to show that they can overcome their increasingly divisive and dysfunctional politics, make the hard social and economic decisions that face them, strengthen the social cohesion and unity of their people, and produce sustained and inclusive economic growth for all. This is ultimately the most effective and enduring counter to the false narrative of the authoritarian state capitalists.

3. How should existing institutions be changed?

a. Reform and revitalize the United Nations

Nothing will better highlight both the need for change—and the fact that change is coming—than a high-profile effort to reform the United Nations. President Trump has signaled his support for such an effort in his recent ten-point declaration on UN reform, which has been endorsed so far by over 140 countries. The current secretary general, who has the background and temperament to take on the task, should lead the effort. He should establish a steering committee of key member states (perhaps modeled on the G-20 group of nations) along with a number of advisory groups, including especially nongovernmental groups (e.g., corporate, philanthropic, civil society, and the like).

The perennial question of Security Council reform should be the last question addressed, rather than the first, for several reasons. First, there has already been significant Security Council reform (adopting the practice of selecting rotating members from regional groupings). Second, further Security Council reform is likely to be quite contentious, perhaps less among the Security Council's five permanent members and more among various regional rivals jockeying for a seat on the Council. Third, changes to the Security Council are unlikely to be agreed upon absent an understanding of what the rest of the revised UN structure will look like.

The objectives of the reform process should be: to adapt to the new global realities that have emerged since the creation of the UN system; to broaden participation of member states; to provide for a more equitable sharing of burdens, responsibilities, and costs; to incorporate and reflect the enhanced role of non-state actors and empowered individuals in the international system; to improve the effectiveness, transparency, and efficiency of the UN institutions; and to update and affirm the basic principles on which the UN system was founded.

b. Embed US alliances in broader regional security architectures

China and Russia have consistently criticized US defense alliances as relics of the Cold War that should have been dismantled long ago. The United States and the other members of these alliances should continue to reject this argument. A revised, adapted, and revitalized international system will continue to require the stability that these alliances provide. They serve to reassure Russia and China's respective neighbors against the potential threat posed by these two larger and more powerful states while at the same time deterring Russia and China from using their power to impose their will by force. In this way, the risk of war is contained and both Europe and Asia are spared the devastation witnessed in World War II. But the preservation of these alliances will be more defensible if they can be embedded in separate security architectures for each region. Chapter VIII of the UN charter expressly encourages such regional arrangements.

China has complained that if these defense alliances are the American system for security in Asia, then it is a system in which China has no place—since China is not a party to any of these alliances. This argument has often been dismissed as disingenuous. But it does provide an opening to create an overarching security architecture for the region—based on World Order 1.0 principles—in which China has a place and in which the US defense alliances can be firmly embedded—and grudgingly accepted—by China.

There is precedent for this idea. The September 2005 Six Party Agreement on the de-nuclearization of the Korean peninsula proposed, as part of the overall settlement, security cooperation in Northeast Asia based on the six-party format (including China, Russia, Japan, North Korea, South Korea, and the United States). The theory was that if the six-party format could resolve the North Korean nuclear issue, it could become a framework for addressing the region's other security challenges.

Europe and the United States tried to incorporate Russia into a European security architecture by creating the NATO-Russia Council in 2002 as a forum for transparency, consultation, and cooperation on common security problems. After some initial enthusiasm and active participation, Russia became increasingly disillusioned with this format, and ultimately rendered it largely obsolete by invading Georgia and then Ukraine.

If the Ukrainian crisis can be resolved in a manner consistent with World Order 1.0 principles (i.e., national sovereignty, respect for existing borders, non-use of force), the time might be right to consider, as part of the settlement, some overarching European security framework in which both Russia and NATO would find a permanent place. Russia has encouraged the idea of such an overarching architecture in the past. It has periodically suggested strengthening the existing Organization for Security Cooperation in Europe (OSCE) (which includes virtually every European country). And in 2008 then-Russian President Medvedev proposed developing an altogether new European security framework.

While these initiatives were viewed as largely disingenuous and were not well received at the time, they do suggest Russia's potential willingness to engage on the subject. Helpfully, Russian experts and some officials still assert that such a framework should be based on Helsinki Principles. These principles embody the principles of World Order 1.0 – and, as importantly, the principles of freedom, democracy, human rights, rule of law, free markets, and open economics.

The reason for seeking broader security architectures in both Asia and Europe is not simply to strengthen the existing American defense alliances against their critics. It is rather the broader purpose of regenerating support for and consensus behind World Order 1.0 principles—and enshrining those principles in a broadly accepted framework for maintaining peace, security, and prosperity in these two vital regions.

c. Open up global economic, financial, and development institutions

Beginning with the creation of the Bretton Woods structures after the end of World War II, the international community has developed a host of institutions to address global economic, financial, and development issues. These include the World Bank, the International Monetary Fund (IMF), and the various regional development banks: the Asian Development Bank (ADB), the Inter-American Development Bank (IDB), the African Development Bank (AfDB), and the European Bank for Reconstruction and Development (EBRD). To varying degrees, these institutions have belatedly begun to be more inclusive and to give a greater role to major global economic players like China, India, Japan, South Korea, and other countries. But so far it has mostly been too little, and much too late.

Emerging global economic players have used this failure as partial justification for creating economic, financial, and developmental institutions outside the established international framework. Examples include the Asia Infrastructure Investment Bank (AIIB) (a Chinese initiative), the New Development Bank (formerly the BRICS Development Bank, an initiative of Brazil, Russia, India, China, and South Africa), the Contingent Reserve Arrangement (a BRICS alternative to the IMF and the World

Bank for developing countries), and China's One Belt, One Road (OBOR) initiative. While sometimes defended by their creators as merely supplemental to existing institutions, they have the potential to become alternatives to them—operating with less transparency, more corruption, and lower professional standards, and advancing blatantly geopolitical objectives.

The sensible approach here is simple.

First, push the existing economic, financial, and developmental institutions to revise and adapt their organizational structures and operational procedures more quickly to better reflect the existing economic and financial realities. But in giving the major emerging economies a larger role reflecting their greater global economic weight, insist at the same time that these countries assume the greater responsibilities and burdens that come with this larger role.

Second, be open and accepting where possible of initiatives like the AIIB and the OBOR. Today's world has enormous infrastructure needs, and countries like China have enormous resources to deal with those needs. If they are willing, they should be encouraged to do so, but in the right context.

China has at least rhetorically welcomed the participation of the United States and other nations in the AIIB and OBOR. The United States should take China at its word and wherever possible encourage its friends and allies to participate in these and similar initiatives alongside the United States. Together they should then use their participation to ensure that these new institutions operate with transparency, without corruption, and truly serve the development needs of the beneficiary countries. They should encourage these institutions to see themselves as part of the international system and help integrate them into that system. And they should encourage the existing institutions (World Bank, IMF, and the regional development banks) to partner and coinvest with these new institutions to help ensure that they operate consistent with the highest international standards.

Most Chinese leaders understand that China has benefited enormously from the international system and its institutions particularly in the financial, economic, and development areas. Their natural impulse is to continue to be part of these institutions but with a bigger role. If the United States does not respond positively to this impulse, it could turn China against these institutions and into an opponent of the international system more generally—to the great detriment of both Chinese and American interests. Given China's enormous economic weight, other countries will undoubtedly follow China's lead. This will make it almost impossible to generate a global consensus behind a single revised, adapted, and revitalized international order.

On the other hand, if China is given a greater role in the existing financial, economic, and development institutions, if the additional institutions it proposes are embraced but then integrated into the international system and helped to meet international standards, and if China is willing to contribute its enormous resources in support of this renovated international system, the entire world will benefit.

d. Revise existing trade and economic frameworks to address current grievances and emerging challenges

This is the principal area in which the international system needs to be revised, less to respond to new global economic and financial realities among states and more to respond to the grievances of citizens within states (especially the United States and Europe). Those grievances result from the perceived effects of globalization: trade imbalances, job loss, inequality, and stagnant wages.

This is not the place to try to resolve the issues of relative causation (e.g., how much of the economic dislocation caused by globalization is due to trade agreements vs. outsourcing vs. automation vs. other forms of technological innovation). But there is a political imperative to revise the international system to respond to these grievances and to address as much as possible the full range of underlying causes.

The trade agreements that are foundational to the current world trade legal order were, in general, written by and for liberal democracies with market economies. This is reflected in the content of the agreements and the structure of the institutions created to adjudicate them. The agreements assume a minimum level of transparency in the domestic legal systems of the countries party to them, so that every country can identify and understand the barriers to trade imposed by other countries. They assume that countries party to these agreements allow their economies to be ruled primarily by market forces and not command-and-control policies.

By contrast, in less transparent societies where the most fundamental features of the economy are controlled by the government, it is difficult, if not impossible, to identify the barriers to trade that the government may be erecting. There is a broad consensus that countries that are not liberal democracies with primarily market economies—and China in particular—exploit the features of the existing trade frameworks to evade the obligations they have assumed under them. This explains the demand that the existing agreements and institutions be revised to better capture the trade-restrictive policies of these non-democratic, primarily non-market countries.

But in the same way that trade agreements are not solely responsible for the economic dislocations from which many people have suffered, revising trade agreements will not by itself provide all the relief they seek. The traditional purpose of trade agreements is to remove trade barriers to create a level playing field and promote fair, transparent, and non-discriminatory competition in goods, services, digital trade, and investment. Trade agreements can except certain trade barriers from the obligations the agreement sets out and thereby accommodate protection for certain sectors of the national economies of the parties to the agreement. But trade agreements cannot suspend the rules of economics or affirmatively provide the benefits that the victims of globalization want or need.

For example, if an industry in a particular country is not a competitive supplier of a good or service, a trade agreement cannot make that industry competitive, either in the domestic or international market. To make the industry competitive would require the government to adopt policies and programs—subsidies, market access barriers, or tariffs, for example—designed for this purpose. A trade agreement could then be revised so that those programs were consistent with the agreement. Thus, revising existing trade agreements—and a revised approach to negotiating new ones—has a contribution to make. But to really address the broader grievances of those who feel victimized by globalizations will require their governments to adopt policies and programs designed for this purpose.

To address both the trade and non-trade aspects of the problem, the United States and other like-minded states need to take a number of steps:

- Use existing legal authorities to address trade-distorting practices by non-democratic countries that, due to the nature of these systems, cannot be addressed in the context of dispute settlement under existing trade agreements (e.g., theft of intellectual property).

- Develop new enforcement tools to ensure better compliance with the obligations that nations (particularly China) have assumed under existing trade agreements and the World Trade Organization (WTO). The widespread perception that China is not complying with its WTO obligations and is a free-rider on the international trading system has severely undermined support for the WTO in the United States.

- Revise existing trade agreements—and structure future trade agreements—to better address the problems of currency manipulation, inadequate protection of intellectual property, unnecessary regulatory requirements, non-tariff barriers, unfair government subsidies, and discrimination against foreign companies, while offering incentives for innovation and job creation, observance of labor standards, provision of acceptable working conditions, education and job/skills training, food safety, protection of the environment, regulatory convergence, and increased efficiency.

- o For example, the Trump administration guidelines for revising the North American Free Trade Agreement (NAFTA) among Canada, Mexico, and the United States call for addressing these and other issues. It is possible that this will be accomplished by incorporating into a revised NAFTA features negotiated in the context of the Trans-Pacific Partnership (TPP)—from which the Trump administration has declared its intention to withdraw.

- Develop domestic legislative programs to address those issues that cannot (or, for good reason, should not) be addressed in the context of trade agreements.

  - o For example, rather than closing plants in Germany and moving German production (and German jobs) overseas to less costly labor markets, many German manufacturers have instead maintained their existing plants and production levels in Germany (thereby preserving existing jobs) while putting new plants and expanded production overseas in lower labor cost nations. This has mitigated the political effects in Germany of increased investment and hiring overseas. The United States might seek to encourage similar behavior by US companies in ways that do not pose major regulatory or financial burdens.

  - o For example, one benefit of a major infrastructure program in the United States—beyond building infrastructure that the country very much needs—is that it would create jobs for people with twentieth century skills who are unlikely to be successfully retrained in twenty-first century skills. These people need the income and the dignity of work until they become eligible for Social Security retirement benefits.

  - o For example, the United States needs to look to Germany and other countries that have been successful in providing job skills and vocational training, particularly for people without a college degree. There are good jobs that go unfilled in America today because of a shortage of people with the training required to fill them. Such training, if broadly available, would allow people to stay in their home communities. In addition, an overall decline in labor mobility could be addressed by identifying and removing the barriers and disincentives preventing or discouraging people from moving to places where jobs are available.

- Put in place other supporting policies to address the lack of reciprocity and equal access for trade and investment between countries—but as much as possible addressing the problem not by closing the more open market but by opening the more closed market—to encourage the vision of an "open and civilized world" that Philip Zelikow has articulated in his chapter.

  o For example, China cannot be allowed to exploit the relative openness of US and European (especially German) markets to Chinese trade and investment (especially in critical industrial sectors like semiconductors and artificial intelligence) while the Chinese market becomes increasingly closed to American and European trade and investment (especially in sectors China has designated as strategic).

- Keep the WTO and its dispute resolution provisions. The world economy needs an adjudicatory framework for resolving trade disputes without the wreckage of unbridled trade competition and "beggar thy neighbor" trade policies that can lead to global recession, financial crisis, and massive unemployment.

- Pursue bilateral trade arrangements where it is in the American interest to do so. At the same time, recognize that multilateral trade arrangements sometimes can achieve US trade objectives while also advancing important American geopolitical and geostrategic interests.

  o For example, even many critics of the TPP support the Transatlantic Trade and Investment Partnership (TTIP) between the United States and the EU not just from a trade and investment perspective but because it strengthens the ties between Europe and America at a time when Russia is trying to divide them.

- Be willing to reconsider initial positions in light of subsequent developments.

  o For example, in the same way that the Trump administration appears to have moved from scrapping NAFTA to joining with Mexico and Canada in renegotiating its terms, the administration should at some point consider whether to carry through on its expressed intent to withdraw from the TPP. An explosion of trade agreements in the region that do not include the United States (and therefore disadvantage US companies) combined with the geo-strategic advantage in Asia that a US withdrawal would give to China argues strongly for staying in the TPP.

Technological innovations (like automation, robotics, artificial intelligence, "big data," and data analytics) that cause job loss and economic dislocations generally first appear in the United States but ultimately travel around the world. A global conversation is needed about how to manage the employment effects of these technologies. The think tank and academic communities are beginning to address this issue under the heading "the future of work." Many experts argue that while technological innovation may destroy jobs in one sector, it will create jobs in others. If true, this will present obvious skills retraining and labor mobility challenges. But other people are asking whether there will still be enough jobs for the world's working age population—and, if not, what does that mean for how societies organize themselves economically?

What New Institutions Need to Be Created?

The international system is made up of a wide variety of international fora, institutions, and other arrangements addressing health, education, environment, energy, culture, security, and other issues. Governments are actively involved but so are non-state actors of various kinds. Some of the arrangements are global, some are regional, and some have an even more limited focus.

These fora, institutions, and other arrangements need to conduct "self-examinations" to see whether they have kept pace with the changes in the world over the last several decades. These self-examinations should address questions of inclusivity, governance, the impact of technological change, and the need for objective measures of effectiveness.

But for many emerging issues of global impact, the current set of arrangements either does not address the issue at all or, more likely, does not address it adequately or effectively enough. New frameworks, practices, agreements, institutions, and arrangements may need to be created in these areas.

Three areas of focus are suggested below—but there are doubtless many others.

1. Develop arrangements to address emerging technologies

Developments in cyber technology, artificial intelligence, genetic engineering, robotics, drones, biotechnology, geo-engineering, and other technologies are at the same time promising, disrupting, and potentially dangerous. They raise serious, difficult, and largely unresolved policy, legal, ethical, and operational issues with potentially global impacts.

Condi Rice and John Deutch have argued in Chapter 7 of this book that the United States is likely to be the world leader in the development of these technologies because of its open, diversified approach to innovation and the unique legal, investment, and regulatory ecosystem that supports it. But other countries are also investing in these technologies and in some instances (as in the case of China) on a massive scale. Many Americans may feel uncomfortable leaving the issues raised by these technologies even in the hands of American and European governments, scientists, engineers, and corporations. They may be even less comfortable about what may be going on in China and Russia in these fields, let alone Iran and North Korea. The way such countries handle these emerging technologies could dangerously and dramatically affect the whole world.

New international frameworks, institutions, and other arrangements are needed to establish standards of safety, transparency, peer review, and accountability in dealing with these technologies. Appropriate mechanisms must be developed to ensure compliance with those standards. This is a textbook case of World Order 2.0: states have a "sovereign obligation" to ensure that these standards and mechanisms are observed within their territories because of the potentially disastrous impact that the misuse of these technologies could have on the rest of the world.

Care must be taken in fashioning these arrangements so as not to burden or impair the development of these technologies and thereby deprive the world of the potentially dramatic benefits. But without even minimal effort to ensure their safe and beneficial development, these technologies present downside risks—like renegade cyber weapons that bring down critical global infrastructure, artificially created and genetically engineered pathogens that become global pandemics, and AI machines outside human control that decide that the humans all work for them.

There is precedent for this kind of cooperative effort. China and the United States have established a bilateral process for addressing at least some of the challenges presented by the cyber age. This effort could be gradually expanded to include other states and over time attempt to develop a common framework or "rules of the road" for dealing with cyber issues.

2. Create a framework for fixing fragile states

From a development perspective, the world has made great progress in the last several decades. Millions of people have risen out of poverty, the global middle class has grown, and interstate conflict has become much less frequent. But this progress will not continue if the problem of "fragile states" is not addressed.

Statistics show that the bulk of the world's extreme poverty, its refugees, and its terrorist incidents occur in a couple dozen of so-called fragile states. These are states where there has been a failure of internal governance such that domestic institutions lack popular support and are unable to provide the security, services, or economic prosperity expected and demanded by their people.

The scale of the problems posed by fragile states is almost without precedent. The world is facing the prospect of four simultaneous famines (in Yemen, South Sudan, Somalia, and Nigeria). The global population of refugees is the largest since World War II (over 60 million people). In recent years 80 percent of global humanitarian assistance was spent to alleviate the problems caused by natural disasters. Now 80 percent is spent on the problems caused by fragile states. And as the world has witnessed, fragile states run a greater risk of descending into armed conflict – armed conflict that then too easily can become internationalized (as in the case of Syria and Yemen).

If the international system cannot find a way to stabilize these fragile states—to end the armed conflicts that are raging in some, and to avoid armed conflicts from beginning in others—the world will find itself in perpetual crisis, trying to manage enormous humanitarian crises for the indefinite future. This enormous challenge will tax beyond the breaking point both the world's humanitarian resources and its spirit of generosity.

To avoid this outcome, the underlying causes of state fragility must be addressed in a comprehensive and more effective way. This will require raising the profile of the problem and dramatically scaling up the time, attention, effort, and resources devoted to it. This in turn will require developing new frameworks and other arrangements providing not just "whole of government" approaches (mobilizing the resources of all relevant departments and agencies across a number of governments and international organizations) but "whole of society" approaches (mobilizing not just governments but businesses, philanthropic organizations, civil society, and ordinary citizens from both within and outside of the fragile states themselves).

To raise the profile of the problem, scale up the effort, and create and revitalize the necessary organizational frameworks and arrangements, the United Nations should begin a process for bringing together representatives of international organizations, governments, and all relevant sectors of society from across the globe to focus on the problem of fragile states. The purpose of this process would be over time to:

- Draw lessons learned from past efforts;

- Identify best practices; and

- Develop a framework for integrating in a mutually reinforcing way effort from all three sectors—government, business, and civil society—to address issues of governance, security, and development.

3. Establish protections for internal political processes

For decades, the world has struggled with the problem of ensuring the integrity of elections from manipulation either by incumbents unwilling to surrender power, or challengers willing to use electoral fraud as a means to seize power. Gradually the international system has developed recognized standards for what constitutes a free and fair election and a variety of election monitoring mechanisms for ensuring those standards are observed. The world increasingly looks to free and fair elections as the way to accomplish a peaceful transition of power and to convey popular legitimacy on a new government.

In the last few years, a new problem has emerged: foreign governments interfering in elections conducted by neighboring (and not so neighboring) states to influence the outcome of those elections or at least to undermine the integrity and legitimacy of the electoral process. Most notably, Russia, especially in the US and European election cycles of 2016, appears to have mounted traditional propaganda and disinformation campaigns, planted and propagated false news stories, helped fund and further the campaigns of favored candidates, hacked private email accounts and leaked the contents to the news media, and used cyber tools to probe and access the election machinery itself.

Because elections are such a crucial part of the political systems of democratic states (and those states aspiring to become more democratic), this problem must be addressed on an urgent basis.

First and foremost, as Tom Donilon has emphasized in a recent report on this subject, steps must be taken to enhance the resiliency of electoral systems and their infrastructure and to protect them from intrusion and manipulation. Electoral systems are "critical infrastructure" just like national financial systems, transportation systems, and electrical grids. States seeking to conduct free and fair elections must harden their electoral systems at all levels of government. The world is now on notice that these systems are vulnerable. If governments do not take steps to fix this problem, they will rightly bear the blame for any future successful attempts to compromise those systems.

Second, steps must be taken to deter future electoral interference. Those nation states, organizations, and individuals responsible for incidents of interference have paid little price for their actions. The perpetrators need to be identified, confronted, punished, and publicly held accountable. The sanctions imposed on Russia by the United States for its activities in the 2016 US presidential election are a good start and need to be affirmatively embraced by the Trump administration.

In particular, more needs to be done to counter and deter disinformation efforts— propaganda, planting false news stories, and hacking and exposing of private email accounts.

- Each of the affected states should establish a blue-ribbon panel to conduct a thorough investigation of election interference in their countries – what was done, how it was done, and who was responsible.

- Based on the work of the blue ribbon panels, each state should then conduct a campaign to educate its public about what happened, who did it, and why it was so serious.

- These campaigns should not just inform the public but also inoculate the public against future disinformation efforts so that it is not misled or taken in by them.

- Each nation should establish a quick-response capability to counter disinformation efforts with the truth, while exposing and publicly shaming the source of the falsehood.

- Governments must seriously consider countering disinformation campaigns by publicly releasing factual and truthful information that will discredit the foreign leaders, organizations, or individuals behind the campaign (e.g., by exposing corruption, illegal activity, and self-interested motivations).

- The more these actions can be coordinated among the affected nations— and the more public exposure and accountability measures are taken by the international community as a whole rather than just by the affected states— the more effective they are likely to be.

Joe Nye has suggested that the problem of electoral interference is an area where the international system might benefit from common standards and a common framework of response. To be effective, this effort must embrace not just the states that are the victims but also those states (especially Russia and to a lesser extent China) that are the perpetrators. Such an effort is unlikely to be successful unless and until electoral systems are better protected, some measure of deterrence and accountability has been established, and the international community takes the problem more seriously. Only then will the perpetrators of this activity have an incentive to abandon electoral interference and accept an international regime designed to prevent such interference in the future.

4. Many other institutions and arrangements are needed

There are undoubtedly other areas and issues that should be addressed as part of a revised, adapted, and revitalized international system. This is not because every subject needs to have a "world government" solution or some global bureaucratic structure imposed upon it. The nation-state will continue to be the basic unit of the international system and most issues of concern to a nation's citizens must be addressed by those citizens' own government. And many issues will be better addressed below the level of the nation-state—by states, provinces, and cities, and by networks of nongovernmental organizations and concerned citizens.

Is Consensus Possible?

As already noted, the world has evolved in such a way that there are a number of critical issues of global impact that can only be resolved by cooperative action among states, non-state actors, and empowered citizens. No state, however powerful, will be able to resolve these issues alone, and every state will have an interest—for reasons of its own security and prosperity—in seeing these issues resolved in some fashion. A revised, adapted, and revitalized international system must find a way to encourage and facilitate broad-scale cooperation on these issues so that they can be addressed in an effective way.

To the extent that it is able to do so, any effort should engage in that process those states (especially China and Russia) that have reservations about—or grievances against—the international system. By doing so, those nations have more incentive to work within that system. In addition, the more these states can be involved in global efforts to address issues of common concern, the easier it may be to address those issues on which their views conflict with the rest of the international community.

Strengthening areas of cooperation can hopefully help in managing areas of competition.

1. Why China might participate in revising the international system

China has abandoned the "hide and bide" approach of Deng Xiaoping and is now actively asserting itself on the global stage. As noted earlier, most Chinese understand the benefits China has received from the international system. And as David Shambaugh has noted in his paper in this volume, China has participated actively and constructively in many aspects of that system (like UN peacekeeping, international development assistance, and stabilizing the global financial system).

But China has complained that it "was not at the table" when the rules of the current international system were written—and has made clear that it wants to be at the table for any rewrite of those rules. It will certainly want to advance its own national interests in the process (as every country does). But many Chinese also understand that the international system can be a vehicle for finding solutions to global challenges that must be solved if China is to realize the "China Dream."

Like emerging powers in the past, China may try to condition its participation in the international system on international acceptance of China's domination of the Asia-Pacific. But there is no reason that the United States or the rest of the international community needs to accept such a deal. Frustrating China's impulse for regional hegemony while still engaging it in renovating the international system is possible through the combination of a regional balance of power (maintained by the active presence of the United States, India, Japan, and China's neighbors), China's dependence on trade and investment with its neighbors (plus the United States and Europe) for its continued economic prosperity, and China's own need for an international system able to solve global challenges.

This optimistic assessment could be threatened, however, by a crisis over North Korea's nuclear weapon and ballistic missile programs. If the United States can make China its partner in resolving the North Korea issue, as Philip Zelikow has suggested, this could facilitate a constructive Chinese role in revising the international system. If this effort fails, the issue is not resolved, and even results in a confrontation between China and the United States, then both US-China relations and a constructive Chinese role in the international system could be at risk.

2. Why Russia might participate in revising the international system

Russia wants a seat that is on par with the United States and China at virtually every international table. So Russia will want to have a prominent role in any reform or adaptation of the international system. But Putin's Russia sees the international system largely as a tool by which America imposes its will on the international community for its own benefit. So while Russia will want to participate, it may not do so constructively.

Russian-American relations are at an almost historic low point, with Russia consistently playing the spoiler and seeking to frustrate American foreign policy at almost every turn. The United States and its friends and allies must push back consistently on Russia's spoiler activity and international adventurism. But once the revision of the international system has gained momentum—and once it is clear that the process can serve the interests not just of the United States and Europe but potentially of Russia as well—Russia likely to become a more constructive participant. In that event, it will be in the American interest to have Russia involved.

Continuation of the Ukraine crisis, however, and especially similar Russian activity in the Baltic States or in the Balkans, would make constructive engagement with Russia almost impossible. For Russia to play a meaningful role in revising the international system, the Ukraine crisis needs to be resolved consistent with the principles of World Order 1.0, and Russia needs to forbear from any further interventions that violate those principles.

3. How the American people might be persuaded to support the effort

For America, domestic politics and foreign policy are inextricably linked. Historically, Americans have been willing to engage overseas only when their political leaders have been able to explain to them why such international involvement is in their interest and how it helps ensure their security and prosperity at home. After almost seventy years, Americans largely take for granted the benefits they have received from the international system. Some in our meeting felt they will need to be persuaded (through concrete examples, powerful stories, and a compelling narrative) that continued global engagement in general—and American leadership in revising the international system in particular—remains in America's interest.

But this will not be enough. Given their current mood, Americans are unlikely to support an effort to renovate the international system unless at the same time the grievances that emerged so forcefully during the 2016 presidential campaign are addressed. This means addressing the dislocations caused by globalization, the unmet social and economic needs, and the growing inequality gap between ordinary Americans and the coastal elites. Only then will Americans support—and have the self-confidence to lead—an effort to reform, adapt, and revitalize the international system.

Conclusion

There is a reasonable prospect that, despite the difficulties, the international system can be successfully refitted for today's world. But if the system is to meet the challenges presented by the recent trend in world politics toward authoritarianism, America and other democratic states will have to promote the causes of freedom, democracy, human rights, and the rule of law within the international system. The more that system reflects these principles, the more congenial it will be to American interests, and the more likely it is to produce a safe, secure, and prosperous future for the world as a whole.

Revising, adapting, and revitalizing the international system will require renovating existing networks, institutions, and arrangements and, in some cases, creating new ones. All nation-states will need to be involved in the effort—including those states (like Russia and China) that tend to compete with or even disrupt the current international system. And it will require addressing in parallel the internal political, social, and economic problems of the United States and Europe—while persuading their citizens that a revised and adapted international system is worthy of their support.

All this can be done. It is more than possible. But only if we begin the effort.

Stephen J. Hadley is a principal of RiceHadleyGates LLC, an international strategic consulting firm founded with Condoleezza Rice, Robert Gates, and Anja Manuel. Mr. Hadley is also Board Chair of the United States Institute of Peace (USIP), and executive vice chair of the Board of the Atlantic Council. Mr. Hadley served for four years as the Assistant to the President for National Security Affairs from 2005 - 2009. From 2001 to 2005, Mr. Hadley was the Assistant to the President and Deputy National Security Advisor, serving under then National Security Advisor Condoleezza Rice. He previously served both in the Department of Defense and on the National Security Council staff. During his professional career, Mr. Hadley has served on a number of corporate and advisory boards, including: the National Security Advisory Panel to the Director of Central Intelligence, the Department of Defense Policy Board, and the State Department's Foreign Affairs Policy Board. He is a member of the Aspen Strategy Group.

"…those committed to the ideas behind the liberal international order cannot be reflexive defenders of the status quo. We should see these challenges as an extraordinary opportunity to shape our world—and the institutions that help it function—for the better."

—MADELEINE K. ALBRIGHT

Modernizing the Liberal Order:
What Needs Fixing?

Madeleine K. Albright
Chair
Albright Stonebridge Group

In recent years it seems as though we have been celebrating the seventieth anniversary of everything, including the end of World War II and the birth of the international liberal order that followed it.

As many members of the Aspen Strategy Group can attest, both people and institutions need refurbishment at age seventy, and it is obvious to even casual observers of world affairs that our institutions are not working as well as they once did. So it is an appropriate time to ask what needs fixing in the liberal order, and how to go about fixing it.

One must also acknowledge at the outset that many political and academic figures, myself included, have at various points already suggested a slew of new programs and institutions—such as a reformed UN, a global NATO, a new Marshall Plan, and revamped financial organizations. These efforts to prepare for the future are laudable and helpful, but often lead to good discussions and little else.

We also have to admit that most of these efforts are, in an odd way, attempts to recapture the past. That is because virtually without fail, when Americans prescribe a global architecture for the twenty-first century, we hearken back to the middle portion of the last one. We yearn to return to the time when America was riding its highest—having won the war, demonstrated unparalleled economic and military prowess, and commenced building new institutions to promote prosperity and preserve peace.

It is understandable why such a memory might appeal to us; it should be equally evident why it does not appeal to others. If we went back to 1947, we would see Japan and Germany under occupation, Western Europe in ruins, Eastern Europe dominated by the Soviet Union, China in the midst of a civil war, and most of Africa, much of Asia, and many Arab countries still chafing under colonial rule.

We might wish to return to the era of Truman and Eisenhower; the world has other intentions. But there is a reason that we admire America's postwar generation: its leaders were not nostalgic. Unlike backward-looking congressional leaders who turned our country inward after World War I, they acknowledged that the globe had changed and that these changes should be reflected in the polices of our country and the nature of international cooperation.

They did not try to re-create an America that had begun to fade, nor did they expect others to stand still. They knew that their way of life had been transformed by the destruction of war, the shock of the Holocaust, the birth of the nuclear era, the rising specter of communism, and the spread of contagious ideas about independence and freedom. They saw that the old order had to give way to something new. But did they have a clear sense of where they were going? Absolutely not.

According to Dean Acheson, this was a period of great obscurity to those who lived through it:

> Not only was the future clouded, a common enough situation, but the present was equally clouded. We all had far more than the familiar difficulty of determining the capabilities and intentions of those who inhabit this planet with us. The significance of events was shrouded in ambiguity. We groped after interpretations of them, sometimes reversed lines of action based on earlier views, and hesitated long before grasping what now seems obvious.[1]

A New Era

The only thing obvious about the world in 2017 is that the old order has once again given way to something new. In countries around the world, the social contract between state and society is broken. The principal drivers of change—globalization and technology—have been welcomed in most quarters but have also caused resentment, anxiety, and massive economic displacement. Gaps have widened between rich and poor, urban and rural, the well-educated and those lacking twenty-first century skills. Rising powers and non-state actors are exerting new influence, and our international institutions are not keeping pace. The unprecedented mobility of people and ideas has rubbed raw feelings of economic and social insecurity, threatening cultural identity and prompting a backlash against immigrants, refugees, and religious minorities. Terror attacks in multiple cities across multiple regions have magnified fear and contributed to a sense that governments and international institutions are failing in their duty to protect.

Perhaps the best summary of today's world comes from Silicon Valley: people are speaking to their governments using twenty-first century tools; governments are using twentieth century tools to listen and nineteenth century processes to respond.*

This lack of faith in institutions has led to deepening doubts about the capacity of democracy to deliver, and a belief by some that democracy leads to chaos. Given the choice between democratic chaos and authoritarian order, many citizens will opt for the latter, and a new generation of strongmen has taken advantage to ascend to power across Eastern Europe, Latin America, the Middle East, and Asia. Meanwhile, President Putin has openly mourned the demise of the Soviet Union while seeking to extend his influence over Russia's near abroad, weaken NATO and the EU, and create a wedge between the United States and its allies.

Seventy years ago, the United States developed a containment strategy to push back against Soviet expansionism and counter the spread of communist ideology, confident that if we put up enough economic, military, and political pressure the Soviet system would ultimately collapse.

Today, Russia is pursuing a containment strategy against liberal democracy—using high-tech tools, such as digital propaganda and disinformation campaigns, to penetrate and undermine Western institutions, while employing hybrid warfare techniques against fragile democracies on their periphery, such as Georgia and Ukraine. President Putin appears to think that if he applies enough pressure, liberal democratic institutions will collapse and the spread of democratic ideals will stop.

Alarmingly, there are signs that his strategy is succeeding, as democracies are increasingly divided. The world was shocked last year by Great Britain's vote to exit the EU and by the election of Donald Trump to the US presidency. Western institutions would have been under stress regardless of those elections, but instead of coming together to defend democracy, Europe is now confronting its own divisions, and the United States has a commander-in-chief who seems temperamentally closer to Putin than to a small-d democrat.

The great strength of democracy is that, unlike communism, it has the capacity to correct its own faults. It is far too early for Putin to claim victory. But Putin is not the only one trying to take advantage of today's disarray. China, for example, also wants to assert a regional sphere of influence, while increasing its global economic

---

* This is based on a tweet from San Francisco civic innovator Catherine Bracy: "Citizens using 21st cent tools to talk, gov't using 20th cent tools to listen, and 19th cent processes to respond." https://twitter.com/cbracy/status/294881170250928128.

and political power and undermining aspects of the rules-based order—for example, in the South China Sea.

But regardless of how this plays out, the old order is not coming back. We are in a new era defined by forces we do not yet fully understand and changes we will not fully appreciate for many years to come. But that does not mean we can sit still. So, as a certain revolutionary once asked: What is to be done?

Embracing Change

To begin with, those committed to the ideas behind the liberal international order cannot be reflexive defenders of the status quo. We should see these challenges as an extraordinary opportunity to shape our world—and the institutions that help it function—for the better.

Where necessary, we must stand behind principles and institutions that have proven their worth over seventy-plus years. But where appropriate, we should embrace change.

We also must admit that there are good reasons that international institutions have grown unpopular. When I was at the United Nations, I used to joke that managing the global institution was like trying to run a business with 184 chief executive officers—each with a different language, a distinct set of priorities, and an unemployed brother-in-law seeking a paycheck.

Similarly, whereas Europeans once directed their hopes to Brussels, they now focus their ire on its unresponsive bureaucrats. There are reasons for this. The European Union has taken on more members, which means more discussion, more rules, a greater likelihood of dissension, and a harder job keeping all countries in line. Voting rules that enable one EU member to block sanctions against another have led to the spectacle of illiberal governments in Poland and Hungary banding together to block action against them, undermining the EU's ability to enforce the rule of law. But the logic underpinning Europe's movement toward unity—including internal mobility, shared regulations, and a common approach to trade—remains utterly compelling. If Europe were to return to twenty-eight borders, twenty-eight currencies, and twenty-eight sets of laws, the result would be more, not less, bureaucracy, and less, not more, money in the pockets of the average citizen.

This compelling logic also translates to the UN and other multilateral organizations. The simple reality is that no one country, even the United States, can tackle the bundle of issues the world faces—from terrorism to nuclear proliferation, economic inequality to environmental degradation. Even if the United States tried to do so, we would have to devote far more resources to these problems, and we would have far less to show for it.

As I often tell my students, decision-makers only have a handful of tools in the toolbox to achieve the kind of foreign policy they want: bilateral diplomacy and multilateral diplomacy; economic tools; threat of the use of force and use of force; law enforcement; and intelligence. That is it. The saying goes that if the United Nations did not exist, we would have to invent it. Fortunately, we do not need to do that—we simply need to make sure it and other institutions stay relevant, and that might include making long-needed, and difficult, reforms. In that endeavor, we have a great ally in the new secretary general, António Guterres.

Adapting Institutions

As we modernize and fix our multilateral institutions, perhaps the greatest imperative is adapting to technological change and the new sources of instability this change has created.

During the Cold War, our greatest fear was that someone with his finger on the nuclear button would miscalculate and trigger what technocrats bloodlessly refer to as a "nuclear exchange." Today, perhaps our worst nightmare is that cyberspace will turn into an arena of shadow warfare, where state and non-state actors subvert our economic and political institutions while putting critical infrastructure at risk. We will likely need to move toward agreed-upon rules of the road, perhaps set out formally in a new international agreement, to provide the tools necessary to manage these challenges.

In addition to technology, another fundamental shift in the international order has been the diffusion of power and the rising importance of regions beyond the United States and Europe. International institutions need to change to reflect these dynamics. Efforts to reform the Security Council, the International Monetary Fund, and other institutions to reflect the changing distribution of power have always been contentious, and they will remain that way. Diplomatic china will need to be broken. But if the United States is going to call on others to step up and take more responsibility, it needs to help establish a framework that will enable them to do so.

Change can also come through regional initiatives, as it has in the Asia-Pacific and even in the Middle East. I recently co-chaired a lengthy Middle East Task Force with Steve Hadley under the auspices of the Atlantic Council; the group focused on the region from a long-term, inside-out, and bottom-up perspective. Our study confirmed that despite the dire headlines, there are positive trends in areas such as citizen engagement, entrepreneurial activity, and regional cooperation. Although the dispute between Saudi Arabia, the UAE, and Qatar has set back some of the progress made by the Gulf Cooperation Council, the overall trend line on regional cooperation is still positive. In many ways it is a fulfillment of the vision of Chapter VIII of the UN Charter, which anticipated the growth of regional organizations and the possibility of them working together in partnership. As leaders across the Middle East take greater ownership and responsibility for the region's security and prosperity, our task force concluded that the United States and other outside powers should support these trends and offer assistance as needed and as requested by regional actors.

A specific area where outside assistance will be needed is dealing with the challenge of *failed states*. As the refugee crisis vividly displayed, problems within countries are no longer contained by borders. The UN has shown it has the capacity to deal with humanitarian challenges, but its efforts have focused more on response than prevention. Going forward, international organizations need to do more to address the underlying failures of governance that produce refugee flows in the first place. One idea worth further exploration is reviving the UN Trusteeship Council under a different name, with the purpose of supporting efforts to reestablish effective governance in failed states.

Another important change to the international order is the growing power of non-state actors. In many cases, large international NGOs and corporations have bigger budgets and more influence than smaller countries on the UN Security Council. They also possess a unique capacity for innovation and technical expertise necessary to solve key challenges in fields such as health, energy, and technology. Governments and international institutions have been able to leverage their contributions through public-private partnerships, but much of their potential remains unexplored. To succeed, *private sector actors need to be at the table much earlier.* Making the public and private sectors work together can be akin to assembling a puzzle out of pieces that do not fit, but it is worth the effort.

Countering Russia's Containment Strategy

If the key institutions of the liberal international order—the UN, the EU, NATO, and others—have something in common, it is that their faults are highly visible and their bureaucracies are easy to mock. Yet they also have a proven track record that is too easily overlooked. As memories of World War II fade, we run the risk of the liberal order being taken for granted and of further emboldening the enemies that seek to tear it apart.

This suggests that internationalists and small-d democrats need a call to action. Those who wish to destroy the liberal order can only succeed if its defenders are too complacent, too divided, too timid, or too stuck in the past to stop them.

The mission for these defenders must be to oppose revisionist forces—led by Russia—that are trying to contain and undermine liberal democracy. To do so, we will need to push back against their aggression using all available tools—including offensive and defensive cyber weapons, economic sanctions, and direct support to frontline states in Central and Eastern Europe. We will also need to invest in making our democratic systems more resilient by adapting to the ubiquity of social media and developing new tools to identify and stop Russian digital propaganda.

Perhaps the most important step we can take is to build a stronger bipartisan consensus in the United States about America's role in the world—a consensus in favor of the global engagement necessary to defend democratic values and advance our interests. In the first six month of the Trump administration, the US Congress has reasserted its prerogatives as a co-equal branch of government in both domestic and foreign policy. While the parties remain deeply divided on domestic policy, a bipartisan consensus has emerged on Capitol Hill in favor of strong international engagement and in opposition to the deep cuts to the international affairs budget proposed by President Trump. A growing cadre of internationalists in both parties and in both chambers of Congress are providing hope that America will emerge from this challenging period. As difficult as things are, what we are seeing in 2017 is the resilience of democracy, the importance of bipartisanship, and the willingness of people of goodwill to come together and solve problems.

The world is utterly different than after World War II, but America remains the only country capable of leading an effective defense of the liberal order and the security and prosperity it guarantees. Despite all the changes the last two decades have brought, we remain the indispensable nation. The biggest risk to global stability today is that America might see itself, or be seen, as dispensable—as just another country operating in a zero-sum world.

We saw a preview of what could be ahead at the recent G-20 meeting in Hamburg, where the United States stood alone while the other nineteen member states came together to recommit to the Paris agreement. The world is not standing still in our absence—we are creating a vacuum that Russia and China are all too eager to fill.

It is not our job to uphold the international order on our own. There is nothing about the word *indispensable* that means alone. What the term really suggests is that we need partners. The United States has never been just another nation competing with every other in a zero-sum game. We are great because we want and need other countries to have the desire and capacity to join us in tackling shared challenges.

Will America Become Dispensable?

The challenges facing the international liberal order cannot be solved by simply launching new institutions, reorganizing existing institutions for the sake of doing so, or by shifting resources from one cause to another.

They also will not be solved by looking only at traditional foreign policy questions, because another defining feature of our era is the breaking of the social contract and the blurring of domestic and foreign affairs. To fix the global order, we need to adjust to the changing nature of our economies, to the ubiquity of social media, and to the thirst that people everywhere have for equal measures of freedom, order, and security.

What is most needed now is a set of guiding principles and a commitment by the key players—governments, international institutions, civil society—to move from talk to coordinated action, even if the precise plan of action is not yet clear. We need to exhibit openness to change, opposition to the false gods of nationalism and tyranny, and a determination to build better, more flexible, and responsive societies as we repair the social contract.

We also need to keep perspective. The seventieth anniversaries of the postwar order have reminded us of a period of grave challenge. Overseas, there was a daunting array of dangers, including the communist expansion in Central Europe, the Maoist revolution in China, the turbulent partition of India, a desperate clash between Arabs and Jews, and tensions on the Korean Peninsula that would soon lead to war.

At home, there were successful examples of bipartisanship, but there were also currents of recrimination, scapegoating, and fear that would produce the McCarthy era—a period of deep division both within Congress and between Congress and the executive branch. In addition, the nuclear era had just begun, bringing with it a feeling that Armageddon might be just around the corner.

Revisiting those times can remind us that democratic institutions are resilient and that problems that appear insoluble often become less so over a period of time. All that is required is leadership of the type that our postwar heroes were able to provide—leadership that understood America was not a dispensable nation, that democracy must be defended, and that the United States was not a prisoner of history but able to shape a better future for all mankind.

Madeleine K. Albright is Chair of Albright Stonebridge Group, a global strategy firm, and Chair of Albright Capital Management LLC, an investment advisory firm focused on emerging markets. Dr. Albright was the 64th Secretary of State of the United States. In 1997, she was named the first female Secretary of State and became, at that time, the highest ranking woman in the history of the US government. From 1993 to 1997, Dr. Albright served as the US Permanent Representative to the United Nations and was a member of the President's Cabinet. She is a Professor in the Practice of Diplomacy at the Georgetown University School of Foreign Service. Dr. Albright chairs the National Democratic Institute for International Affairs. She is also the president of the Truman Scholarship Foundation and a member of an advisory body, the US Defense Department's Defense Policy Board. In 2012, she was chosen by President Obama to receive the nation's highest civilian honor, the Presidential Medal of Freedom, in recognition of her contributions to international peace and democracy. She is a member of the Aspen Strategy Group and a Trustee of the Aspen Institute.

[1] Dean Acheson, *Present at the Creation: My Years in the State Department* (New York: Norton, 1969), 3.